The Theology of Death

The Theology of Death

Douglas J. Davies

t&t clark

Published by T&T Clark
A Continuum imprint
The Tower Building, 11 York Road, London SE1 7NX
80 Maiden Lane, Suite 704, New York, NY 10038

www.continuumbooks.com

All rights reserved. No part of this publication may be reproduced or transmitted in
any form or by any means, electronic or mechanical, including photocopying, recording
or any information storage or retrieval system, without permission in writing from the
publishers.

Copyright © Douglas Davies, 2008

Douglas Davies has asserted his right under the Copyright, Designs and Patents Act,
1988, to be identified as the Author of this work.

British Library Cataloguing-in-Publication Data
A catalogue record for this book is available from the British Library

ISBN-10: HB: 0-567-03048-2
　　　　　 PB: 0-567-03049-0
ISBN-13: HB: 978-0-567-03048-1
　　　　　 PB: 978-0-567-03049-8

Typeset by Newgen Imaging Systems Pvt Ltd, Chennai, India
Printed on acid-free paper in Great Britain by Athenaeum Press Ltd,
Gateshead, Tyne and Wear

Contents

Chapter 1

Introduction

This book is for Christians who do not believe in 'life after death', for those who do, and for that silent majority who do not know what to think, or are too embarrassed to express their thoughts. It is also a book that complements what we think with how we feel and how we live. Not all questions possess definite answers, certainly not questions over details over death and afterlife, but life consists in more than questions and there are ways of 'knowing' that extend beyond verbal proposition. It is to those 'embodied' forms of knowing as much as to formal theological argument that the following chapters are devoted.

Certainly, contemporary Christianity holds many opinions over life, death and life after death. Formal orthodoxies expressed in creeds do not pass unqualified because now, more than ever, tradition-shaped knowledge grounded in ideas of revelation engages with modern discovery-based knowledge of the natural, human and social sciences. That interplay comes to sharp focus in contests over 'playing God', a phrase often deployed in debates over human conception and birth at the start of life, and over euthanasia and doctor-assisted suicide at life's end. 'Playing God' pinpoints profound issues over knowledge, its source and responsible use and becomes a two-edged sword in the hands of those competing for the moral high ground in the new ideological wars between and within 'ethics' and 'religion'.

Many tradition-focused Christians implicitly trust God over all matters of life and death, holding the death and resurrection of Jesus as foundational for their own post-mortem destiny. But, it is not long before interpretations bring increasingly considerable differences to conceptions of that destiny and the processes generating it. Earliest Christians probably awaited a returning Christ and a transformed earth as its own regenerated Kingdom of God. Some expected this in their own life-time such that they would not die at all but be transformed in the twinkling of an eye. Others anticipated death followed by a transition into that new world-order while, yet others, looked forward to a future resurrection with a new life not on earth but in a heavenly realm. Souls, resurrected bodies and spiritual bodies were all elements in this conceptual chemistry of Christian destiny.

In today's world various ideas of soul and spirit still play a part in the way some believers conceive of the human self, even when the notion of embodiment – of being as a body – has gained enormous intellectual popularity. Some Christians press the embodiment idea, abandoning ideas of soul or spirit, to focus attention not on human fulfilment of destiny in some other world but in this material world. For them, traditional ideas of resurrection take on a different kind of interpretation, one focused on their own transformation in this life amidst the

1

community of the church. Though it is easy to press these different types into stark opposition they tend to co-exist in any single church, they may also exist within the same individual at different times in their lives as experience and retrospection influence understanding. Regular liturgies as well as funeral rites, hymns, and ongoing pastoral theology all play a part in what has become a mixed religious economy of the human 'self' and its place in society and in the church.

Theology of death

To speak of 'theology' in the singular as far as death is concerned only makes sense if we think of theology as the actual process of quest and reflection in the ongoing life of believers rather than as a singe set of answers. Much the same holds for other major areas of Christianity such as Christology, Ecclesiology, or of the Trinity, for considerations of Christ, the Church and God are ever ongoing. It is in this sense that this book sets out to be a sketched theology of death. While neither a systematic nor historical theology it offers a series of theological reflections on life and death drawn from each. There is no intention here to cover the standard topics of biblical eras, church dogma and established theologians that are available in other books. The goal, by contrast, is to be highly selective of theological thinkers, several who are currently out of fashion, and of cultural issues to prompt thought and foster a link between 'life-style and death-style': an expression that will recur throughout this book.

Unlike some formal theologies that can easily appear philosophically abstract this book is deeply concerned with what we make of life and death. Especially with what many think but seldom say. It takes its cue from Albert Schweitzer's militaristic and economic shaped questions of 'whether death reigns inside you? Whether 'you have conquered it within and settled your account with it?'[1] Whether we prefer such aggressive interrogation or more peaceful reflections on life and death this book will seek to ground itself in concrete issues lying between the 'war and peace' polarities of a Christian concern with living and dying. This will include some familiar theological and historical afterlife beliefs of heaven and hell, contemporary rapture beliefs of Armageddon-interested America, private rituals with cremated remains and developing interests in British woodland burial. Whether in ideas of raptured believers caught up to meet their Lord in the air or in those seeking return to an earthy bed of a woodland glade, human desires express a sense of identity and of the purposes of life itself.

Life-style and death-style

Such images capture moods, express ideas, and create a style of life. And it is precisely this issue of style that underlies this book and is focused in the relationship between life-style and what we will call, 'death-style'. 'Style' is a useful term

---

[1] Albert Schweitzer ([1907] 1974: 67). Sermon on 'Overcoming Death' of 17 Nov. 1907.

because it has an easy, everyday, sense to it as a reference to the values people choose and choose to express in a great variety of ways. Though it would be possible to adopt the sociological ideas of *habitus* and *gestus* [2] to analyse in a more technical fashion the deeply embedded ways people live I choose to remain with the more direct notion of style because it makes it easier to discuss the interplay of life-style and death-style. Such styles within a society affect us all, some we inherit and favour, others we change as opportunity, market-forces, aesthetics and personal circumstances permit. Indeed, the contemporary world is especially interesting for thinking Christians because it is, as 'contemporary' moments have always been, a place where tradition is negotiated, where, as far as 'ceremonies' are concerned, 'some be abolished and some retained.'[3] That expression, still found in editions of the Church of England's *Book of Common Prayer,* comes from one of the most interesting brief and self-reflecting treatments of ritual in British culture history, one that understood issues of 'innovations and newfangleness' as well as the need for cultural appropriateness of ceremonial form. That balanced realism is sought in what follows, especially when appraising the diversity of commitment of Christians whether to traditional afterlife beliefs or to quite a different and this-worldly appropriation of 'eternal' life.

Method and intent

Numerous other issues embracing liturgy, doctrinal history, and the changing practices of bodily disposal also find some theological analysis here as part of a Christian self-reflection on how the ideas, values, beliefs and behaviours that constitute our life-style also relate to our death-style. I stress this mirroring of styles because it pinpoints the concerns of many people in a contemporary world where change and the negotiation of change through abolitions, retentions and innovations of beliefs, practices and the way people relate to each other is a basic reality.

Amidst the constraints and opportunities of social change the essentially traditional nature of aspects of religion are challenged. It is no wonder that the later twentieth century witnessed considerable disturbance between religious conservatives and liberals, whether within churches or between entire cultures, indeed, the very notion of a 'clash of cultures', was apt for all such contexts. Secularists, too, have entered debates of how to think and live in the twenty-first century. All have to engage with the changes wrought by science, technology and medicine and whilst some conservative traditionalists simply deploy advances in technology to communicate an essentially anti-modern message others sense a truthfulness about life in scientific developments. The speed and complexity of change often makes for unbalanced movement and uncertain control. At the very time

---

[2] Douglas J. Davies (2000: 108–138) for the sociological background of these concepts as well as an extensive application to Mormonism.
[3] *Book of Common Prayer* (1662) 'Of Ceremonies, Why Some be Abolished, and Some Retained'.

when religion has resurged as a social and political interest – including American interests in Israel and Islamic responses to that; the extensive Protestantization of South America; the re-traditionalizing of Russia and of some eastern European countries- religion has tended to be replaced by the rise of a generic 'ethics' in western Europe and allied developed cultural situations. The very issue of the nature of life and of the process of death has come in for a hitherto unknown scrutiny. Indeed, the very idea of 'playing God' serves as a verbal touchstone for the competitive territories of religion and 'ethics' in the twenty-first century as the ability to sustain life in the near-dead and to foster life in the infertile by mechanical and chemical means outruns the capacity of theologians, philosophers and the new generation of ethicists to define life and death.

And yet we all die. It is precisely in anticipation of our own death and in the experience of the death of others that this book sets out to be a pause for thought, a dwelling upon life and death issues in relation to the deeply abiding human themes of survival, fear and love. With that in mind the following chapters focus on the work of selected theologians, an eclectic group of some familiar and unfamiliar names, chosen as conversation partners with a variety of theological, historical and social scientific views.[4]

Genesis bodies

The key focus of our reflections lies with the body, this matrix and medium of our beliefs and values. This is not simply the temple that enshrines our prime values but is the very basis for them, a view that warns against the overly abstract nature of either theology or philosophy and of how they talk about doctrine and belief. The intuitive self-knowledge of our embodiment lies behind the affinity we sense between our own 'life' and the 'life' of Jesus. The Victorian penchant for literary 'lives of Jesus' that set an integrated and harmonious narrative of the Gospels within some geographical knowledge of the Holy Land was but an example from one era of the emotional sense of attraction to Jesus as an embodied person. The knowledge of ourselves and others close to us as bodies born, living, suffering, dying and sometimes sharing in 'glory' is, itself, one reason why we are drawn to the embodied person of Jesus. While the doctrine of the Holy Trinity or of the Church as the Body of Christ may have an intellectual appeal to those whose trained minds may gain a thrill from the beauty of ideas they do not always enthral Christians at large. For that immense fellowship it is 'heart that speaks to heart', and body that knows what another body undergoes, that powers devotion and the insight of faith. It is just such a body-affinity that undergirds the spirituality of life and death explored in this book.

Examples are legion but one will suffice. A Pieta from Pernio Church in Finland dating from the 1420s, now relocated to the State Museum in Helsinki, offers a telling example of just how the blessed Virgin, holding her dead son, offered mothers of earlier days solace when they, too, lost their own children, as

---

[4] D. J. Davies (2002).

4

many regularly did. This possibility of identification of emotion within human life – body to body, grief to grief – furnishes an ongoing backdrop from Christian tradition not only for the funeral liturgies of churches but also for the private devotions of each individual woman coming into church to share her grief with God and engage in some sympathetic prayer with Mary. Art and statuary of this type are, of course, extensive within the Catholic world and I mention this particular one precisely because its decontextualized location, from church to museum, throws its precise message into even sharper analytical relief.

Such an image, speaking directly of survival, fear and love experienced as emotion, allows us to acknowledge the importance of embodiment within this book and easily highlights the theological importance of the ideas of creation and salvation that are brought together throughout the following chapters. Though closely interrelated in historical theology, creation and salvation show deep trends of their own as to the direction of thought they prefer. Creation speaks the positive language of birth and development, of fullness, and the divine imagination set upon a widening relationship of God and the world in the broadest of cosmic senses: survival comes by expansion. Salvation, by definition, begins in the domain of negative forces too with survival coming by deliverance. Of the two Genesis myths of creation, for example,[5] the first follows our model of 'creation', involving a world created and deemed by God to be 'very good'. So good that God rested after his six days of work, leaving the male and female within a teeming world and with the command to be fruitful and multiply so that a new humanity might have dominion over all that was already made. The second myth changes the scene with its dramatic barrenness of the newly created earth watered by that mist which allows the Lord God to form man and to breathe life into his moist clay form. He is transported to the newly planted garden and is confronted by the tree of the knowledge of good and evil whose presence promises death if once its fruit is eaten in disobedience to the divine command. This epic tells of that eating, its fall and the shame of nakedness it brings before the disobeyed Lord God. They are banished from Eden and there stands the angel with the flaming sword preventing return and any possibility of reaching to 'take also of the tree of life'.

Yet that tree would reappear, not in a creation narrative but in the epic of salvation, as the cross, as the tree of life that would, indeed, witness a hand 'put forth' to take of it, the hand of the one Christians saw as the second Adam. The process of survival in this history of salvation had become a social covenant. The self-survival grounded in the fear of nakedness and expressed in fig-leaf aprons was replaced by the divine promise of survival revealed in the garments of skin with which the Lord God dressed the errant and expelled pair. Those skins would, in turn, be echoed in the protective mark placed upon Cain, murderer that he was, and also be symbolized in the Ark, made by righteous Noah but with the Lord as the one who 'shut him in'. After the deadly flooding-out of evil humanity comes a repeated command to be fruitful and multiply and to fill the newly resurfacing earth. This time, however, it is not a tree that is forbidden,

---

[5] Gen 1.1– 2.3, and Gen 2.4 ff.

a tree in a world of vegetarian eating, but the life-blood of animals in the new world of carnivorous humans. God's blessing of Noah involves a fear of humanity that will lie upon the animal world. Noah's blessing comes to shape in an explicit covenant of survival made by God and displayed as a rainbow. All these survival motifs of skins, mark, ark and rainbow would come to their much fuller covenant expression in the circumcision of Abram.

As the biblical epic progressed the human desire for survival came into its own in the account of the Tower of Babel yet it, too, is a failure and incurs the divine wrath because motivated by self-help; it is not a mark of covenant-survival. It falls and yet another form of dispersal occurs. Adam's exit from Eden, Cain's alien-ation from the earth, and the flood that was its own separation of humanity from its earth-base, is now encountered in humanity's scattering across the earth's face until the LORD calls Abram and sends him on what would become the great covenant journey of a covenant people of great number, and all to be marked once more when the near hundred year old Abraham is circumcised. Only after this is Isaac born to Abraham's postmenopausal wife, Sarah: and Isaac becomes the ongoing source of the covenant people. Though so much more could be said of this remarkable epic of the Hebrew Patriarchs the point is clear that death and extinction partner life and the flourishing of a people. Indeed, death as tragedy now fades from the scene as the promise of a multiplied posterity takes over in the emergence of the people of Israel. For centuries the issue of an afterlife is entirely subsumed by the issue of descendents filling the promised land. In Christian terms it is only relatively soon before the time of Jesus that afterlife beliefs and the emergence of ideas of resurrection emerge. Though acknowledging a series of cautions, Tom Wright, for example, locates the real transition point of Jewish belief in 'human beings themselves actually dying and actually being given a newly embodied life at some point thereafter' in 'Isaiah's servant passages'. From there he takes us to Daniel and Ezekiel and the idea that Israel's belief in a creator God who could punish disobedience through exile and yet offer life from the dead in response 'to his people's martyrdom'.[6] Irrespective of its precise origin it is this resurrection option, familiar by Jesus' day in the outlook of the Pharisees, that frames his life and death and the belief in his resurrection by the earliest Christians.

From Genesis to Genes

I rehearse this Jewish mythical epic at some length to highlight its influence on so much Christian thought and also to induce a sense of its limitations in a day when the story by which many live does not begin in Eden and proceed by marks of covenant. From Darwin's nineteenth- century evolutionary insights to twentieth-century genetics, a new narrative of the way things are has emerged and death occupies a different place within it. The transition between such powerful narratives involves a sense of disquiet and of conceptual fear. Many conservative

---

[6] Tom Wright (2003: 123–127).

Christians feel it but express it as an issue of revealed truth versus secular scientific hypothesis. Death has yet to play the important role awaiting it as one key symbolic focus of this debate. Death for Genesis–Adam is not the same as death for Genetic–Adam. So, too, for the way in which both the doctrines of creation and salvation take their form and for the place of death in each.

'The land of everlasting life' [7]

To love one another and to possess eternal life: these two themes developed in the *Book of Common Prayer* epistle and gospel readings for Trinity Sunday offer a challenging entry into any modern theology of death. But, the great harmonies intrinsic to Trinity Sunday are not those heard at all times and in all places. On the contrary, the general voice of Christian theology, following the Jewish narratives, speaks of death as a disruptive evil whose enmity towards humanity lies close to the very heart of the divine engagement with mankind. The growth of Christian narrative, founded on the Genesis myth of death as punishment for disobedience towards God, soon interprets even the myrrh presented to the infant Jesus as symbolic of his coming death, itself interpreted as sacrificial of an incarnate deity. While the dusty destiny of the first Adam, so marked by the skull at the foot of many an artist's cross, is transcended by Christ, as second Adam and his resurrected triumph, yet death retains its sting as controller of the story. Standing in the wings, mortality prompts the lines of life's actors, both great and small: not least in the microcosmic dramas of the universal purposes of God, in Eucharist and Baptism, death stands deeply firm in discourse demanding conquest. In his seminal theological work Oscar Cullman offered a classic and tight orthodoxy for the salvation-history framing these events with Christ's resurrection as 'the centre point' of redemption and with believers possessing hope for their own future resurrection. He, importantly, set the Holy Spirit, as the dynamic factor underlying that hope as also of the state of tension as this world-order awaited its future divine transformation. Even the departed dead, still awaiting their future resurrection, 'live in a condition in which the tension between present and future still exists'.[8] His future directedness, framed as an eschatological tension between 'times', now seems quite dated when compared, for example, with Christians who also deem the present to be transitional but who deploy ideas from physics to ponder a spiritual futurity, as we will see in a later chapter.

Natural death

Yet, look in another scientific direction and perspectives arise in which death is natural to life, where the theological judgement that makes death both evil and unnatural is rendered redundant. Here death and the destruction of biological

[7] *Book of Common Prayer*, Baptism Service.
[8] Oscar Cullman ([1946] 1951: 240).

material is an integral part of the process of procreation within a wider biological environment. Millions of sperm live and die in the very process of reproduction, a scenario played out in many other ways as those who are successfully produced go on to live and die. Life and death become inevitable partners of life. The eye of the scientific mind, whose mental concern is with how the material world works, sees death as a fundamental phase of living things. Religions have taken up this process and sought to make sense of it, not least through their myths and doctrines of how things are born, live and die and, as part of the natural bonding of partners and communities, engender the pain of loss and of the knowledge of loss in the process. Bereavement is no less severe for the biologist than the theologian, but the pain of natural consequences is, itself, a fact of life and need not be a moral evil even if it is a psychological one. How we classify our pain is, itself, a social issue that defines our style of humanity: even the fear of death is not universal.[9]

Against these varied backgrounds Christianity may itself, be defined in at least two ways, one positive and one negative. The positive perspective takes Christianity as humanity's helpmeet. Its definition of death as the outcome of sin and its offer of salvation from death through a resurrected future is good news indeed. All is deeply personalized, from the tragedy of Adam, the heroic love of Christ, the comfort of the Spirit's sympathetic groans that are too deep for words,[10] to God's ultimate faithfulness. Here we find succour and help in times of trouble and, in the history of a frequently hostile world, an answer to the pained questions of millions. One reason for Christianity's success lies in its strength in meeting death and life's pain with many a form of personal comfort.

The cross

But there is also a negative aspect of this kind of Christian perspective. It is one that establishes death as the central moral pivot around which God works with the cross as its symbol. Whether in the Catholic theology of the Mass or the Protestant theology of the Cross Christ's death is manifested. And while it is easy and even theologically necessary, to argue that it is always death conquered by life that is theology's duty – the grave below the empty tomb – there remains a certain Christian romantic commitment to death as evil that can be adjudged as less than valuable. And it is here that the scientific vision needs invoking, for Christianity also possesses a commitment to creation, albeit one that is not generally as romantic as is its commitment to death, a lack due to the sinful overlay of the Genesis myths and of the biblical literalism that then develops a spiritual psychology of human guilt proceeding from Eden and the banished pair. The sin of Adam is used to weave a fabric of a fallen world and a fallen humanity:

[9] Joanna Burke (2005: 3, 25–50).
[10] Rom 8. 23.

the romance[11] of the cross then speaks to the latter more immediately than the excitement of the microscope to the former.

What I am arguing at this point is that Christian theology can and should set the fall-focus on death more firmly alongside a redemptive attitude to the world and our life within it. And I say 'alongside' rather than 'replace' because the potential for moral evil in humans remains and benefits from mythical narratives that express it. Still, it is within a world-view involving a scientific perspective of and upon nature that death could and should be given a place of its own, and one that is not evil. In other words, death needs to be understood in terms of doctrines of creation much more than it ever has been in the past. But there are consequences following such an adjustment, and one of them would involve a repositioning of the sin-death link established in Genesis and that has been dominant for much of Christian theological history.

Here, then, we arrive at a foundational paradox, that death can be framed as either natural, albeit still fraught with grief and potential anxiety, or as a supernatural evil to be countered by a supernatural good. This very question pinpoints the relationship between science and religion that highlights the nature of myth and doctrine in religion and of the observation and analysis of the world by science. To say this is not to privilege science over theology or vice versa, and it is certainly not to assume that by approaching death as a natural process we avoid the human domain of loss and the pain of grief, and certainly not the experience of evil. But it is to approach death as natural to life and not as alien to life. In this sense death is part both of creation and salvation.

Faith

At the outset this makes it important to speak of faith and its framing, of the way in which people's insightful dedication to how they live encounters and engages with death. For here we immediately find ourselves caught up in strong differences of opinion amongst different churches and people within churches, and find traditions and contemporary values variously embracing and rejecting each other. On the one hand the Christian tradition is, formally by its creeds, firmly and absolutely rooted in the resurrection of Jesus from the dead, his ascension into heaven, his coming again in glory to establish new realities into which the resurrected dead will pass after judgement. On the other hand some Christians would interpret that tradition and its doctrines in this-worldly terms to offer a way of life quite apart from any expectation of an afterlife. For some traditional Christians such an apparently this-worldly outlook denatures the Christian faith, indeed, it would be hard to find a more poignant disagreement over the identity of Christianity than this core topic of death and afterlife, yet it exists and its existence provides an opportunity for considering the dynamic forms that Christian religion may take at different times and places and amongst individuals of the

---

[11] Though here I am deeply aware of the intense difficulty of even referring to 'the romance' of the cross from a Protestant theological perspective.

same day and age. It is this creative polarity that fires this book rather than any embarrassed and forced recognition of diverse beliefs on the one hand or polemic against either view on the other.

Death in Safe-Society

To acknowledge differences is important not only to foster mutual understanding amongst contemporary Christians but also to do justice to Christian history with its numerous variations on thoughts of death. In so doing, however, we need to face the fact that, despite death's centrality to the very structure of Christian history, liturgical practice, and ethical concerns, by the early twenty-first century death has become marginalized in everyday conversation and regular Christian teaching. While history furnishes many theologies of death this is not an age overly rich in them. Indeed, it is a time of scarcity, most especially in churches within developed and stable societies where death holds an uncertain place and where people live much longer, making frequent experience of bereavement rarer than in countries where birth-rates and death-rates are much higher through infant mortality, the ravages of disease and warfare. Still, even within the 'safe societies' of economically developed worlds, issues of war, terrorism and famine ensure that the news media constantly present depictions of death just as the entertainment media regularly dwell upon the detection of murder with the almost mandatory scene of post-mortem forensic pathology. The sudden death of someone, most especially if they hold celebrity status, becomes newsworthy because it encapsulates the intrusive nature of death into life, so, too, with the relatively rare untimely death of someone, issues to which we return in Chapter 3.

Each era brings its own topic of belief to the fore as the spirit of the age provokes or is provoked by Christian tradition and we will, for example, analyse two instances of such cultural interplay in the cases of cremation and green burial in a later chapter. More broadly, however, I want to explore phases of relative silence and innovatory speech over death with the heart of the book coming to beat with a demanding intensity as we turn to our own day and to the thoughts and emotions that frame our longer silences and briefer utterances of faith. This is all the more important given the fact that we all die, that we all have to live through the death of those we love, and because the strangely distant deaths of hundreds of thousands are carried to us daily by the media. On a spatially vaster scale there also remains the once almost unimaginable death of the cosmos, now pressed more urgently in ecological concerns for the viability of human life within changing environmental conditions.

Death in diverse lives

More immediate, and yet with their own form of strange distance, we must consider the theology implicit in the underlying motifs of death that run through the regular rites central to Christian denominations not least those of baptism,

Eucharist and matrimony considered in Chapter 3. That flow extends into wider theological issues of life making the complex interplay of life and death central to the rationale of Christian understanding and ensuring that liturgy and ethics are of a piece within daily existence. This interplay of death and life constitutes a crucial feature of this book, given my assumption that the entire grammar of discourse of death is only intelligible in relation to pre-existing notions of life. This is a complex topic since 'life', so easily named as a singular abstract noun, is given many different emphases at different times and places. To have 'life' as a slave in an early Mediterranean Christian church would have been quite unlike 'life' in a post-modern professional or a poor member of an underclass. The expectations and constraints framing 'life', in all of its versions, enter into what death also means in those lives. Any number of studies from autobiographies to histories could exemplify this obvious but easily ignored fact. Studs Terkel, for example, offered an exceptional collection of interviews with ordinary Americans whether actor, airline steward, bus driver, dentist, farmer, football coach, mason, miner, piano tuner, professor, prostitute, receptionist, solicitor, or any one of some eighty occupations, male and female.[12] His descriptions furnish a practical demonstration of the variety of forms of 'life' in one complex society. One might complement it with Max Weber's considerably more theoretical and sociological engagement with the varieties of salvation that the different forms of living of, for example, bureaucrat, merchant or soldier, seem to demand.[13] Sociologically speaking, salvation is not the same for everyone as liberation and other forms of theology have also made very clear. While such studies offer a distinctive challenge to systematic theologies that tend to offer rather formulaic accounts of life and death they speak powerfully to pastoral contexts where the mixed diversity of individual circumstance engages with the more abstract simplicity of doctrine. It is this interplay of cultural perspectives and shifting individual opportunities in the opening decades of the twenty-first century that catalyses the complexity of lives as seldom before. Local, national and international economics, politics, philosophy, science and religion exert distinctive forces on 'life', its constraints and opportunities, and upon 'life's' refraction in ideas of death.

To speak like this raises the very particular issue of priority or causality. In other words, do ideas of life drive ideas of death or ideas of death drive ideas of life? The parallel of the life-style and death-style relation is similar. While no single answer is possible this sharp dichotomy can serve a useful cautionary purpose whenever we ponder any specific historical era. It might, for example, be an important question when comparing a 'religious' age that views this life as a preparation for the afterlife with a 'secular' age in which the only concern is with this life. Each context bears its own constraints as, for example, in contemporary anticipations and risks associated with wide-ranging anxiety over terrorist attack, global warming, natural disasters and potential epidemics, as also in the much more personal issue of old age, sickness and death. In developed societies even the benefits of increased health and long-life bring in their train concerns

---

[12] Studs Terkel (1974).
[13] Max Weber ([1922] 1963).

focused in issues of death with dignity and even the right to die through assisted suicide. Previously firm Christian cultures in which, for example, suicide was both criminal and sinful, as even forms of art made clear,[14] are now pressured to ponder such issues within the new-born value-expectations fostered by the notion of human rights making 'death rights' in relation to assisted suicide a strange social presence and prompt for theological response.

As historical theology engages with such contemporary situations there is a pressing need to consider the current paradox of Christianity's triumphant doctrinal proclamation over death set alongside the churches' relative doctrinal silence, though here some caution is needed since 'theology' is a multiplex activity. I do not, for example, assume that 'theology' exists as a free-standing activity, as might be suggested when it appears as a distinctive subject in the syllabus and departmental organization of, for example, British universities for there is usually extensive overlap between what is taught as an apparently free-standing academic subject and the religious biography of its teachers. While the confessional stance of Protestant, Catholic and Orthodox Faculties of Theology in parts of Europe and in many seminaries and theological colleges across the world, not least in the USA, makes faith-influences formally apparent this is also the case to varying degrees in British state-funded departments of Divinity, Theology, Religion and Religious Studies. Theology, more extensively than most other academic subjects, possesses an intricate relationship between faith and scholarship just as it does between academic and ecclesiastical professionals and between them and an extensive laity of deeply engaged people as well as a broader public. For all these reasons ritual practice, ethical concerns and public opinion all relate to formal theology and require that some attention be paid to funeral rites, bereavement issues and pastoral practice, alongside explicit texts, reports and discussion documents.

Social focus

In much of what follows it is important to emphasize the contemporary British context and, within it, some emphasis upon the Church of England. Those familiar with other religious contexts will be able to compare this with their own situation, for Christianity is now so extensive and varied that no book of this type can hope to be comprehensive. In seeking to be exemplary, however, we can expect to address key issues with common historical roots and significant contemporary application to contemporary life. I am aware that some will, quite rightly, point to millions in the Americas, Africa and elsewhere in flourishing Christian communities where traditional ideas of death and afterlife dominate. That is as may be, but the western European context cannot simply be ignored as an 'exceptional case' of secularization as some sociologists do with some dedication. While this is not the place to argue secularization let it be noted that as the twenty-first century opens there is some evidence of atheist and strong agnostic voices being raised in

[14] Ron M. Brown (2001).

what is a religiously political-correct USA. It is much more likely that America
will come to resemble western Europe than the other way around and death and
attitudes to it should be kept in mind as an index of this secularizing tendency,
something that most sociologists have not yet pondered sufficiently.

Traditionally, of course, Christianity, as a Jewish Messianic movement, became
a religion born out of the death of Jesus. Belief in his conquest of death engendered the new community and lay at the core of its key rites of Baptism and
Eucharist. The creeds framing these depict Jesus as one whose incarnation
embraces death and proceeds into resurrection. Despite that, practical Christian
teaching on our own death or that of those we love is often silent. Here the
diverging experience of priest and people needs some clarity, for many a minister
reading the above might well respond by numbering the funeral services conducted over the last month, rehearsing what might have been said in a funeral
address and noting the numbers of people present. Those same ministers, however, are highly unlikely to have preached on death or anything concerning the
afterlife within their regular congregation at ordinary services. While this dual
activity of religious leaders may give them a sense that they do engage much with
a theology of death the picture is likely to be quite different for the average
churchgoer.

The frequent silence

This frequent silence over death within western churches could be read by traditional Christians as the result of lack of faith and of disbelief in long-accepted
images of the after-world. And that may be true despite the fact that millions of
Africans, Americans and others adhere to long-established belief in a post-mortal
heaven and hell much as did many European Christians in recent times. Times
change and so do the ways in which Christian beliefs are appropriated and even
transformed.

The key issue here concerns formulae of Christian identity. Traditionally this
has involved creeds with churches interpreting them in the light of scripture, previous doctrine and contemporary circumstance. The fact of interpretation lies at
the heart of change and of this book. Within liberal groups there is an open
acceptance that interpretation is of the essence of faith seeking understanding
while conservative groups view interpretation with deep suspicion even though
the stance of those groups is, itself, rooted in a particular form of interpretation.
Conservative Protestant evangelicalism and conservative Catholicism are often
rooted in their own presuppositions in such a way that they tend to be hidden
from those holding them. This makes it possible for devotees to speak of themselves as possessing 'the truth' whilst others have 'interpretations'. The assumptions of this book are that doctrine emerges in and through social and cultural
forces and changes with time as new appreciation and knowledge grows.

A classic case of this affects the creedal assertion that Jesus will come again in
glory to judge the living and the dead. That such a millennial view was present
in early Christianity is evident, it is equally obvious that Jesus did not come
again. But what then? One logical step is to assume that early Christians were

misguided over the timing of his advent and that he will come one day. Another is to accept that he will never come and that times have simply changed in terms of how to view the world and interpret ideas of a Jewish Messiah and Christian Saviour. These issues have their own theological history associated with theories of eschatology.[15] It is at this point that the conservative is likely to advance the 'slippery slope' argument and indicate that the liberal, disbelieving a key interpretation of traditional Christianity, is likely to go on and disbelieve many more of them until there is nothing left that can be properly identified as authentically Christian. And that is a fair point, not least over the resurrection, here the issue of interpretation demands honesty over how churches work and teach.

Mid-range doctrine

Christian Churches, as all human groups, actually function at what might be called a mid-range of communication deploying language that allows us to engage with each other and create worlds of meaning that do justice to aspects of the material world and to our social groups. We survive and flourish as and when we remain within this middle range of agreed values and beliefs. Many are lost, for example, when physicists tell of mathematical formulae that may explain how space and time are related in ways that may seem counter-intuitive. The mid-range acceptance that a chair is a solid that holds my weight serves well compared with the counter-intuitive 'fact' that it is composed of electro-chemical activity. We thrive when we remain within a suitable range of descriptive explanation. And so it is with religious ideas. To use the Bible in church or in devotional life is, also, to operate on an agreed-upon level of understanding. The textual, historical critical and social-contextual forms of biblical analysis that have flourished for much more than a century are easily ignored in ordinary congregational life and teaching even when clergy have learned and know their significance. The politics of church leadership combined with the defence of personal identity forged in the acceptance of mid-range interpretations sometimes makes the acceptance of technical levels of understanding difficult, unwelcome or impossible. To speak of these things is, often, to be deemed to attack the identity of the believer. But, and this is the crucial fact, these perspectives have, most usually, been developed by people who are believers in search of the way things are and who cannot deny what they have found. The peculiar irony of religious debate is that it is those in search of the truth who can come to be deemed unfaithful to the truth when they can no longer accept what has been passed on to them for truth up to that point.

Still, there is a wisdom that can emerge from such considered opinion influenced by scholarship and alert to the fact that Christianity is much more than a simple sect, for the birth and expansion of the Jewish cult into a world-religion has fostered beliefs and practices of a breadth that most members of any

[15] Albert Schweitzer ([1906] 1910), C. H. Dodd (1938).

one church can hardly imagine. Once set-free in the world its potential became enormous. The fact that the early twenty-first century is a period of growth amongst conservative forms of Christianity, often quite different from each other in doctrine, as also of conservative forms of other world religions, must, itself, be interpreted and not simply accepted as proof that 'conservative is true'. From a sociological perspective a great deal of conservative and fundamentalist religious life exists in direct response to a globalizing secularism, commercial consumerism and forms of imperialism that breed a sense of uncertainty, marginalization and fear. At the personal level they challenge people's sense of identity.

This book aims to ponder these issues in relation to death. For death awaits us all and interpretations of its significance must stand amongst the most important facts of life. Christianity holds some interpretations of death that no longer appear sensible to many people. If Christianity depends totally upon one particular interpretation, and one that is not intelligible to people who, otherwise, find their life deeply informed by Christian values and practice and, indeed, by a sense of God, then it will fail itself as well as them. It is with them in mind that this book pursues an understanding of death in relation to life in a way that seeks to make sense of each. This is better than leaving the situation in which many people simply ignore what Christianity says because it seems senseless.

Life and Death: kinds of knowing

A major aspect of any theology of death, then, is that it must also be a theology of life. To say this is not to play with words but is to highlight the place of self-reflection within our experience of being human. It is also to raise the crucial topic of the method by which theology works. This is highly problematic and must not be ignored because it concerns the source and means by which we discuss the profound issues of our existence.

One of the clearest traditional examples of this double-action feature of life and death surrounded the death of Pope John Paul 11 on 5 April 2005. Having already been ill and then seriously ill for some weeks he returned from hospital to the Vatican where, after some days, he died. Public statements made it clear that it had been his choice to remain in his private apartment and die with his staff around him in what was to be a classic catholic death. Whilst the presence of medical staff was noted much more emphasis fell upon selected cardinals and staff who answered his charge to hear passages from the New Testament. The day before he died he received the Sacrament for the Sick and Dying: it would be a 'good death'. In the surrounding media commentary an interesting form of discourse emerged in which reporters raised points of social, pragmatic, political, historical or even ecclesiastical import only to be met, on occasion, by responses grounded in confessional aspects of faith. As the Pope lay dying one Cardinal spoke of him as already reaching and touching the Lord, another spoke of the Lord as opening the gate of heaven for him. A recurrent theme was that this Pope, who had sought to affirm life and its value at every point, including his opposition to abortion, now showed the value of death as the path each Christian needs to follow. He who was 'Pro-Life'[16] was also pro-death. Here was life affirmation as a frame for death. In the brief days of serious illness and physical decline spokesmen talked of the path on which the Holy Father was now set and on which, through prayer, the faithful could accompany him.[17]

Revelation and imagination

This example teaches the fundamental lesson that death befalls individuals in their own death and impacts upon the living through the deaths of others. This truism is requisite and necessary lest we, too, slip easily into an attempted systematic theology of death that might reify death, making it abstract and removed from the realm of experience. In the history of Christianity, as in our personal biographies, we may think of death rather abstractly but we encounter death not as an abstract philosophical idea but as the death of a person. Our direct response is, primarily, one of grief: but that most immediate of human reactions is, itself, soon framed by cultural ideas and customary emotional responses that may be deeply influenced by religious beliefs or by their absence.

In contemporary western society it is relatively easy for this fact of grief to be blurred by the relative lack of experience of death many have until well into adult life with the result, as John Hick noted some thirty years ago, that 'it is the course of death of our contemporaries that most powerfully brings home to us the fact of our mortality.[18] In the absence of experience it is all too easy for people to seek 'professional' or 'expert' knowledge over death and grief. Even theological knowledge might be counted as such a category, but that would be unfortunate in the sense that bereavement is one of those life experiences that comes with its own impact and character. One cannot receive preparatory tutoring for new experience. Bereavement is a fact of biography that divides a population into those who have or have not encountered it at a particular point in life. Similar things can be said about specific forms of bereavement and, indeed, for other aspects of existence. Experience is also at the heart of theology and of the tradition of Christian churches, not least the experiences of the earliest disciples of what they took to be the resurrection of Jesus, a prime example of the idea of theology as a reflection upon experience after the event.

This way of thinking is reinforced through the experiences that subsequent generations of believers have within their own lives, not only in the context of worship or explicitly religious activity but in life at large. Often there appears to be a degree of congruence between the way in which formal doctrines were generated in the past and the way people experience life today. The sense of God, experienced in life, is proof enough for many of a divine authority fully capable of revealing things to humanity. By contrast, philosophical and sociological

---

[16] Pro-Life: the well-known name of the anti-abortion movement.
[17] Archbishop Michael Fitzgerald commenting on BBC Radio Four's *News at Ten* on the day of the Pope's Funeral – 'A pope of life and a life that goes on through death.'
[18] John Hick (1976: 82).

thought speaks of knowledge as humanly generated and socially constructed as human imagination engages with the world around it in a complex play of meaning-making. On this basis the different religions of the world came into existence under different cultural, geographical and historical constraints and disclose these birth-marks in their conceptions of the world.

To set up the issue of knowledge in this stark fashion of opposition between revelation of the divine mind and the projection of humanly originating ideas is both problematic and yet helpful within this study of death. It is problematic in the sense that it can be taken as an affirmation of a great divide between theology and other forms of human knowledge. One historical response, powerfully present in the philosopher Feuerbach,[19] demands that all theology must be translated into anthropology, on the assumption that no divine revelation exists. But, the distinction can also be helpful if we see the process of 'coming to knowledge' as a feedback between the human drive for meaning and the nature of events that both provoke that drive and furnish information allowing it to take shape in particular ways as John Bowker insistently argued.[20] The now rather dated theological idea of salvation history was one way in which such an interpretation of events, or the bringing of meaning to situations that beset particular individuals and communities, allowed an interaction to emerge. In practice, many theologians still operate on the basis of some kind of reflexive pondering of events to discern their significance, even if that process is restricted to their personal experience.

Faith and hope

Ultimately, however, the dramatically complex way in which human beings gain a sense of meaning in the world is oversimplified, if not rendered banal, by any simple dichotomy between revelation and human meaning-making. It is a faulty model of knowledge. The very nature of faith is such that it brings a wide frame to bear upon life's experience in which issues of human identity, imagination and creativity interplay, all within the multifaceted nature of the world as an arena of human operations. In this book we will not ignore these more pragmatic processes within a pondering of death, in the belief that a firm this-worldly theology of death may be as telling as any traditional other-worldly approach to human destiny in bringing a sense of depth and worthwhileness to life, worship and ethics. Indeed, in many of today's churches and spheres of religious influence a major subject of discussion concerns the way in which traditional ideas of received wisdom should relate to contemporary social, psychological and scientific insights.

Here much care is needed over the very mode of speaking, over a certain tone of faith, that which proclaims and exhorts as it describes and reflects upon itself. Karl Rahner's closing paragraphs *On the Theology of Death* offers a classic

---

[19] Ludwig Feuerbach ([1841] 1957).
[20] John Bowker, (1973, 1978).

example. It concludes: 'And just as, amidst the weakness and misery of men, the Spirit, through his own victorious strength, provides that man's cowardly laziness should not extinguish the Spirit in the Church, he also provides that in the Church, again and again death is that terrible and blessed event, in which glorious testimony is borne that man freely believes and by such an act of total freedom in faith, enters by grace into the infinite freedom of God.'[21] While such a passage provides a sense of power through testimony and a fellowship in life amongst believers its tone is not the only, and often not the prime, tone that rings through reflections on death.

Nowhere, perhaps, is this emotional charge upon ideas as obvious as when we speak of 'hope', or of its negative partner, 'despair', in relation to many aspects of life and death. Indeed, the whole of this book is, in a sense, a study of the dynamics of hope in relation to human identity. Hope expresses a belief in the meaningfulness of life. In terms of formal disciplines 'hope' is enormously suggestive as an arena within which the sociology of 'meaning', the psychology of identity, and the theology of salvation meet. In essence 'hope' is a bridge phenomenon in the classic sociological problem of the relationship between individual and society. Nowhere is it more germane than in matters of death, that fundamental challenge to society itself, and in the capacity to turn the grief stricken towards life.

When writing his *Sociology of Protestantism* Roger Mehl cited Berdyaev's view that 'The organization of society is an objectivization of human existence and an oppression of the human person.' He cited this both to acknowledge that what is true for society at large is true of the church as a formal institution and in order to replace 'oppression' by 'to make a community live'.[22] This element of 'objectivization of human existence' was, of course, at the heart of Schleiermacher's theological view that ideas of God were, in effect, forms of human self-reflection.[23] This became a recurrent theme in the sociology of religion, widely known from Berger's sociology of knowledge, but less familiar in Georg Simmel's important style of sociology in which existentialism was married with a form of Christian theology to yield a distinctive socially rooted mode of human self-reflection. Victoria Lee Erickson aptly described this: 'Society is the product of human movement towards its Being.'[24] It is just that 'movement towards its Being' that can be exemplified in the dialectic between life-style and death-style. It is worked out both in how we ponder issues in a rational way and come to see their merit through our forms of life. In so doing Christians, and those curious about the faith, find themselves caught up in great traditions from the past, in the pressing influences of our own day and age, and in the personal biographies where we seek to make sense of our lives and live them as we may.

---

[21] Karl Rahner (1972: 119).
[22] Roger Mehl (1970: 144).
[23] Schleiermacher, F. ([1864] 1975: 86).
[24] Victoria Lee Erikson (2001: 112).

Chapter 2

Corpse, Coffin and Cross

The whole of life can be described as a movement into 'being'. For Christians this progression is deeply influenced both by a tradition rooted in a sense of life as a shared venture of faith and by innovative creativity amongst believers and people at large. All of this is a deeply embodied process, indeed the very notion of embodiment lies at the heart of this life-style of faith and of its consequential death-style. To speak of embodiment is to stress the place of the human body as the medium in and through which various kinds of experience are acquired and come to be 'known'. To emphasize 'embodiment theory' is also to ensure that established forms of logical, rational and philosophical thought of an abstract nature are firmly complemented by the fact that we are bodies much influenced by emotional dynamics of life. While contemporary interest in embodiment in a wide variety of academic disciplines[1] is valuable it is, in many ways, secondary to the long-standing Christian theological preoccupation with the human body[2] and with the church conceived of as a corporate body of believers, both perspectives grounded in the deepest interest in the body of Jesus. The fact that Jesus died and that subsequent believers have identified with his death just as they have identified with his resurrection makes this whole topic one of inescapable importance.

Depth of embodiment

One reason why embodiment as a theoretical perspective is important for theology is because it complements or offsets the unduly abstract and philosophical nature of much theological debate. The philosophy of religion and the systematic theology that it often undergirds demands some caution for the issue of 'belief' has as much to do with feeling states as with 'thought'. Indeed a major value of embodiment theory can be to show us that we often 'think' through our senses. The example of smell, perhaps, might be instructive to show how body-based 'knowledge' may be teased out from 'rational' forms of knowledge. To engage in such teasing must, of course, be taken as something we do for the sake of argument, fully aware that in the practice of life, all kinds of knowing work together in profound intimacy. But, for the sake of argument, let smell pinpoint the power of experience and lead us into a consideration of death in the form of dead bodies.

[1] Malcolm MacLachlan (2004). For an interdisciplinary spectrum of embodiment theory.
[2] Carolyn Walker Bynam (1995). For extensive treatment of Christian body and bodies.

Sensing life and death

Smell is one of the most basic human forms of knowing the world. It involves a dramatic intimacy between the material molecules of things and our brains as the olfactory nerves conduct messages from the very 'stuff' of the environment to our brain. In terms of experience, to smell a smell is to be taken back to some previous situation in an instant recall of memory. The smell is an end in itself: it 'means' our experience of a person, place and time. If it is our first smell of that smell it becomes a momentary resource in memory now awaiting future recall. For most people it is practically impossible to 'recall' a smell in its absence, unlike recalling a face. We need the smell to have the smell 'in mind'. Reinforcing this point, most cultures of the world do not have names for smells in the same way that they have names for colours or for most other 'things'. Smells are 'like' or 'of' a particular object, place or event yet, the power of a particular smell is not denatured by its not possessing a name of its own: its power lies in our embodied memory of it.

This case of smell is valuable when considering the kind of knowledge aligned with death or, more particularly, with how we 'know' the dead. Here we encounter two major issues, the first concerns the desire to remember a deceased person as he or she was 'in life' and the second to recall them as a corpse. To wish to remember someone as their former, living self can be to wish to avoid the ultimate fact of their death. It is a wish not to know them as a corpse and, in some contexts, not to enter into the bitterness of life that such memories can provide. With the very roots of our own sense of self set in the past our embodied knowledge of others provides a substantial portion of our own sense of self. Our memories of being with them, of having done so many things together; our sense of their touch, look, voice, smell and the very ways in which they moved are compounded within our own constitution. All these are memories of a living person and because it is that person we most often wish to carry with us into the future it is perfectly understandable that many might not wish these living pictures of memory to be overlaid by pictures of the same person when dead. And this is increasingly likely to be true in a culture where death is largely marginalized.

But what of those 'pictures of the dead'? Here it is worth drawing a distinction between those who have just died and those who have been dead for days. This is an important distinction as far as embodiment is concerned because of the different pictures they can present to memory and because of the way in which different religious traditions keep or rapidly dispose of their dead. In Jewish and Islamic traditions, for example, the dead are buried very rapidly, preferably within twenty-four hours of their death, a custom that most of these groups wish to maintain even amidst dominant cultures that retain their dead for longer periods before a funeral. And the same applies to Hindus and Sikhs in their preference for cremation. The picture presented by the very recently dead can be one that still closely resembles the former, living, individual. It is relatively easy to speak of them as 'asleep', or of 'being at peace' or 'at rest', especially if their death was preceded by much pain and illness. Certainly, the one distinguishing feature of the dead is that they are very still, do not move and, in that, are radically different from their living mode characterized above all else by movement.

After some time, however, the onset of the marks of death appears as the corpse is distanced from its former state of life. Death becomes a more obviously active presence. Now it is not so easy to say that the 'person' looks asleep: they look dead unless funeral directors engage in particularly extensive cosmetic activity as in parts of the USA where the dead are made to look very 'life-like'. To the fact of looks can be added that of touch. The very recently dead are, for example, unlike the longer dead in terms of how they feel to the touch. The idiom of being as 'cold as death' is a telling expression of human experience contrasting, as it does, with the 'warmth of life'. To whichever of these cases we refer the issue of embodied knowledge is important. The way the dead 'feel' to us is reflected in how we feel towards them in later days. Perhaps such issues should not be entirely ignored in biblical exegesis as, for example, in John's Gospel and its albeit difficult to translate verse when Jesus is depicted as asking Mary Magdalene not to touch or, perhaps, not to hold on to him, in his transitional state of 'not yet ascending.' [3]

For many people these 'touching' experiences become part of that wider memory of the dead in a positive and more rounded sense of the past but, for some, that picture and sense of the dead can present an ongoing negative memory, one swallowing or overshadowing the memory of the living person. These difficult issues embrace[4] complex questions of relationships and personalities and are enough to give pause for thought when encouraging or discouraging other family members to 'view the dead'. That very phrase, involving the rather impersonal verb of 'to view', will often not do justice to what is really involved for people in a viewing that may help bring a period of human relationship to a fruitful pivot for some people but, for others, a painful focus of future memory.

In theological terms a great deal is involved in all this. The fact of a cold corpse can, more directly than any verbal description in a powerful sermon, assert a variety of ideas. For some, it asserts the belief that death involves a bitterness and a firm, clear end of a person, for others it is stark proof that the soul has departed. Indeed, the very deadness of the body demonstrates the power of the belief in a soul as an animating energy, once present but now in some other realm. Seldom can the power of a presence so denote the power of an absence. Such a view of death is, itself, a potentially significant source of belief in an afterlife domain of a heaven.[5] It is no accident that theologians, as with Calvin in the Reformed tradition, have explicitly noted the tendency of the ordinary believer to opt for ideas of the immortal soul and abandon belief in the resurrection of the body. In other words, he takes seriously the practical knowledge of people that the dead simply rot and are not likely to be resurrected.[6] Against that, Calvin wished faithful Gospel ministers to advance the biblical belief in resurrection as did later church leaders including Archbishop William Temple from a more systematic

---

[3] John 20: 17. Cf. C. K. Barrett ([1955] 1975: 470). R. Bultmann ([1964] 1971: 687).

[4] It is not accidental that such 'sensory' verbs as 'touching', 'embracing', 'holding', 'grasping' etc. are used for forms of knowledge and attitude.

[5] E. B. Tylor ([1871] 1958). Rooted religion's origin in 'animism' and a theory of souls.

[6] John Calvin (Institutes, III. XXV. III).

philosophical standpoint, and Tom Wright, Bishop of Durham, from an emphasis upon a biblical-historical theology.[7]

Reversed symbols

My earlier question of how a smell and a corpse might be similar was intended to highlight the immediacy of experience, an immediacy that now faces us in relation to the theological affirmation of resurrection. Belief in the resurrection of the Christian dead involves, dramatically, a hope against hope. Here two key elements of our discussion reinforce each other, viz., the contradictory sense of death as the end of everything and of the corpse as a soul-deserted body. On the first count, much traditional Christian emphasis upon belief in the resurrection accepts the deeply negative experience of the corpse as the end only to confront it with the assertion that, in God's good time, that earthy emptiness will be transformed into a new and divinely planned body. In hope against hope, with joy in the face of despair, the impossible is believed.

This, at least, is one matrix of faith, one context that allows the lineaments of one form of faith to be manifest. It is precisely because of our experience of the harsh negativity of life ending in death, in the reality of a corpse, that we believe we will 'rise to the life immortal'. The theological importance of this affirmation would not be as powerful as it is if the corpse was taken to be a deserted-shell. Indeed, this is the very reason why numerous scholars, not least those of the New Testament, argue forcefully for a doctrine of the resurrection, interpreted as a divine act of recreation, and argue against beliefs in an immortal soul. To believe in an immortal soul, in the sense of some 'stuff' that carries the identity of a person, is to sidestep the terminal sting of death's ravage upon the body. For some, as with Wright, it is the very existence of New Testament texts of encounters with a post-death Jesus that serves as a foundational element of Christian faith rooted in the 'revolutionary doctrine' of the resurrection.[8] In terms of human psychology there is also some sense in which hope – itself the fundamental emotional basis for survival and flourishing – takes shape upon the hopeless. Here hope is not a risk factor in which the evidence suggests that perhaps I may win a prize in a draw. Hope is light that takes its nature above the deepest darkness: it is not born out of shades of grey.

So it is that the doctrine of the resurrection involves a focused reversal of symbols. The corpse will, somehow, be the basis for a transformed individual for the person that it was will live again. To bury someone in 'sure and certain hope of the resurrection' is to set one's understanding of life on a fascinating complexity. It affirms the reality of God as both creator and redeemer, as one in whose overarching providence the events of life transpire and whose re-creatively redemptive powers will bring about a state that we cannot even imagine. Of all this the corpse is the symbol. It brings to the discussion its own cold value to challenge whatever

---

[7] William Temple (1935: 461), Tom Wright, (2003).
[8] Tom Wright (2003: 138).

may be said in hope. In a wider framework it gains its symbolic power from the corpse of Christ.

One of several reasons why the theology of the cross is of paramount importance is because it embraces the corpse as the physical outcome of the life of Jesus. Here I use the phrase 'theology of the cross' in a general way, albeit embracing the Protestant sense of the phrase with its emphasis on the glory of Christ revealed in his passion and salvation-achieving death. His death through crucifixion highlights the body that has died and which is taken down with its 'descent from the cross', depicted by so many artists, recognizing that the body has its limits within the material realm in which human beings live their life. It is also the recognition of suffering in life and of its moral and immoral components. Jesus is the one who embraces the experience of all. Human life is so mixed, there have been so many deaths and different kinds of death. Doubtless, there have been deaths involving more pain, much longer suffering, even greater indignity than even crucifixion but that is not the point. The death of Jesus stands as the death of all deaths, it is the prime symbol of all deaths, totally participating in what it represents. It is death as the end of life that comes to focus in his death. His descent from the cross is a mark of that greater descent of life into death. It is not a movement of life and certainly not of deliverance and salvation, as Mark's Gospel makes clear in the voice of those who call to the crucified Jesus to 'come down' from the cross and save himself.[9] His death is representative death; it is the obvious example to us that we will all die. In this aspect of his death there is no point in trying to make it out to be the most painful or the most degrading or the most significant: it is a death that draws the believer's attention to focus on death itself. Its own particularity marks the particularity of everyone else's death, its symbolic power lies in the fact that each death is particular. Though few have been crucified all die. That descent from the cross has also, however, been used in Christian tradition to evoke the sense of pain, loss and wondering over destiny present in Mary as she receives her son's body.[10]

Coffin to the Cross

There is, here, a depth of reflection that bears pondering, whether privately for one's own mortality, or publicly for congregational use. The great symbols of the faith came to exist because they fostered faith and flourish when that fostering remains.[11] It is with that in mind that I pause to highlight one issue that some might find worth dwelling upon, to accept or reject or simply to find a prompt for wider reflection. I pinpoint it because it occurs in a document specifically aimed at funeral officiants by the British Churches Group on Funerals. In its brief *Guidelines for Best Practice of Clergy at Funerals* it begins its short section on Liturgy with the terse assertions: 'A funeral is a religious ceremony. A coffin is

---

[9] Mk 15. 30–32.

[10] Ladislaus Boros ([1973] 1976: 62).

[11] Paul Tillich (1953: 266) spoke of 'dead symbols', obsolete when no longer germane to life experience.

presented to the cross. Human death is set in the context of the worship of God.'[12]

That a funeral is religious goes without saying in its context. Just how 'human death' relates to the context of worship is more interesting and relates, for example, to liturgical contexts of baptism, marriage and the Eucharist as explored in subsequent chapters. But it is that middle sentence that gives pause for thought: just what does it mean to say that 'a coffin is presented to the cross'? Is it of deep significance or simply vacuous and on what basis might that be decided? Certainly it is an expression worth pondering oneself or indeed, using in a group discussion. Positively speaking, it has all the merits of a symbolic statement that hides as much as it displays, conceals as much as it reveals. Its highly condensed format evokes a sense of many-layered significance. The cross element allows people to bring their own traditional sense of that symbol into play which inevitably unites suffering, death, and the dynamics of sin, forgiveness and love. It activates their own experience of the cross from a physical object in architecture, art and personal jewellery to the sign of the cross in liturgy. But what of the 'coffin' element? Here some telling problems arise for, while the intention would seem to use the word to indicate 'death' it is a strange way of doing so in British society. For a symbolic construct to work its constituent parts need to complement each other: they need to be of the same type with like echoing to like in the generation of mutually expanding meaning. It seems to me that this does not quite happen here, instead a kind of jarring occurs. This may be because, in Britain, a 'coffin' is not a full symbol of death. Here, of course, I am on dangerous ground because different people will, quite properly, have interpretations of their own on this matter. Still, it is worth considering as one way into much wider issues of death, faith and cultural influences upon theological exploration. If, then, the expression is not a 'full symbol' could it be a 'partial symbol'? At the risk of creating a rather dubious notion I press this idea of a 'half symbol' because there are phenomena that either begin or end their life as a symbol in this way.

So, what of a coffin? Is it a utilitarian object for holding a corpse or something more? If it is something more, what might that be? Certainly, it is more than a container, a mere box. Its additional value comes from what it contains and why it contains it. On the one hand it holds the valued, respected or loved remains of a relative. Its significance comes from their significance, and that is understandable. It also reflects that relationship as well as the status the deceased held in a family or in society at large. This is well expressed in the popular idea of giving someone 'a good send-off', or of 'giving the best' for the person. This has often been observed and, as often, criticized by those thinking that some people spend too much money on a coffin, especially amongst poorer people for whom it is a significant expense. In the consumerist individualism of the late twentieth and early twenty-first centuries many different kinds of coffins and coffin-decorations are available at a price. Are such highly individualized coffins readily 'presented to the cross'? There is a problem here as the grammar of popular grief engages with the grammar of Christian tradition. This is an issue that will emerge in

[12] Churches' Group (1997: 6).

subsequent chapters in the analysis of what I call the eschatological and the retrospective forms of fulfilment of identity. Here my suggestion is that the more decorated and individualized the coffin the less likely it is that people will want it 'presented to the cross', or the less appropriate will be that symbolic partnership.

I spoke earlier of the 'revealing-concealing' aspect of symbols and this is very appropriate for coffins in both a literal and more metaphorical sense, we will return to it when considering cremated remains in Chapter 8. Throughout the second half of the twentieth century the increasing professional management of the dead in Britain witnessed their removal from the home and the hospital to funeral directors' premises where they might be 'viewed'. Decreasing numbers of people tended to take that opportunity so that the actual dead person became less familiar to more people that was hitherto the case. For those who had so seen their dead it is likely that it is that memory that remains, for a longer or shorter time depending on a multitude of factors. But for others, perhaps less close kin and for most friends, neighbours or workmates, it is the coffin that stands for the deceased person. In this strange sense the coffin conceals whilst also revealing someone. To offer such 'a coffin to the cross' is, perhaps, to give voice to emotions and desires that are equally vague or that at least allow a play of the imagination and memory unconstrained by images of the dead it contains. The very nature of a coffin as the focal form of the material culture of a funeral allows for a wide play of imagination and memory in forms of decoration and as a base for floral decorations when it may become entirely hidden or surfaced by additional symbolic expressions of status and relationship.

Symbolism is always related to pragmatic considerations and this certainly applies to coffins, not least in association with cremation and crematoria as we show in Chapter 8. Though there is the obvious demand for minimal furnishing of coffins and any decorative additions for reasons of incineration and gas output there is another profound aspect of the coffin and the crematorium, that of potential depersonalization of the dead discussed in Chapter 8. In this crematorium context the 'coffin to the cross' motif could offer a powerful contrary message, one that serves to personalize not only the deceased but also all others present in relation to the deceased and to God through the life and death of Jesus and of resurrection life within the church community. This raises the practical question of whether a literal cross exists within a crematorium that could serve as a focus within the rite. If not already contained within the fixed decoration of walls or windows crosses are usually available for temporary use, a factor of real importance in what are, essentially, civic buildings not owned or run by churches and in an era when Hindus, Sikhs or Buddhists and others including Humanists and Pagans use cremation but would not wish the iconography of the cross.

However, more significant for coffin symbolism and its affinity with the cross was the late twentieth century's small but significant development of what has variously been called 'green, woodland or natural' burial in Britain. The issue here is directly with the nature of the coffin and its relation to the body and to the earth. Generally speaking, people desiring a 'green' funeral also think of the corpse as something that is to be returned to the earth through decay rather than kept from the earth in some idealized sense of 'preserving' the body from decay through expensive coffins or, in the classic American context of brick-lined graves with hermetically sealed caskets containing embalmed corpses. The 'green' coffin is likely to be made of relatively easily decaying organic material. The theological tendency, where it exists, is likely to relate more to the earth than to the cross as such. On a doctrinal spectrum the issues involves in woodland burial are more likely to engage the doctrine of creation than of salvation and to envisage salvation in terms of the natural processes of life and death. In such a context to 'offer the coffin to the cross' prompts inappropriate symbolic imagery. Or so it might seem at first glance for, in most Protestant theological thought the theology of the cross has focused on Jesus as a sacrificed Saviour. The sacrificial language, with its deep roots in Old Testament ideas of animal sacrifice and, possibly, of messianic and suffering servant motifs, combined with New Testament elaboration of these themes as focused in Christology tended to eliminate wider theological ideas associated with the cross.

Different from the intention and ethos of the strong atonement base underlying the theology of the cross there is another approach possible whose foundations lie in early Christian thinking and its developments in association with the much wider religious symbolism of the tree of life. Here there are various traditions that identify the cross as the tree of salvation, and locate Christ's place of crucifixion with the site of Adam's death. Artists have often portrayed Adam's skull, the outcome of his sinful disobedience, at the foot of the cross, the site of the second Adam's redemptive triumph. In an extensive cavalcade of comparative symbolism the cross now becomes the tree of eternal life, reminiscent of the tree depicted in the Book of Revelation as being in 'the paradise of God' whose fruit would feed the faithful and whose leaves were for 'the healing of the nations'. [13] Early Christianity also spoke of new converts as neophytes or the new-planted, horticultural motifs whose life-affirmation is obvious. This apocalyptic Jewish-Christian tradition, with its own background in middle-eastern paradise-garden symbolism has a parallel in neo-pagan ideas that have included the motif of the 'green man'. This wide sphere of reference could facilitate a sense in which the 'coffin to the cross' motif could engender much new meaning.

Israelite elements

What of ancient Israel as a major root of Jewish-Christianity? It seems to originate with ideas of the dead having a very shadow-like existence in some afterworld that did not commend itself to the living. In other words the main emphasis fell upon this life, upon the need for obedience to God and divine commandments with the result that God would bless me and my heritage. The prime focus was upon the individual as a family member, as a kinsman and clansman. The promise to Abraham was not that he should have an immortal life in some heaven but that his children should be as the sand upon the seashore in number. To live a long life, with many children and much cattle was the goal of a blessed life.

---

[13] Rev 21. 7. and 22. 2, both echoing Ezek 47. 12.

To these pastoralists, and to the urban dwellers who followed them and developed the temple cult of Israel the prime focus was this-worldly success including the flourishing of families through their offspring. It was also upon a single deity who was to stand over all others and receive human worship. Here it is worth pondering something of the dynamics of afterlife and this-life beliefs in relation to a deity. Let me do so through an interesting assertion of Girard in his *Violence and the Sacred* where he argues that:

> In certain cultures the gods are either absent or insignificant. In such cases Ancestors, or the dead, take the place of the missing divinities and are seen as the founders, guardians and, if need be, disrupters of the cultural order.[14]

His suggestion is that an opposition is likely to occur between belief in a god and in ancestors. The mutual relationship between the two will vary depending upon the emphasis placed upon each. Great emphasis on a god, little upon ancestors: little emphasis upon a god, great upon ancestors. Here we are dealing with the economy of relationships between the living and supernatural power. Here, too, we are also dealing with the relative identity of the living in relation to supernatural powers. Ancestor cultures tend to subsume the individual in group responsibility and to diminish individual responsibility. They would tend not to accentuate individualism. God cultures, I speculate, develop individual responsibility and individualism. This is exemplified, perhaps, in the famous text of Ezekiel[15] in which he denies the idea that people are punished for their ancestors' sins rather than for their own.

So it was that, in ancient Israel ancestors, the founding fathers, were important but were not to be worshipped. There is no ancestor cult it would seem yet perhaps the commands against calling up the dead were, in fact, an expression of opposition to any such thing. Any ancestor cult would, necessarily, detract from a focused monotheism and whatever else the prophets of Israel wanted it was just such a monotheism. In accordance with that it does not seem foolish to speculate that any attitude towards the ancestors that might have tended to worship, would also have been opposed.[16]

Some believe that it was the Babylonian captivity of the sixth century BCE and the deep encounter with Hellenism in the second century BCE that affected much change on these ideas, introducing ideas of a personal judgement after death along with a resurrection. Certainly, a variety of resurrection ideas developed in the two centuries preceding Christ and, as David Catchpole expressed it, 'A single systematic scheme is just not forthcoming, and to look for one is to ask for the impossible. That way lies nothing but confusion and frustration.'[17] He unites Jewish and Hellenistic elements with an eye to different political times and

---

[14] Rene, Girard (1977: 254).
[15] Ezek. 18.
[16] Joseph Blenkinsopp ([1995] 2004: 175–191). Mary Douglas (2000: 4, 98, 106–7).
[17] David Catchpole (2002: 141).

social classes. As for the Jewish base, he begins with the notion of resurrection and the bones from decayed bodies collected in an ossuary. These would be the basis for a future resurrection and a life on this earth. What is more, this resurrection was grounded in the political-national belief that resurrection vindicated the righteous dead in the form of martyrs and was related to the life experience of 'disenfranchised classes'.[18] Indeed it was the very violated bodies of martyrs, especially during the 'Seleucid persecutions in the 160s BCE', that fostered the idea of their this-worldly resurrection.[19] The notion of the immortality of the soul, by contrast, he assumes, entered into Jewish thought through high class Hellenistic reflection 'unrelated to the painful theological and personal challenge of the martyrdom of faithful loyalists'. With time and in changing social-political circumstances these combined in the new Christian community. From the second century BCE, too, the rise of mystery religions also reinforced ideas of a soul and its personal afterlife.

Evidence for the difference between Sadducees who did not accept resurrection and the Pharisees who did is clear in the gospels. Other evidence suggesting that Greek ideas of the soul had also influenced Hebrew thought, as it did early Christianity, comes from Philo (20BCE–50CE.) who devoted much thought to the soul as the prime medium of communication with God. It seems that people believed the soul lingered near the body for some three days after death hoping to reanimate it, until at last it saw that the body began to decay. This may, perhaps, explain why John's account of Jesus and the death of Lazarus involved a three-day wait before visiting the tomb, on the fourth day[20] as Kraemer indicated.[21] This might have echoes in the case of the women seeking to anoint Jesus' body as soon as they could to aid the very process of 'death' and the separation of soul and body. For Jews, certainly shortly after the time of Jesus and probably then too, considered death to involve the departure of some kind of life-force, or spirit that might even remain around the corpse for a while and which should be borne in mind and paid due respect during the practice of mourning. This view, elaborated by Kraemer, might even help explain why the women visited the tomb to anoint Jesus. Kraemer dwells on the traditional view that all Jewish deaths involved a process of atonement for one's sin, a process reckoned to be a painful one for which anointing would help or aid what we might call the 'post-corpse dying person' to cope with his suffering. In Rabbinic texts this even extends to what would appear to Gentiles as counter-intuitive, viz., that it could be a good sign for a dead person to be 'not buried . . . or dragged by an animal' because such experience of disgrace would engender suffering in the 'dead' person, and since 'suffering effects atonement,' it would assist that process for the individual concerned.[22] This potentially significant aspect of what might be called death-dying is seldom considered by Christian theologians for Jesus once he is removed from the cross. For them death is death or else he is deemed alive and

[18] David Catchpole (2002: 141). Quoting G. W. E. Nickelsburg (1972: 95).
[19] John Dominic Crossan (2006: 175).
[20] Jn 11.6.
[21] David Kraemer (2000: 21).
[22] David Kraemer (2000: 98).

with other work to do as some theologians argued, for example, both in the reformation and in nineteenth-century frontier America. As Chapter 5 shows, they debated issues such as that of Christ's 'Descension,' the idea that he went in 'Spirit' to an afterlife world (a pre-resurrection one in Wright's terms) to engage with the departed there. Though that was a lively issue, for example, in sixteenth- century Cambridge it is probably only among groups such as contemporary Mormons that such topics would even be familiar today.

It is certainly wise to consider the Jewish basis of early Christianity in and through biblical and other theological texts as, for example, in Tom Wright's extensive study *The Resurrection*. There he develops the idea of the 'transphysical' to indicate a unique phenomenon of 'transformed physicality' that can neither be described as 'resuscitation nor the abandonment of a physical body.'[23] Wright's 'transphysicality' was 'an event, for which there was no precedent, for which indeed in very precise terms there was no prophecy as such and of which there remained in their day, and remains in our own day, no subsequent example.' This statement of faith, proper for a bishop of the Christian church, naturally engenders an apologetic genre that is not the same as most historical forms of interpretation of the past. He seeks the 'best explanation' of texts as we have them, always alert to the possibility of those who might have wanted an artfully constructed text announcing that Jesus had come to life again.[24] Wright stresses resurrection as 'life *after* "life after death,"' viz., 'a fresh living embodiment *following* a period of death-as-a-state,'[25] and does so, partly, in order that we should not project some contemporary ideas of resurrection back into a historical and cultural context in which some two-fold process rather than a single event occurred. He offers a valuable corrective to the long and rather amateur traditional theological idea that Jews 'believed in resurrection, while Greeks believed in immortality'.[26] The error lying in the assumption that Jews pondered only a body, leaving ideas of souls or spirits to Greeks and other Gentiles.

Wright's is, of course, not the only approach to resurrection, as his own discussions show when treating theologians such as Schillebeeckx.[27] Though differing from the traditional Christian view aptly expressed by Wright's coinage of 'transphysicality' others also have a place as members of the ongoing Christian tradition offering their own sense of the resurrection appearances, empty tomb and dynamic nature of the early Christian sect. Many of these views may benefit from the long-standing anthropological argument of Robert Hertz[28] concerning the two-fold nature of many funeral rites, the one dealing with the decay of the body and demise of a life-focused identity and the other with the dry bone remains as the basis for an other-life focused identity, say as ancestor. I mention this here to reinforce the idea that both life and death, and 'afterlife' too are

---

[23] Tom Wright (2003: 543, 612).
[24] Tom Wright (2003: 723, 718). But see also note 21 p. 694.
[25] Tom Wright (2003: 31).
[26] Tom Wright (2003: 129).
[27] Tom Wright (2003: 703).
[28] Robert Hertz ([1907] 1960).

process-related entities. One is seldom 'born' in one act, nor does one die in 'one act,' nor does one's afterlife occur in one act. These events are, rather, staged in various ways, both socially and psychologically. Hertz argued this at length for the double-burials that involve a stage of decay (whether slow in burial or fast in cremation) followed by rites that give new identity to the dry remains, processes that also allowed for the living to adapt to living without those who had died, or living in a different relationship with them as ancestors. The ossuary burials of Jesus' day would have involved just such a scheme and in its own way the very idea of the empty tomb could be analysed as part of the transition in identity of Jesus in the disciples' minds. Rowan Williams describes it as providing a 'structure of presuppositions within which subsequent experiences could be organized'.[29] He was no longer the earthbound Master but the heavenly Lord, a sentiment and belief behind which a great deal of theological energy would be expended in pursuit of an explanation. In this sense, the empty tomb was the equivalent of an ossuary, it symbolized the new identity of Jesus in relation to which the disciples would now live. To it was to be added the new sense of vitality that turned a core community of loss into a dynamic group set upon expansion. That fact of corporate life would also attract its own theological energy of explanation in terms of the Holy Spirit. The empty tomb and the Holy Spirit marked that absence and presence that brought early Christians to their own sense of themselves as the Body of Christ.

One aspect of both resurrection and soul motifs that ought not to be ignored here concerns psychological aspects of grief and 'visions' of the dead sometimes linked to them. Catchpole, for example, rehearses well-known arguments of people like Lüdemann[30] suggesting that disciples, not least Peter, may have had such a grief- driven sense of a 'risen' Jesus. There is no doubt that today a considerable minority of people in Britain, approximately a third, especially women, gain a sense of the presence of the dead, with some 'seeing' their separated loved ones.[31] This is as close to a normal spectrum of human behaviour as one may find.[32] Catchpole is astute, however, in questioning whether such a grief experience of Peter, for example, would have attracted 'resurrection language' at that time. The degree of fit or kind of affinity between various experiences and the cultural categories available for their explanation is a complex issue and no simple solution should be too easily grasped. Today, for example, some who 'sense' their dead may be quite at a loss to explain it by any readily available belief or doctrine, even if they wished to do so. Indeed the Christian churches are rather poor in providing any such explanation and are far from happy when Spiritualist

---

[29] Rowan Williams (1982: 97).

[30] G. Lüdemann (1994: 97).

[31] Douglas J. Davies and Alistair Shaw (1995: 96), practically a third of a large population survey. Douglas J. Davies (1993) for sensing the dead at the Eucharist by active Anglican churchgoers.

[32] A timeless experience perhaps. 'Pliny the Younger once wrote that that he sometimes felt as if he could still see and hear and touch his deceased mentor Vergilius Rufus'. Byron R. McCane (2002: 131).

Churches describe the passing of people from this world into the world of spirit, a shift quite independent of resurrection motifs.

More definite than such speculation is the recent research suggesting that early Christians followed and shared a largely Jewish pattern of funeral rites and attitudes to the dead for some time. McCane, for example, considers that no real change occurred until the fourth century when instead of burying the dead, who had been identified as ritually impure, outside the range of normal habitation, they were brought into 'an emerging vision of an ideal Christian society', largely in association with the influence of the cult of martyrs.[33] Indeed, the very idea of Christian martyrs, in all its complexity, reveals the extent to which death can be used as a vehicle for doctrine as well as for defining orthodoxy and heresy. [34]

Drawing from texts of the third and fourth century[35] McCane argues that some Christians, especially in Syria, were encouraging other Christians, in Palestine for example, to change their outlook on the 'dead' as 'dead' and therefore ritually impure on the Jewish categorization of things, and to consider the 'corpses of the Christian dead' as harmless 'because they are not really dead' . . . (but are) 'asleep' or 'at rest'. By the fifth and sixth centuries he shows that reliquaries had embedded at the very centre of Christian places of worship in Palestine 'directly under the altar'. Given the political changes that had also transformed Christianity's social status we now find that 'the Christian dead had become, as Greek and Roman dead had been for some time, valued members of the social network.'[36] Their presence as part of the ritual life of the community in which the resurrection of Jesus was celebrated amidst rites of eating and drinking brought Christian identity and commensality to a focus.

Contesting the soul

Just how Christians went on to ponder the identity of the dead in relation to the living is a complex affair not least when comparing different Catholic and Protestant theologians. Catholics asserted the immortality of the soul as a dogma in 1513 at the Fifth Lateran Council. Many Protestants shared that general belief with Calvin, for example, being perfectly happy to speak of the body as an earthen vessel and 'the residence of an immortal spirit'.[37] With time, however, Protestantism came to play down this perspective and to affirm the resurrection of the body as its prime locus of discussing eternal life. The role of Spiritualism in the nineteenth century and its revitalization after the First World War as so many people sought some insight into the post-mortem existence, especially of young dead sons or husbands, reinforced this change of emphasis.

---

[33] Byron R. McCane (2003: 110–112).
[34] Arthur J. Droge (1995: 155–169).
[35] Respectively, the third century *Didascalia Apostolorum* and fourth century *Apostolic Constitutions*.
[36] Byron R. McCane (2003: 121–122).
[37] John Calvin, Institutes (I. XV. 1).

Paul Tillich's Protestant theology, for example, viewed the human desire for 'the immortal substance of the soul' as an understandable response in the face of death but one that was also unfortunate.[38] That was because of his strong existentialist base and desire to see the body as the basis of the self. From a different source of origin, William Temple argued forcefully for belief in the resurrection because he wanted to assert in the strongest possible terms that eternal life was something God gave to people on God's own terms: people did not hold a claim on eternity because they possessed an eternal soul. As he put it, 'Man is not eternal by nature or by right; he is capable of immortality and there is offered to him resurrection from the dead and life eternal if he will receive it from God and on God's terms'.[39] From yet another standpoint, that of the process theology of the 1960s, Norman Pittinger also expressed the thought that 'we cannot be satisfied with the notion that the "soul" is the persisting reality in man'.[40]

The Catholic theologian Yves Congar explicitly marked this difference when he affirmed belief in the immortal soul: 'for the soul is immortal, as appears expressed or implied by Holy Scripture itself, whatever many Protestant writers may too readily assert'.[41] While, from a strong confessional perspective, he affirms that 'faith is faith' and 'stands by itself in its own order . . . without need of props or explanations' he is fully alert to the fact that we all live in cultural contexts whose environments are such as to raise questions about these affirmations. Faith should, as a 'condition of its full honesty' address these and not ascribe blame to those asking. So, for example, he is not worried about the cremated remains of Joan of Arc that were cast into the river Seine, nor of the hundreds of thousands of the incinerated of Hiroshima. He recalls that some theologians see the problem as overcome because the soul itself 'ensures identity to the body', or because the almighty power of God can make it so. But his main emphasis falls upon Thomas Aquinas and the philosophical view that just as the soul 'makes the body, and keeps on making it, borrowing elements from the external world' during life so too in the afterlife. Spelling out his position a little we find that there is no question of bringing together again atoms from the decayed body, not even glorified or transformed atoms. Whatever the material available in that domain of a 'world to come' and not of this world or in any aspect of this cosmos, the soul will have the capacity to make itself as an embodied being, but one with a quality 'transfigured' through resurrection. His acknowledgement of our limitation of thought as to how all this may be is full. Philosophical or scientific means of explaining this statement of faith is beyond us: he says we are not 'deluded into thinking, as the middle ages were in part' that we have the capacity to explain these things.[42] This is precisely where his confessional base is important.

[38] Paul Tillich (1953: 219).

[39] William Temple (1935: 472).

[40] Norman Pittinger (1967: 86).

[41] Yves Congar (1961: 175). He cites, Matt. 10. 28. Phil 1. 21, 23. Heb. 11. 40. And the Apocalypse where, 'From end to end, the elect live on during the continuance of earthly history'.

[42] Yves Congar (1961: 177).

Ladislaus Boros also possesses some insightful confessional views on these issues. He argues for the most intimate of pervasive alliance of soul and body – 'man does not consist of two things. He is one, matter and spirit are indissolubly united in his being.' So much so that 'the moment of death . . . must be regarded as the moment of resurrection'. All this takes place against the background of the 'sin of life', a state of 'wrongness' parts of which we may be aware but parts of which may lie beyond our grasp until the time of death when, perhaps for the first time it may become possible for us to act 'fully as a person' and to 'encounter Christ and decide about his eternal destiny'. Whilst encouraging people not to 'take offence' when he encourages his hearers not to 'cling stubbornly to the idea that the human soul is naturally immortal',[43] he condenses traditional Catholic notions of purgatory, judgement and hell to this point of each individual's death. Death becomes 'our breakthrough to God', all is lost to us with 'only our selflessness' remaining. Purgatory is 'defined as a momentary process of becoming truly ourselves in the deep abyss of death'. At that point of totally honest self-encounter 'we behold Christ himself', and 'this meeting with Christ may be called, quite simply, the judgement'. A dual aspect of Boros' account is of considerable interest for this book as it interprets our knowledge of what we have done in life as having been 'God's impulses', a 'dimension of Christ', and that, 'Nothing else counts at that moment, and nothing prevents man from entering a state of complete joy'. He reinforces this point: 'In the last judgement, all things are put right. How simple things are ultimately if judgement is seen as a message of joy'. This robust theological assertion cuts against the images that the very word 'judgement' has accumulated in the judicial models of ethical religion and through the art depicting punishment. Hell, for Boros, is similarly personal and non-locational, it is not a place: 'it is the everlasting state of a man who has no more and desires no more than himself alone'. It is, above all, Boros' acclamation of joy that characterizes his deeply personal and relational vision of life and death and life eternal, and to it we return in Chapter 5.

Tents, temple and body building

Although almost too obvious to state, whatever else the Christian idea of resurrection is, it is a church-focused doctrine whose significance derives from and, in turn, shapes each particular church community. L. S. Thornton, one of the most thorough yet almost forgotten Anglican theologians of the twentieth century exemplifies this in his *Incarnate Lord*,[44] a study of the Incarnation in the light of evolutionary thought: the two volumes on *The Form of the Servant*[45] are especially insightful. He transformed a biblical theology into a powerful systematic theology fired by the kind of sacramental ideals expected from a member of Mirfield's

---

[43] Ladislaus Boros ([1973] 1976: 49–56).
[44] L. S. Thornton (1928).
[45] L. S. Thornton (1950, 1956).

Community of the Resurrection.[46] He sought to overcome the failure of liberal theology through a church-based resurrection theology grounded in the belief that religion is neither solely the product of its cultural environment, nor something that 'transcends' it but which 'masters it'.[47] His extensive descriptive analysis of the resurrection interplays themes derived from all parts of the Bible in a unitary vision whose richness cannot be conveyed in this sketch. The 'ascending and descending' scales of Genesis creation themes and Paul's resurrection teaching passes into accounts of the 'body-building' and the 'body-garment' analysis in which images of earthly tents and earthly and heavenly temples engage with the dress of Adam and Eve, with Paul's desire to be 'clothed upon', and with the blood-cleansed robes of the heavenly martyrs. Pervading such images is the baptismal union with Christ, of Christ and the church, and of the Holy Spirit in sealing and effecting these creative and progressively developing bonds in what is, essentially, 'the redemption of creation as a whole', all governed by the 'apostolic thesis that in the Christian way of living death is simply a function of life' in which operates the 'Pauline belief . . . in a hidden process going on in the earthly "tent-house" which was vitally connected with the building of the risen body'. [48] Seldom, perhaps, is the Holy Spirit as the Lord and Giver of Life more directly important than in this context.

Imagined eschatology

Far from Thornton's traditional biblical theology with its influence of evolutionary thought is the philosophical theology of John Hick influenced by eastern religious ideas. Noting statistical shifts in afterlife belief in the second half of the twentieth century and seeing it as evidence of the power of personal experience and the influence of 'accredited sciences' that left the afterlife to be 'dismissed as a fantasy of wishful thinking', he described a spectrum of theological response from strong traditionalists who advocated resurrection, judgement, heaven and hell, through moderate traditionalists retaining an afterlife but devoid of hell, to radical theologians embarrassed by eschatology afterlife beliefs.[49] Unhappy with these accounts Hick sets out his own vision of the human future in what is a remarkable and unusual scheme for a philosopher of the Christian religion.

Seeking a global and not a 'one-tradition theology of death' and influenced by his time in India prior to the book's publication in 1976, it was driven by a firm teleological conviction to present 'our life in time as a movement towards a goal'.[50] His global theology adopted a three-fold model of human life, 'body, mind and atman' and explored the changes they required beyond death as the

---

[46] The Community of the Resurrection, founded in 1892 sought to relate belief to modern life.
[47] L. S. Thornton (1950: 1).
[48] L. S. Thornton (1956: 117, 121, 125, 130, 141, respectively).
[49] John Hick (1976: 92–93).
[50] John Hick (1976: 15, 407).

essential 'need or unsatisfactoriness' of the embodied life, marred as it is by various forms of egoism self-evidently preventing most of us from getting anywhere near salvation in this life, is transformed into a 'right relation to . . . Ultimate Reality'. This scheme of change is different from both a heaven-hell afterlife and the reincarnation model in which we experience a 'series of lives, each bounded by something analogous to birth and death, lived in other worlds in spaces other than that in which we now are'.[51]

Hick presents this vision as an 'eschatological speculation' deploying the best of appropriate ideas he has been able to gather from a long analysis of Jewish, Christian, Hindu and Buddhist traditions.[52] Hick comes as a refreshing change for those who wish that theologians affirming an afterlife should actually say something about it rather that simply emphasize its necessity because Jesus rose from the dead. Such biblical inevitability often ends as soon as biblical verses terminate. Not so for Hick. He works from the assumptions that existence does possess a meaning whose sense has to do not only with the moral conditions of individuals in community but also with the meaning of all things and with an ultimate reality. These last points are important for he chooses to 'reject' the Indian perspective of a simple oneness of all things to arrive at a final state of some ultimate community 'which is probably not embodied and probably not in time'.[53] He tellingly adds that the alternative Indian choice, and the one he adopts, resembles the Christian idea of a relation with deity and denies an absorptive unity with the absolute. This leaves him with a relation between all the selves that have been developing through their various worlds and with the possibility that embodiment may no longer be necessary for this to occur. This marks a radical departure from most Christian theology in which the personality of selves is deemed of fundamental importance whether in this life or an afterlife, but he retains the sense that personality is of prime importance for understanding 'selves'.[54]

In evaluation of this approach Hick must be commended for attempting what most ignore, the tremendous challenge of writing about that unknown but important intersection of life with death. Here we have an abstract scheme whose deployment of long-established philosophical notions of self, identity, moral value, the flawed nature of current experience, and the teleological goal of a meaningful reality, produces a clear argument of possibilities. In that he achieves his goal. A critical appraisal might suggest that this account forgets to explain that it is, itself, a form of myth about death, though that might be a slightly unfair description since its philosophical essay-format lacks the narrative form of myth. Hick's philosophical analysis gives the sense of being a demythologized account

---

[51] John Hick (1976: 451, 453, 454, 456).

[52] John Hick (1976: 464). Also pp. 22–34 for his method and for 'para-eschatology' or 'near-eschatology'.

[53] Technically speaking, he prefers the *vishishtadvaita* to the *advaita vendanta* school of thought.

[54] John Hick (1976: 463). See p. 45. 'The myth of the soul expresses a faith in the intrinsic value of the human individual as an end in himself'.

of the afterlife. It is, of course, an attempt at 'a tantalizing mystery' as his very first section clearly states, and it highlights just how humanity, whether in folk-telling myth cultures, theological preaching, or philosophical essays, all engage as best they may with life-death quandaries.

Novel developments

Hick is not alone in offering creative ways of thinking about human destiny. The development of modern technology and information systems, for example, has prompted some to wonder whether the memory capacity of computers might be a model for a human future after death. If all the information that constitutes a self could be transferred to a computer then, *in a sense*, that person could survive the death of his or her body. However, the issue of embodiment and of being 'as a body', rather than as information on embodiment held in a machine would still be questionable, as would the idea that uploading such information on to a computer might constitute a 'resurrection'. Aligned problems have also not passed unnoticed.[55] A more directly Christian version of this 'knowledge' model of self and destiny can be found in the physicist-theologian John Polkinghorne's work which invokes the idea of God as using this person-originating information when recreating new afterlife worlds.[56] When it comes to attitudes to death and potential afterlife existence contemporary studies in cognitive psychology have their own contribution to make, especially when discussing the interplay of fear and hope as key elements in human motivation, and in what one scholar sees as the 'tragedy of cognition' – the human's sense of self-awareness in the face of death.[57] Indeed, there is a great deal of work still to be done in other places on the interplay of such cognitive psychology and anthropology in relation to theological ideas of death and death's conquest. Theology, however, is seldom closer to the human condition than when pondering death. The ancient Jewish laments that integrated 'mourning and rejoicing behaviours'[58] still have their echo in the passion and resurrection of Christ and in the life of Christian believers as they participate in Christ today. The engagement with death is ever complemented by that with life. It is hardly accidental, for example, that Rowan Williams concluded his meditative study of the resurrection not only by expressing a frustration with an element of vagueness over final conclusions over 'what actually happened', but also with an affirmation of his own humanity as 'healed, renewed and restored' spoken in the 'language of worship and active discipleship'.[59]

[55] Herzfeld, Noreen (2002: 192–201) 'Cybernetic Immortality versus Christian Resurrection'.
[56] Polkinghorne, John (1994: 163).
[57] Atran, Scott (2002: 62–79).
[58] Olyan, Samuel M. (2004: 131).
[59] Rowan Williams ([1982] 2002: 110, 112).

Here embodiment comes into its own and reminds us of the complexity of that kind of 'knowing' through our bodies and through what we do compared with the 'knowing' through logical thought. Embodied knowledge is less definite, often blurred and imprecise in propositional terms but often tremendously powerful in effect as it conducts us 'into being'.

Chapter 3

Baptism and Marriage

Christianity is the most death-focused of all major religions because the death of Jesus lies at the heart of its epic gospel narratives and the interpretative theologies of its epistles. These turn the dark reality of death into the promise of life through belief in the resurrection of Jesus from the dead. This dialectic between death and life was taken up and developed theologically in Christianity's key sacraments of baptism and Eucharist, rites that remain challenging in today's world as they present a focused opportunity for pondering ideas of mortality. It is this very conjunction of death with life and of life with death which came to provide a significant part of the symbolic power driving Christianity as a religion touching the heart of human existence.

Ritual forms

This chapter explores baptism but will leave the Eucharist for separate treatment in Chapter 9. However, this present chapter will have a dual focus as we bring marriage alongside baptism as key rites of passage involving many people within society and which reflect significant aspects of the death-life continuum. For, unlike the Eucharist, both baptism and marriage bring sexual and reproductive aspects of human life within a divine order of meaning and significance in quite a distinct fashion.

Rites: of passage, of intensification

From a different perspective, though one that is also technically based, another reason for treating baptism and marriage separate from the Eucharist is because the former are, properly speaking rites of passage, while the latter is a rite of intensification. This useful distinction, derived from social anthropology, has seldom been recognised within theological or liturgical studies, despite the popularity of 'rites of passage' in many theological treatments of ritual. They differ in important ways. Rites of passage deal with events in which people pass from one social status to another with their social identity changing in the process. Following Arnold van Gennep, who first described this scheme of things, people often refer to a threefold process beginning with a separation from the pre-existing status and its patterns of behaviour leading into a period apart. This seclusion involves training in which new ideas, truths, values, perspectives and duties are learned both in a formal and abstract sense but also through body-based rites and new forms of behaviour. The final rite returns initiates to mainstream society albeit with new ideas and educated emotions available for practice in and through the new status that has been conferred upon them and recognised by society at large. Often this threefold scheme is explained in terms of crossing a threshold or, in Latin, a *limen*, with the three elements described as pre-liminal, liminal, and post-liminal phases of change. Van Gennep stressed the social aspect of all this though later anthropologists have brought the actual experience of initiates more into the picture and, as such, have incorporated a psychological dimension to ritual change. Contrasting with the strict emphasis on social status and giving more credit to psychological factors, rites of intensification are not about changes in status but change in state. Beliefs and values that are important to us are brought to sharp focus and our relationship to our beliefs is intensified. Many means help achieve this goal including, singing, chanting, music, silence, special postures, places and clothing, as well as formal instruction.

As it is possible to think of many rituals as events in which we leave behind one 'world', enter into a special place in which the intensification happens and leave again to rejoin the 'ordinary' world, albeit rejoining as an inspired and re-motivated person, it is tempting to speak of such a process as a 'rite of passage'. By avoiding such a temptation and leaving rites of passage for real periods of change of status and not simply of mood we can gain a clearer sense of what different rituals are and of what they aim to achieve in life. It also allows us to see the complexity underlying occasions such as baptism and marriage and can help those with pastoral responsibility for them. While a standard church service of baptism and of marriage is, for example, clearly a rite of passage for the bride and groom, and for all those present who now must come to see the wedding couple in the new light of their new status, it can also be a rite of intensification for those already baptised or married and who can now re-affirm their allegiance to the basic beliefs and values that once they took on themselves and now watch others adopting for the first time. It is as though they are being 'baptised' or 'married' again. Churches do, in fact, provide a variety of ways for the explicit renewal of vows – baptismal, ordination and marriage– without any formal reference to, or perhaps knowledge of, the useful technical notion of rites of intensification. The *Book of Common Prayer*, for example, has a preface to its service for the Publick Baptism of Infants that presses its use on a Sunday or other Holy-days when as many people as possible may be present, not only as a proper way 'to receive' someone 'into the number of Christ's Church' but also so that 'every Man present may be put in remembrance of his own profession made to God in his baptism'.[1]

The great majority of church services involve rites of intensification, a notion that also provides a valuable means of exploring such practices as confession and absolution, recitation of creeds, and the enjoyment of hearing familiar words and concepts in readings, sermons and hymns. Private prayer too follows this pattern of the impressive power of key beliefs to inspire and re-mediate Christian living. Such rites of passage and of intensification are also a means of affirming

---

[1] Present also in the *First and Second Prayer Book(s) of Edward VI* (1549, 1552).

life, they identify the structured aspect of social existence and of the creative possibilities it creates. Leaving the intensification capacity of the Eucharist until later we now consider baptism and marriage as their own form of life-affirmation in relation to the limits and constraints of death, all within Christianity's life-death partnership.

Baptism and marriage have, for centuries, furnished the great majority of ritual in and through which many people engage with Christian belief. They also provide an important background for our consideration of funerary rites in the following chapter. To treat baptism and marriage together is intentional and necessary both because they lie at the heart of the processes that bind together the life-death-life vision of this book, and because they provide the major point of contact between many people and the organizational life of mainstream churches.

Baptism

Baptism may be considered at a variety of levels, as evident in much contemporary liturgical language. Its symbolism includes the death of the 'old' sinful self of the 'flesh', and the birth of a new life grounded in forgiveness and lived in 'the spirit'. As the prime 'water-rite' of Christendom it appropriately embraces Old Testament motifs of Noah's flood, itself one of the most dramatic biblical scenes of destruction, death and the blotting out of life yet also of deliverance of the chosen few, as well as the similar destruction of the captor Egyptians as the captive Jews passed through the Red Sea to their deliverance in the promised land. It also embraces the baptism of Jesus in the River Jordan as an expression of the manifestation of Jesus as the divine Son upon whom came the Holy Spirit in the symbolic form of the dove[2] explicitly aligned with the Holy Spirit in one of the strongest traditions of all the Gospels.[3]

Indeed, properly speaking, baptism needs complementing by the rite of confirmation as one integrated ritual scheme in which the Spirit, the Lord and Giver of Life, is clearly manifest over the negative domains of evil, as once evident in the exorcism integrated into the baptismal rites of early Christianity and followed by many into recent times. The Church of England, for example, included an exorcism in its rather Catholic–Protestant compromise Prayer Book of 1549[4] only to remove it both in the more firmly Protestant book of 1552 and the 1662 *Book of Common Prayer*, where Godparents were, however, still asked whether they forsook the devil and all his works. So, too, with the rite of Confirmation. In 1549 the minister signs the candidate with the sign of the cross and

---

[2] The symbolic layers are capable of wide extension, with the dove, for example, being much involved in the Noah story as the creature bringing the 'freshly plucked olive leaf' back to the ark as a sign that land, and deliverance, was now at hand (Gen 8. 8–12).

[3] Mt 3. 16. Mk 1. 10. Lk 3. 21. Jn 1. 32.

[4] *First Prayer Book* (1549). The rubric has the minister looking upon the children and say: 'I command thee, unclean spirit, in the name of the father, of the son, and of the Holy ghost, that thou come out, and depart from these infants . . . '

lays hands on them in the threefold name of the Trinity while in 1552 'grace' replaces the sign of the cross as the bishop says, 'Defend, O lord, this thy child with they heavenly grace', and asks that the child may continue with God and 'increase in thy holy spirit more and more.' Despite the changes due to theological preferences we find death aligned with evil and the devil in these rites and contrasted with the positive and salvation-focused goal of the ritual action.[5]

In these rites there is a strong sense that ordinary human existence is one thing and a negative a death ridden thing at that, but that it may be transformed or transcended by a spiritual existence. Here we find a primary key to understanding the Christian theology of what might be called 'life, death and life'. For, just as we argued at the beginning of this chapter that Christianity is the most death-focused of major religions so, too, do we find its accentuation on life to be correspondingly great and these come to clear focus in the theological cluster of ideas uniting doctrines of creation and salvation. The creation is filled full of life, in the heavens above, on the earth and in the seas. But this dynamic vivacity is overshadowed and flawed by disobedience, murder and sin in general.[6] A series of covenant opportunities give promise of life amidst this world of death, at first grounded in the promise of many heirs and an increasing progeny and later in a restored world and a resurrection from the dead. With the emergence of Christianity this Jewish sense of life despite death's constraints becomes focused in and through a resurrected Messiah who is to become Lord of a new creation. Accounts of the Jewish based baptism of Jesus at the hands of John the Baptist as a prophetic herald of the Christ validates the baptism of those who would become his followers through and at the hands of his initial disciples. But Jesus was not only baptized, his ongoing life – marked by the divine spirit as it was – became subject to death. And there sin and the great negativities of existence resurged to take his life, sometimes interpreted as a battle with the devil who claimed some right over him, sometimes as a response to a god outraged by his rebellious creatures and variously as a sacrifice in relation to these evils.

Death in the life-giving community

The baptism of Jesus is central as a model for the baptism of believers with the waters representing the grave of his death out of which they 'rise' as they exit the waters of baptism. The new Christian moves from death to life in association with Jesus but with the added power of the Spirit that attends life in the new community of faith. Here the biblical account of the Day of Pentecost,[7] finds its place as a time when the community is granted the outcome of Christ's conquest

---

[5] It is not intended to trace liturgical changes in any detail in this book. The historical Anglican base is used simply to outline broad theological issues and prompt analysis for those familiar with recent liturgical changes in the major denominations.

[6] Gen 3. 14–23. 4. 10. 6. 11–14.

[7] Acts 2: 1–47. Or its Johannine equivalent of Jesus 'breathing' the Spirit on the disciples (Jn 20. 22).

of death. Deaths that now occur in the early Christian community assume a new significance with two standing out and demanding comment, viz. the death of Ananias and Sapphira on the one hand and of Stephen on the other. Ananias and Sapphira enjoy membership among the earliest Christians in a period of success when 'great grace was upon them all.'[8] In this period of spiritual dynamism and a sense of life illuminated by Christ's resurrection this pair seek to deceive the community by selling land and passing off part of the proceeds as the whole of their gain. This deceit is uncovered and their betrayal deemed a lie to the Holy Spirit: on its discovery they each drop dead. A lie against the Lord and giver of life ends in sudden death. This is a kind of double-death since it is death within the life-giving community. In many respects it resembles the spirituality of the Epistle to the Hebrews and its notion that all is lost if once people have 'been enlightened . . . tasted the heavenly gift and have partakers of the Holy Spirit' they then 'commit apostasy'.[9] So much seems to hang on the new experience of death's conquest in and through the Holy Spirit that 'death' now assumes a new meaning.

So it is that the case of the death of Stephen fills a symbolic opposite to that of the deceitful pair. Stephen is chosen as a faithful and dependable servant of the new community in practical ways. Accused of blasphemy within the Jewish context he is brought to trial where he takes opportunity to describe the gospel message in one of the fullest sermons presented in the New Testament. This provokes his hearers who set about stoning him to death. But his death is to be far from ordinary, for 'he, full of the Holy Spirit, gazed into heaven and saw the glory of God'. He proclaims that he can see the 'Son of man standing at the right hand of God' and prays to 'the Lord Jesus' to receive his spirit and not to hold this sin against his oppressors – words highly reminiscent of those of Jesus at his own crucifixion – and then Stephen 'fell asleep'.[10] Often described as the first martyr, that designation framed his death as special and pointed to the transcendent outcome of the death and resurrection of Jesus, itself the basis of the new life in the Spirit experienced by the emergent Christian community. Against such a rich scriptural background, baptismal rites allow for a plurality of symbolic associations of death to life motifs that also include deliverance from captivity as well as birth into this new family of believers which is also the mystical 'body of Christ'. L. S. Thornton's biblical-sacramental theological study, introduced in the previous chapter, is one of the best Anglican theological examples of this theme being worked out.[11] In Baptism death is transformed into life by Spirit as the Holy Trinity frames both death and life. The baptism of Jesus occurs before the Father – the heavenly voice guaranteed it, while the symbolic dove marked the Spirit's presence. That practical Trinitarianism underlies a great deal of theological interpretation of baptism. What is more, the once for all nature of baptism, with its symbolism of dying and rising with Christ, also carries with it

---

[8] Acts 4. 33. 5. 1–11.
[9] Heb 6. 1–8.
[10] Acts 6.5–7.60.
[11] L. S. Thornton (1956. NB. pp. 111–143).

the theme of a constant 'dying' with Christ and 'living in the Spirit'. Here we have the basis for a Christian spirituality to which we return at the close of this chapter. Before that, however, we turn to marriage and to the role of this pattern of human life that provides another basis for 'dying to self' and 'living for others.'

Marriage

To consider marriage within an exploration of the theology of death is to recall that 'death' is ever the death of 'someone' and that 'someone' is a person set amidst relationships, usually family relationships and in this case, of a spouse. Here I take marriage to be the normative form of committed relationship that Christian ethics favours as the context for personal development in the flourishing of man and woman together, embracing sexual relations and the birth and nurture of children. To this must be added the vital social context of marriage as partners and their children relate to wider family, friends, work, education, health and leisure networks. It is this networked world that is affected when a family member dies and turns the abstract topic of 'death' into the concrete world of grief. The fact of bereavement can, of course, be as profound for unmarried partners, single-sex relationships and friendships among single people but, for simplicity's sake I focus here on 'traditional' family forms.

Family

To speak of marriage is to speak of family, terms reflecting the same reality in different ways. Marriage can be both the rite that creates the legal partnership and the state into which they enter to create a 'family' of their own. When such a context provides a meaningful and fruitful life for the partners it becomes an optimum base for fostering meaning in children. It is precisely because emotional and rational forms of meaning may develop in deeply integrated ways within a family that death strikes its members so hard. The loss of a member reverberates in many and often quite different ways for husband, wife, brother, sister, grandmother, grandfather and other relations.[12] The family, as the prime social base for individual grief, is also a prime context for learning to live with and beyond grief. Here traditional liturgical formulae come into their own as they talk about husband and wife committing themselves to each other 'for better for worse, for richer for poorer, in sickness and in health, to love and to cherish, till death us do part'.[13] That final phrase is extremely telling as it brings death to the fore in a rite that is a rite of life and procreation.

[12] Marc Cleiren (1991).
[13] The familiar *Book of Common Prayer* 1662 words in 'The Solemnization of Matrimony.'

Double fertility

One reason why death is so poignant within families is because that group of parents, children and siblings forms the prime site of that 'double fertility' of reproduction and personal flourishing. Here there is considerable complexity at work. Death and biological fertility, for example, are symbolic opposites within life, forces that contend and oppose each other, with each gaining in power the closer they are juxtaposed. In contemporary Britain this is very obvious when a family suffers the loss of a new-born baby or a young child. But the personal flourishing aspect of 'double fertility' must also not be ignored in such a context where the personal hopes and longings of mother and father, as well as grandparents and friends may become enshrined within the baby, even as a foetus before it is born, and can be dashed so mercilessly if it dies just then. For some, biological infertility can also be a kind of prevention of a flourishing of the self that involves a kind of secondary shadow of a deathly kind. While the flourishing of a society depends upon its breeding population to reproduce sustainable communities, the quality of life within those communities depends to a large degree upon the personal flourishing of its individual members. And that is precisely where the place of nurture, trust and love amongst family members enters the human scene.

Commitment scenes

Christian social theory is grounded in the idea of society in covenant with God in such a way that individual development within community is conceived of as a process of salvation. Such a grand vision requires concrete expression and in British religious history, it takes the prime form of Monarchy that, in practical terms embraces ideas of a royal family, including the troubles of that family and the deaths it experiences. While this is not the place to analyse royal funerals it is important to think of them as one expression of the life of a family with which many other families may empathize. Just as in soap operas, novels, the lives of celebrities or the Bible, we find here a point for the potential projection of the loves, hopes and fear, and also of the grief that many commoners experience. And it is royal marriage that maintains 'royal family' which, in turn, furnishes the stage for public grief.

The marriage ceremony, which in Catholic traditions is sacramental and in Protestant a more civic legality of pair-bonding blessed in God's name and presence, exemplifies what the anthropologist Rodney Needham described as a 'paradigmatic scene'. Such a scene is an enacted expression of values and emotion that captures the goals and ideals of a society. Such was the marriage of the Prince of Wales to Diana and such was the scene of her funeral. Magazines and shops devoted to wedding dresses provide a niche market all of their own and it is no wonder that marriages of all are increasingly depicted as camera technology advances. Marriage is to family life what the Eucharist is to the community life of sacramental Christian traditions. This is, for example, why a nuptial mass or Eucharist at a wedding, is such a telling event: it combines two paradigmatic scenes in one making more than the sum of the parts.

As for the marriage rite in relation to death it is worth rehearsing the well known expression that has entered into popular culture in the deepest way, viz., the 1662 Prayer Book expression 'till death us do part'. It comes in the affirmation made by each partner to the other as they take each other as husband and wife with an expression summarizing the contrarieties of life whether it be better or worse, richer or poorer, beset by sickness or enjoyed in health. Each promises to 'love and to cherish, till death us do part'. That phrase echoes the earlier question of the priest when asking the partners if they will have each other as spouse 'so long as ye both shall live'?

Interestingly the 1549 English Prayer Book had this phrase as 'til death us departe',[14] as also in the 1552 version 'tyl death us depart'.[15] Whether in departure or in parting and some difference in theological significance could be made over those images, the legal nature of these vows is deeply influential in these time-limited expressions, for once one dies the other is free to marry again: ignoring here all issues of divorce. Aspects of biblical theology express similar thoughts with Jesus responding to questions on the afterlife and the Jewish practice of the levirate by saying there is no marriage in heaven.[16]

In folk-theology as in aspects of pastoral theology, however, there has long been a sense that in the after-world spouses will be reunited. Innumerable memorial stones and texts speak of meeting-again in heaven with a fine pictorial representation in Robert Blair's notable early nineteenth century, *The Grave, A Poem,* whose series of fine engravings included, 'A Family Meeting in Heaven.'[17] Two pairs of small children hug while husband and wife hold each other in a most intimate embrace and two angels hover to frame the happy scene of a reunited family.

From a philosophical perspective some would argue that since heaven entails a fulfilment of life, including a flowering of individual personality before God, it would require an ongoing presence of and relationship with those whose lives had been part of each other on earth. This makes sense when the dominant issues in a particular case include love and that kind of mutual commitment and union that underlies the 'one flesh' motif running from the Genesis epic of Adam and Eve[18] through to Mark's words of Jesus that a man leaves his father and mother and becomes joined to his wife so that 'they are no longer two but one flesh'.[19] Life experiences that include active memories, dreams, visiting graves, prayers for the dead, and the sensation of experiencing the dead after their death, may all conduce to this sense of the departed 'other' as an ongoing part of one's self. But, equally, there are Mark's gospel-based words of Jesus in response to 'the question that really interested the Pharisees (who) wanted to know what the resurrection

---

[14] The *First Prayer-Book of King Edward VI* (1549: 234–35. Sic).

[15] The *Second Prayer-Book of King Edward VI* (1552: 191. Sic).

[16] In the levirate brother married his deceased brother's wife to raise children to the dead man's name (Gen 38. 8. Deut 25. 5. Mk 12. 25).

[17] Robert Blair ([1808] 1813, Plate 11, with engravings by Luigi Schiavonetti (1763–1810), after style of William Blake).

[18] Gen 2. 23.

[19] Mk 10. 8.

would be like',[20] viz., that in the resurrection people 'neither marry nor are given in marriage, but are like angels in heaven'.[21] These have informed a mass of theological opinion including, as David Brown noted, 'Augustine, Aquinas, Luther and Calvin' and that 'it is only in modern times that heaven became thoroughly domesticated': to which he added the gloss, 'and thereby lost its credibility'.[22] For him heaven would not restrict people to the lives they lived on earth, not even to developing them on that same model in heaven. There, rather, all sorts of creative openings would emerge as the ways of infinity lay forever before us to explore and never to exhaust. This is a valuable approach because it begins to press ideas and explore possibilities in contemporary ways that take ideas beyond the potentially static images of a crippling literalism whose city of golden streets and angelic harp-filled air many find unattractive. In criticizing the idea that heaven will not involve an extension of earthly family life it applies an appropriately sharp break to casual thought that heaven will simply 'make everything all right'. Here pastoral theology on the one hand and philosophical theology on the other have a useful opportunity of examining their own and their mutual rationales. The idea that heaven will develop the earthly self will, for some, demand the presence of the earthly spouse since it is the very fact of partnership that has 'made' each partner what they are, indeed, they may even think of themselves as existing as a partnership and not as single people. Here pastoral and philosophical perspectives might cohere on the theme of identity and its heavenly evolution. There are those, however, including many who have been divorced, who would certainly not wish to continue earth-partnerships in heaven as serial divorce and remarriage shows. Such speculation reveals the power of the process of projection of human desire and patterns of thought on to a postulated heaven, a process, David Brown acknowledged and to which we return in Chapter 5.

Betrayal as death

The power of marriage, with all its ideals reflected both in the expense of organizing a 'perfect day' and in liturgical forms, can become inverted as affection becomes bitterness. This sad reality demands some pondering in terms of the reversal of processes of flourishing. In John's Gospel we find a marriage the occasion on which Jesus turns water into wine, a text embedded for centuries in the Anglican marriage service,[23] as was the early Christian idea that Christ is to the Church what a husband is to his wife.[24] The image of water transformed to wine is, perhaps, something of a symbol of man and woman transformed into husband and wife with a bond of love that makes two into one. To read this on the level of a sense of shared identity is to establish a goal of trust and shared living that makes the topic of betrayal as brutal as the theme of loss through death is potentially dehumanising for a life-long partner.

[20] Eduard Schweizer (1970: 247).
[21] Mk 12. 25.
[22] David Brown (1995: 49).
[23] Jn 2. 1–11.
[24] Eph 5. 23–32.

It is precisely such betrayal of marriage bonds leading to divorce that justifies the use of 'bereavement' language for the 'loss' involved. Though the potential for deploying 'bereavement' as a model for many kinds of loss can easily be over-done and weaken the real sense of the word, the very nature of the betrayal of love may justify its use since it describes the disruption of identity that partially denatures a person. The 'loss' of part of a self, that 'dying a little' that naturally shares in the inevitable partings brought by death, may also follow the betrayal of love and make it quite understandable why some partners have felt the need to get rid of their marriage ring in a definite way. Indeed, the whole issue of wedding and engagement rings in relation to divorce and in different ways in relation to ordinary forms of bereavement, is one of interest to Christian pastoral theology. The similarity between private, if not secretive, 'rites' of disposal of such rings or other symbols of relationship and the private disposal of cremated remains of loved ones should not be ignored. The capacity for individuals to be helped express themselves alongside another, or even, to engage in a slightly more formal fashion with the life-changes surrounding them, can be something of interest to pastors in an age when rites are far from defunct.

Loss of a child

But, beyond partner betrayal or death there is another aspect of life that increases the complexity of individual and partner identity, viz., the death of a child. Throughout human history many have not survived childhood, let alone their infancy, with birth also being of potential danger for mothers. The clarity of this proximity of birth and death was reflected in the rite variously called 'the Purification of Women',[25] 'The Thanksgiving of Women after Childbirth'[26] or the 'Churching of Women' included in the various prayer books of the Church of England. In 1549 there is a telling phrase, omitted in subsequent editions but italicized here, where the priest addresses the kneeling mother, stating that

> Forasmuch as it hath pleased almighty god of his goodness to give you safe deliverance, *and your childe baptism*, and hath preserved you in the great danger of childbirth: you shall therefore give hearty thanks unto god and pray.

This address reflects the theme of survival expressed as deliverance, itself a form of salvation in this context and reminds us that death, whether for mother or child, was far from unknown in the sixteenth century as Britain began its move into early modern times. John Hick dwelt on these issues in his far reaching study on death and immortality citing, for example, the fact that as recently as 1870 'the number of people who died in Britain before reaching the age of twenty was

---

[25] The Prayer Book of 1549.
[26] The Prayer Books of 1552 and 1662: 'The Thanksgiving of Women after Childbirth commonly called The Churching of Women'.

equal to approximately 32 per cent of all the children born in the country in that year'. In contrasting that with 1970, when the figure was just under 4 per cent, he pondered the almost inevitable change in attitude towards infant death in recent times, citing a variety of historical figures commenting on their own sense of grief or relative lack of it.[27] Tellingly he also rehearses Philippe Ariès familiar work on childhood to the effect that modern notions of childhood had not developed in medieval Europe because the mortality rate was so high. More recent British statistics show a 'huge fall in infant mortality' over the twentieth century itself so that, for every thousand live births there were approximately eighty four children dying before they reached the age of one in 1921, but only just over five by 2001.[28] These modern statistics also indicate that children born inside marriage show a lower mortality rate than those born outside marriage.[29] Such changes help interpret the rubrics of the early Anglican Prayer Books as they advocated rapid baptism for children on either the Sunday or other holy day immediately after the birth and their legal, printed service provided for emergency baptism not conducted by a priest entitled, 'Of them that be Baptized in Private Houses in Time of Necessity'.[30] Though, for normal circumstances, parents were to be admonished to bring their children to church for baptism and not 'without great cause and necessity' to baptize them in their own home, it was still appreciated that a need existed for 'one of them', obviously a layperson, to name the child and baptize it. If the child survived, it was later to be brought to church where the minister would question the parents as to how it had been baptized and if he decided all was in order he would validate their action: 'certify you, that in this case have done well'.

Here, our intention is not to dwell on those historical features but simply to note the recognition of the dangers surrounding pregnancy and birth in relatively recent times. One aspect of this within the context of marriage concerns the impact of infant mortality on surviving parents and their mutual understanding amidst grief. Recent decades have witnessed an enormous rise in a more public expression of the variety of grief occasioned by children's death that, in previous days, may have been borne in silence or against a public attitude of fortitude. Mutual support groups of many sorts have emerged, books and poems have windowed hidden feeling. And it is to a poem that we turn here to pinpoint the issue of mutual understanding or rather the lack of it, of partners committed to their own grief and only wishing the other could see and feel as they feel themselves.

In his telling essay '*On Grief and Reason*' the Nobel Prize-winner, Joseph Brodsky, pondered tellingly on Robert Frost's poem 'Home Burial'.[31] He viewed

[27] John Hick (1976: 82).

[28] *Social Trends* (2003: 131).

[29] *Social Trends* (2003: 131). Between 1991 and 2001, inside marriage fell from 6.3 to 4.6 per 1000 live births, compared with 8.8 to 6.1 outside marriage.

[30] The title, in modernized English here, from the Prayer Book of 1549, pp. 223–227.

[31] Joseph Brodsky (1997:223–266): Brodsky, Russian poet (1940–1996); Robert Frost, American poet (1874–1963).

Frost as being in pursuit of 'grief and reason', of seeking to reduce the influence of these elements, since they were 'poison to each other', whilst also being 'language's most efficient fuel'. The poem has a narrator who reports on husband and wife. This narrator describes how the husband catches his wife looking from an upstairs window onto their family's funeral plot. 'He saw her from the bottom of the stairs, before she saw him.' He wants to know what she has been looking at, she doesn't want to say that it is the grave mound of the child he has just buried, just before coming in with soil-marked boots – 'Of the fresh earth from your own baby's grave' – and with the spade placed by the door. For she believes he cannot understand what her looking meant to her or what she has seen. She wants to get out of the house, he doesn't want her to go:

He said twice before he knew himself: "Can't a man speak of his own child he's lost?"

'Not you! – Oh, where's my hat? Oh, I don't need it!
I must get out of here, I must get air. –
I don't know rightly whether any man can.'

She can't understand how he could possible dig the grave of his own child: – 'How could you? – his little grave?'

And as for others, she voices the thought that so many have expressed elsewhere:

No, from the time when one is sick to death,
One is alone, and he dies more alone.
Friends make pretence of following to the grave,
But before one is in it, their minds are turned
And making the best of their way back to life
And living people, and things they understand.
But the world's evil. I won't have grief so
If I can change it. Oh, I won't. I won't

The wife and bereaved mother thinks and speaks in grief and of grief and believes that such grief does not admit of the practical talk in her husband's mention of 'Three foggy mornings and one rainy day', and of how long it would take a birch fence to rot. What on earth had that to do with 'what was in the darkened parlor?' Her grief could not tolerate his 'reason'. His 'reason' could not understand her inability to speak with him:

You-oh, you think the talk is all. I must go-
Somewhere out of this house. How can I make you-.

How, indeed, can she make him see, feel and understand as she does? For the narrator it is all too obvious that he does so see and feel but his talk is different from hers.

My words are nearly always an offence.
I don't know how to speak of anything

49

So as to please you. But I might be taught,
I should suppose. I can't say I see how.
A man must partly give up being a man
With womenfolk.

As she opens the door still wider, to leave, his question is still that of reason, 'Where do you mean to go? First tell me that.' His final word and the close of the poem, hints at a shift in mode of communication, perhaps what she desires:

"I'll follow and bring you back by force. I *will*!-".

In this complex, allusive, yet often deeply clear composition the human bond of emotion and of the distress of loss is played out before our eyes. They long to communicate but some form of established habit of relating to each other, expressed here in alignment with gender, serves as a form of double-bind magnetically keeping them apart. The poem touches on that wider human experience of people living intimately and yet, at some level, at a distance from each other, with depths that perhaps are only partly accessible to themselves let alone to their spouse or closest friend and which events such as bereavement throw up as fault lines within togetherness. Many have known this over bereavement and, for not a few, it has contributed to a growing distance and even, divorce. There is something in Frost's lines on minds being turned and people at funerals 'making the best of their way back to life' that is reminiscent of John Betjeman' s poem 'Aldershot Crematorium'[32] with its:

But no-one seems to know quite what to say
(Friends are so altered by the passing years):
'Well, anyhow, it's not so cold today'–
And thus we try to dissipate our fears.

Such fear-stained embarrassment contrasts vividly with his private sense of the cremation event that only the medium of the poem allows him to vent in the lines:

And little puffs of smoke without a sound,
Shows what we loved dissolving in the skies.

Of quite a different nature are those many poems and memorials in which a spouse uses the literary form as one powerful means of pouring out the heart's grief, whether speaking to others or, for example, speaking to the departed one. Here one example will suffice, the rather special and almost entirely unknown case, of Alfred Lambourne, an American, who published a memorial edition of one hundred signed copies for his dead wife and prefaces it thus: 'I attest my signature, inscripture in meo sanguine'[33]; and it really seems so to be, for that

---

[32] John Betjeman (2003: 302).
[33] Alfred Lambourne (1917) 'Inscripture in meo sanguine' : Latin for, 'written in my blood'.

sentence is written in red and in what does appear to be in blood. He not only speaks of his wife who has 'gone and left me to the years, Grief dazed and weak', but also of those experiences familiar to very many:

Yet do I listen as I roam the house,
Thy step I wait to hear upon the stair;
From my dejection startled oft I rouse,
Yet think it was Thy voice, I may not dare.

It has been worth citing these lines to highlight the very fact that poetry allows the depths to surface in ways that many long for at times of loss. It is no accident that very many folk, much like Lambourne removed from the compositional skill of a Frost or Betjeman, write lines of verse or choose poetic couplets of greater or lesser literary merit for use at funerals or in memorials. For there is, at least, a widespread cultural acceptance of poetry as a medium of the heart at times of loss, a medium that can bridge the middle-range of silence and of 'not knowing what to say' even when there is so much to say. The apparently most simple of social customs, like the writing of a label for a wreath, can afford a moment for personalized expression and of deep emotion. Theologically speaking, such lines, rhymes and expressions of personal love are sacramental in their way and, at their best, allow a truth to be spoken that otherwise might lie silent. Their sacramental nature depends, above all else, on their being a channel for the depth of human life to find its communal place. Matter, albeit a label or a back of envelope poem, becomes a means of human grace. The inward moves out towards the inwardness of others present. They are lines that display the power of embodiment.

Laws of the mortal body

We began this chapter by justifying its dual focus on baptism and marriage on the basis that each brought sexual and reproductive aspects of human life within a divine order of meaning and significance. We also promised a return to this theme through a more technical perspective. That we now do through the briefest of descriptions of Richard Hutch's creative work on the place of biography and autobiography in 'the spiritual quest' and, specifically, through his concept of 'the Laws of the Mortal Body' in relation to the 'formation of saintliness'.[34] It is work of deep relevance for death. Hutch is concerned with how human beings cope with life, tell their story of that coping to others, ponder it themselves and with how we may engage with their narratives and relate them to our own. For him 'saintliness' is no formal status awarded on the basis of merit but an evaluation of how we may come to a sense of life and of living it in what he describes as 'a process of *ongoing human sacrifice*'.[35] Here death and our living towards our death is of paramount importance. This, he thinks, can be best interpreted

---

[34] Richard A. Hutch (1997: 87–90).
[35] Richard A. Hutch (1997: 119. Original emphasis).

through two laws of the mortal body which are, first, 'the turnover of generations' and second, 'active biological/gender complementarity'.[36]

First Law: *The turnover of generations*

These deeply- related 'laws' touch the basic needs of human beings and the responses or reactions to those needs. The need underlying 'the turnover of generations' is the need 'to make way for the next generation'. He finds some inspiration from the work of Erik Erikson and his sense of the 'wisdom' that lies in something of a 'detached concern with life itself, in the face of death'. Certainly, it is through a sense of our own body and its purposes that we are moved to reproduce in the first place but there is another need and that is to become aware that the rising generation requires ours to give way to it. Our sense of personal autonomy and the egoism of desiring control of life needs to give way to the knowledge that our own power and position must, perforce, give way to the rising generations because that is precisely the nature of existence. As Hutch sees it 'sexuality is located within mortality' both in reproduction and in cultural replacement of parent by child, but sexuality is also fundamentally expressed in his second law, that of gender complementarity. It is through the 'practical sexuality' of reproduction that the turnover of generations is achieved and through which past and present contribute to the future. In this sense, sex helps generate a social time dimension, it links ancestors and descendents as each particular individual moves through this spectrum of relations in their own life-time: now as a child, a parent, grandparent and ancestor. Coming to terms with natality – the fact of sexuality in producing birth and new generations, and with mortality – the fact of passing out of the living world, involves a process that can be spoken of as a kind of self-sacrifice. To this self-sacrifice we return in the conclusion. Though there is a great deal that could be said about the rest of Hutch's evocative and stimulating study, enough has been said to bring a new perspective to the interplay of baptism and marriage in relation to death. For baptism offers a prime example of Hutch's first law on the turnover of genera-tions, just as marriage typifies his second law of gender complementarity.

There is, still, in some places a popular idea that a birth follows a death in a family. Though, doubtless, some would regard this as a superstitious trifle it expresses the fact of generational turnover as does the more concrete practice of naming children after deceased or elderly relatives. Most infant baptisms, for example, will witness a group of mixed-aged people where grandparents, parents, and mixed-aged children surround the babe in arms. The deep desire of many people to have some sort of baptism, blessing or naming ceremony, or even a party as such, reflects not only the pleasure of a new birth and an addition to the family, but also a deep sense of change in the family's development. This is as close as British society now gets to a formal ceremony for becoming either a parent or a grandparent, with the formal marking of 'God-parents' itself

---

[36] Richard A. Hutch (1997: 88).

providing a valued marker of friendship and trust and also creating a formal relationship to a child for those many in contemporary society who are single or
childless. For all these people baptism reflects natality and its power to mark the
shift of time that older people must accept. And to accept it is to engage in a form
of 'self-sacrifice' and to gain a degree of 'wisdom'.[37]

It is precisely this emergence of a sense of change with time and in relation to
the lives of others that fosters a maturity of character and a degree of 'understanding' of death. Here, too, we find ourselves better able to grasp the significance of
'mid-life crises' or of the desire to 'remain young' and not to 'grow old'. In this
context these represent an unwillingness to accept the mortality at the heart of
the turnover of generations, they deny the 'self-sacrifice' that can help foster the
wisdom of 'saintliness'.

Though that natural sense of change allied with generations is different from
what we are now going to take up with baptismal theology it is not alien to it.
Earlier, when speaking of baptism, we alluded to the fact that whilst baptism is
a single event – a rite of passage, in which the Christian is said to die and rise with
Christ, it is followed by the regular, daily, possibility of dying and rising with
Christ. This may take the formal context of rites of intensification in Eucharistic
participation or other kinds of prayer or of a more personal prayerful minded-
ness. This outlook is itself a dialectical process involving an ongoing 'dying' with
Christ and 'living in the Spirit'. The basis for this patterned Christian spirituality
is very firmly rooted in the synoptic gospel tradition of discipleship with its
injunction of self-denial, taking up one's personal cross and following Christ.[38]
This particular gospel sequence is particularly crucial for it pivots on Peter's confession that Jesus is the Christ and on Peter's rejection of the notion that Jesus
should suffer. It is here that Jesus addresses Peter as 'Satan' because his perception
and desire were contrary to the path Jesus had set before himself. While there is,
almost certainly, a strong eschatological sense driving those gospel passages the
message of the opposition between the motive of saving and losing one's life
remain without it. Hutch's notion of life as an ongoing human sacrifice finds a
natural reflection in the Christian ethical truth that self-seeking preservation
results in destruction whilst self-sacrificial service results in salvation. This notion
of salvation is not rooted in any idea of merit–that one merits 'salvation' because
one has given up certain things – but in the intrinsic consequence of not
living in self-protection. It is the moral dynamic portrayed in the Epistle to the
Philippians with its account of Christ and the love-humility of Spirit participation in which 'Christ Jesus . . . did not count equality with God a thing to be
grasped',[39] but humbled himself as a servant. Such biblical passages and injunc-
tions are often deployed when exhorting the faithful to lives of service and mutual
regard and carry a profound sense in relation to the life and death of all. To know

---

[37] In technical terms this could serve to answer Jean Baudrillard's philosophical assertion that
Christianity, in baptism, 'has done nothing more than . . . to define the *mortal* event of birth',
and that 'life' needs to be 'returned' to death. ([1976] 1993: 132).
[38] Matt 10. 38–39. Mk 8. 31–37. Lk 9. 23–25.
[39] Phil 2. 5–11.

and in some preliminary way, to sense that we will die is to engender an attitude that does not banish that perspective. By dying to the belief that I may save my life I am saved from having to do so. The gospel injunction, however, sets this within a community base and advocates a life lived for others. For it would be close to moral apostasy to seek to develop an attitude of self-loss in the hope of experiencing self-salvation. That would mirror the common view that altruism operates because of a self-satisfaction derived from generosity. Again, Hutch's scheme is helpful in maintaining a balance within this rationale, not least when it is related to his second 'law'.

Second Law : gender complementarity

That second law, concerning gender complementarity brings marriage firmly into the picture of life and death. Its ritual form specifies the need and response of man and woman and builds upon the first law of generational change. It sets the ideal of child-birth and child-rearing into a scheme acknowledging the 'better and worse' aspects of life and the movement towards death as that which will cause one of the partners to depart. For Hutch there is a potential process of wisdom and saint-making inherent in all this, precisely because it involves degrees of self-sacrifice within marriage and within parenthood. The partners vow to give themselves to each other and to 'forsake all others' in the process. Paradoxically, the demands of parenthood may also require that they allow their own children to 'forsake' them in due course as they gain a sense of their own identity and make their way in the world, 'leaving their father and mother' for their own spouse. Here, too, there is an element of parental self-sacrifice. The love of free-dom that would keep some, perhaps an increasing number in early twenty-first century western Europe from marriage can be interpreted as a fear and avoidance of self-sacrifice. The desire for autonomy in an individualist and consumerist society would thus militate against the wisdom-outcome of self-sacrifice. Here the desire for personal control is, fundamentally, antipathetic to ideas of old age and the 'loss of dignity' let alone to ideas of death.

Before leaving Hutch's perspective, at least for the moment, it is worth under-lining the very fact that he spoke of 'laws', for there is a certain oddness in this since we normally expect to find 'laws' of this kind in scientific rather than in philosophical or theological texts. Certainly, we are familiar with laws or commandments in the Bible as also with rules governing social and cultic life in the Old Testament, but his 'laws' are different, for they do enunciate principles of operation of life.

Ritual and style coherence

It is with this very notion of principles in life that we now conclude this chapter, focusing on the theme of what I will call style-coherence, a specific issue emerg-ing from the life-style and death-style relationship, an underlying theme of this book. The ordinary Christian rites of baptism and marriage easily exemplify this idea and indicate how it may also apply to funerals.

Formal ritual offers a complex pattern of behaviour in which conventional beliefs and social values are, as we argued above, intensified. The success or failure of such rites depend upon the degree of assonance or dissonance the participants experience in the ritual process. For people who are deeply involved in church life, for example, we may expect a high degree of assonance between what they believe and the nature of church rites in which they participate. The clergy are likely to be in sympathy with their intentions and they with the clergy. When more peripheral people are involved, as is often the case in mainstream denominations, things may not be so easy. I once wrote of this in terms of dual-purpose rituals in which the officiant and participants saw a rite in different terms.[40] The baptism of a child may, for example, be viewed by a priest in strongly sacramental terms of church membership and Christian identity while the child's relatively unchurched family see it as some kind of family celebration and expression of a general gratitude for having a baby. Such a ritual event can take itself in several directions. The depth of sincerity of the family may be intuited and understood by the priest in such a way that the use of the set ritual form along with informal welcome, asides and any address, serves to evoke a strong positive response, even in respect of theological ideas that may be relatively unfamiliar. By sharp contrast a priest may intrusively assert what he discerns as absent in the family and cause them a degree of unease or even of downright dismay. And there is a spectrum between those stances of a sense of assonance or dissonance between participants and the leaders of a rite. It is precisely here that a person's ordinary life-style may embrace or reject the rites of churches or other institutions.

The role of funeral directors, for example, sets out to empathize with bereaved families and to serve their needs, even if it is sometimes done in a pattern ultimately desired by the professional director. The rise of individualist consumerism within a culture of choice has fostered this attitude. And it is here that life-style and death-style coherence emerges. At the heart of ritual practice lies the experience or lack of experience of what has been called 'flow', of the sense of a unified integration of individual experience and the action of the rite at large.[41] When a person comes to feel at one with the others involved or in accord with the purpose of the event in hand much is achieved. Here lies a sense of satisfaction and of being taken out of oneself, of a degree of transcendence of the mundane with all its fragmentation and torn qualities.

The event of baptism, for example, can embrace the vicissitudes of relationships, conception, pregnancy, birth and adaptation to a child just as marriage focuses innumerable preceding events. The desire of people to have a 'perfect' wedding day is one popular expression of a desire to bring things to a completion. Though the sense of 'flow' is grounded in a psychological capacity for ritual participation it is related to the many social events preceding a rite and anticipated as following it. For flow to contribute to a style-coherence there needs to be a degree of sympathy with the goals of the event rather than an inbuilt antipathy.

---

[40] Douglas J. Davies (2002: 120–123).
[41] Douglas J. Davies (2002: 132–136). The term derives from M. Csikszentmihalyi ([1974] 1991).

Pastoral theology might benefit from attending to such issues as 'flow' and how it conduces to style-coherence and the wellbeing of people. Indeed, the very concept of worship as the deep substance of faith-communities effective within rites of intensification draws precisely from such experience. Occasions that cause dismay in the collision of divergent beliefs and attitudes tend to be destructive rather than creative and that can occur when an officiant engages in theological language that is simply not accepted by those present. A case in point would be the strong liturgical belief in resurrection when most people may think in terms of an immortal soul and not of any kind of resurrection related to the dead body.

It is with that in mind that 'style', as pursued here, should not be interpreted as a superficial and ephemeral preoccupation of marketing gurus promoting brand names but as an aspect of human embodiment, of people within communities. Of course, there are vital concerns of theology and belief involved in all this since some Christian leaders would wish to convert one 'worldly' life-style into another whilst others might seek to align themselves with the style of those they serve and so on. Whichever is the case, the topic of ritual assonance and dissonance cannot be ignored most especially when differing sets of cultural values meet. This is a particular problem of traditional churches in times of social change and, in particular, as far as death rites are concerned since it is here, above all, that church leaders meet non-church people.

Chapter 4

Liturgies, Life and Death

Our life-style challenges our death-style. That coherence of belief and life just discussed is increasingly evident in the way funerals relate to death. People choose hymns, music and readings, some write their own funeral services in 'living wills', cremated remains are disposed of with personal intention allowing the final death-style of the deceased to match his life-style. Just how these styles may cohere is a question that grows by the day as our desire to survive and flourish takes new forms, as social patterns of relationships in families and between clergy and people change, and as new fears emerge to challenge love. In theological terms ideas of creation and salvation have their axes in an ongoing state of realignment as we discover more about the world and about ourselves. The 'revelations' of science and the 'ministry' of medical technology influence our sense of coherence within our life-styles and any anticipation we may have of a style of death. It is here that the very fact of Christian funeral rites, their alliance with other rites of faith and their consequence for ethics furnish a resource hard to surpass.[1]

Theology as resource

The fact of our death and of the deaths of those we know and love occupies a place on the spectrum of reality of our lives that sometimes is invisible and sometimes blinding. Whether in the teenage sense of personal immortality or the flourishing life of a new family or job opportunity, death may often seem a world away while the next moment, as bereavement strikes, the bottom seems to fall out of our life leaving an emptiness hardly worth living at all. As we have seen, for many in our unusual era fewer die young and many are not troubled by death until elderly parents die. Even professionals whose medical or clerical work brings regular encounter with death often find themselves strangely moved when it comes to their own immediate kin. Both in and beyond grief, death remains a factor that enters into our formula of life with Christian theology offering a rare contemporary opportunity to engage with it rather than ignore or repress this demand of mortality. As an exploration of life in relation to God, within ongoing communities of faith, theology is a human resource of considerable worth, when manifest in liturgy its significance increases further still.

---

[1] See Geoffrey Rowell (1977) for a valuable insight into liturgical aspects of burial.

The power of liturgy is closely allied with the way in which we make sense of everyday life, with what we have described as life-style. Indeed, liturgy is the formal expression of how, theologically, we make sense of life, it raises the prime question of coherence and consonance with which we concluded the preceding chapter. Systematic theology, whose strong philosophical tradition easily makes it appear distant from daily life, exists for others when it comes alive in liturgy and helps motivate pastoral action. When Adam is given the task of naming the world the theological brief is written for understanding it. Meaning-making flows from naming as evening and morning framed each day of the Genesis myth and as each morning and evening frames each day of Christian living. Christian identity emerges over time and achieves a sense of reality when the meaning of daily life, liturgy and ethics cohere. There is a flow[2] within existence that sustains a sense of salvation and copes with life's problems by having some means of embracing them. The difference between a coherent and a fractured existence is probably more acute today than ever whether interpreted as a post-modern shift from shared interpretations of the world or approached from economics and the freedom or captivity that wealth and poverty establish. This is, for example, a more important way of approaching what is often called the 'secularization hypothesis' than is any concern over levels of church attendance. For many people life can be viewed as a series of encircling domains of competence within which a degree of control is experienced and comfort gained. Though, for a few, it may be focused within the privacy of their own self-identity for many it is externally based in a family, friendship, work or leisure context. Traditionally, we suppose that in Christian societies the church provided a satisfactory sense of the meaning of life across many of these domains. Yet, in saying this, we are all too aware of millions for whom poverty, war, social and psychological distress make life anything but coherent and for whom a Christian ideal enshrined in ideas like the 'Kingdom of God' or 'Body of Christ' is something to be pursued. The poverty that produces an 'underclass' within a wealthy society also yields a death-style related life-style within which the cheapness of life is set against its worth – often controlled by the strange notion of 'respect'.[3]

Life focus

Just how and where to discuss life and death in a much divided world is one significant issue in many contemporary contexts. Clergy and leaders of funerals occupy one of the few available though fragile platforms where 'the meaning of life' can be approached at all in a public fashion. A dramatic increase in the role of family and friends at funerals makes this opportunity all the more public. And through this increasingly open social window there is emerging a focus on life, on its celebration and the place of the dead in the memory of the living. Relatives choose readings and music favoured by the deceased or that express their

[2] As described in the previous chapter.
[3] Richard Sennett (2003).

relationships with them. In much of this the people prompt innovation and lead the church. Just how 'life' appears in these events is what I now consider in the three models of 'life through death', 'life in life' and 'reverence for life'.

Life through death

We begin with 'life through death' as the traditional Christian view that our existence has two components, one in this earthly life and one in some post-mortem state, often conceived of as being 'in heaven', 'in God's presence', 'with Jesus' or the like. The life and resurrection of Jesus serves as its own double component model for believers. Just what this resurrected double-life means, however, is far from known. To discuss it is to become dramatically aware of the way in which particular cultural images feed the very notions of resurrection, eternity, immortality and life after death. Here we find much of Christian doctrine operating in a middle-range of meaning. This allows things to be said that make sense as long as they are not pressed too far. The Resurrection of Jesus, for example, makes sense because the idea of resurrection had emerged within later Old Testament times and by Jesus' day, it was widely held by many Jews that a future day of resurrection would come. Christians believed that such a day had dawned in the specific case of Jesus and that believers would be resurrected at a due date to come. When early Christians wished to press the question of just what such a resurrection would mean for them it prompted Paul to write of the qualitative difference between 'physical' and 'spiritual' bodies in this and in that life, using analogies for the different kinds of flesh present in fish, birds, other animals and man, on the one hand and the different degrees of light shed by sun, moon and stars on the other.[4] For Paul, resurrection made sense as part of an entire Jewish scheme of creation, fall, divine covenant and the enactment of that covenant through a promised Messiah whose resurrection vindicated his life's mission: it also underlay his own conversion experience of Jesus. To press the question of what the heavenly body might be like was to raise a different sort of issue, yet one to which he felt able to respond through the 'physical-spiritual' body classification. A key feature in all this was death, its origin and conquest, but it was hardly concerned with just what those spiritual bodies would do for all eternity. The 'glory' involved in resurrection and in the forthcoming divine kingdom was such an overarching concept that to ask pedantic questions of heavenly existence was inappropriate.

Just what resurrection might mean in different cultures is quite a different issue. For much of Christian history, converts and the societies they engendered have been taught schemes of Jewish-Christian religion. This is not to say that such societies have been transformed into a mirror image of that thought, but they have often produced some amalgam or complementary sense of it as pre-existing beliefs have found an affinity with the incoming gospel message. This is one reason why ideas of an immortal soul have often flourished in alliance

[4] 1 Cor 15. 38–41.

with Christian ideas of resurrected and transformed bodies. Indeed, as we see at several points in this book Christian theologians differ as to their acceptance or rejection of this alliance. This is understandable given that ideas of souls of some kind have been practically universal, often related to ancestor beliefs or to various conceptions of deity. The local culture, as well as the influence of particular religious leaders and thinkers, can never be ignored. Two examples in this chapter will illustrate this, Charles Kingsley and Albert Schweitzer.

When Charles Kingsley, the English social reformer and author of the *Water Babies* and much besides, preached on death to the village congregation of Eversley that he served for much of his adult life, his scope was vast.[5] The week past had witnessed five deaths, 'the death-bell has been tolled in this parish three times, I believe, in one day – a thing which has seldom happened before.' Three had died on Ascension Day, 'the day on which Jesus the Lord of life, the conqueror of death, ascended up on high . . . to send down from the heaven of eternal life the Spirit who is the Giver of life'. 'That', Kingsley added, 'was a strange mixture, death seemingly triumphant over Christ's people on the very day on which life triumphed in Jesus Christ Himself'. How could these things be? He answered this question in a remarkably indirect yet focused fashion and with a style revealing his colloquial grasp of life-questioning. God had created all things and given them all a life of their own. 'This is a deep matter, this; how there is a sort of life in everything, even to the stones under our feet.'[6] God has allocated a place for everything and when in place it lives in its own fashion. When displaced it may be said to die and yet through its death new possibilities emerge. 'Living rock', for example, exists when in the earth, but when displaced it decays, yet through its decay produces soil for the growth of other things.[7] Indeed, 'what is now your bone and flesh, may have been once a rock on some hill-side a hundred miles away'. So it is with people. They have a life that is God-given and 'the moment He withdraws His Spirit, the Spirit of life, from anything, body or soul, then it dies.' And that was how death entered human experience at the beginning, for sin made the human being 'unfit for the Spirit of God'. Thus he interprets Paul's assertion that 'the body is dead because of sin'. Though his logic may not be complete, Kingsley's argument that God's Holy Spirit of life sustains life and that sin frustrates this leads him to interpret the whole of existence for his people, as he calls them, to decide to live according to divine commands so that, in the hereafter they may gain a reward at 'the gate of everlasting life and glory' rather than 'suffer in eternal woe' at the 'gate of everlasting death and misery'. From all this they should see that Christ's ascension transforms one level of existence, through death, into another existence of heavenly life; albeit with the threat of hell as an alternative possibility.

[5] Charles Kingsley [1819–1875], (1886: 18–24).
[6] At about this time E. B. Tylor (1871) whose ideas would help forge the emergent discipline of anthropology, was also pondering ideas of such powers which he termed 'animism'. He preferred 'spiritualism', but it had been adopted by the new 'Spiritualist Church'.
[7] Paul Tillich (1959:128) notes the established 'theological doctrine that God acts in all things according to their special nature . . . in stones according to their organic nature'.

Kingsley died in 1875, few village or even city congregations would hear anything like this today. The shift to a post-modern existence in which many competing explanations of life are on offer can easily challenge that kind of overarching 'sacred canopy'[8] as individuals are given the uneasy privilege of choice within a known explanation of things. This is especially problematic when it comes to death and the ritual of death. One of the arguments of this book is that we interpret death in alignment with how we interpret life, if life possesses a variety of optional meanings so will death. But, those very options have the capacity to reduce the significance of any one of them. It takes an additional sense of commitment to a belief to accept it and live by it when it is an option and not simply a 'given' within a social world.

In this sense funerals are odd. People come to them with different attitudes, unsure of the value of what will be on offer and of how they may respond to it. Certainly, they may share a common sense of a public response to someone's death, but after that much differs. This makes liturgical assertions about life and the afterlife of uncertain value and it brings us to the theme of memorial services and to the category of 'life in life'.

Life in life

A feature of the closing decade of the twentieth and opening years of the twenty-first century concerns shifting attitudes to death and how to think of those that have died, not least in terms of their life in this life and not their life after or life through death. To speak of their 'life in life' is to offer a descriptive explanation of the growing practice of engaging in memorial events of various kinds. Here we take memorial events in two senses. The obvious sense is that of a formal service, held either very soon or some time after death, in which a group of people gather to focus their attention on someone who has died. This may occur in a school or similar institution in sharp response to the accidental, tragic or maliciously caused death of a pupil or pupils, or within a local community, or at a sporting event when thousands mark the memory of a sporting legend. The emphasis varies from shock to sadness to warm regard. The point is that it is a shared response to a death irrespective of the afterlife beliefs of those involved. Interestingly people may display their regard either by silence, deploying the socially available practice of 'a minute's silence' or increasingly, giving applause through handclapping, a response already familiar in respect of celebrities and celebration. Indeed, the difference between silence and applause is itself an interesting example of social change in which life-style and death-style cohere.

The less obvious sense of a memorial event lies in its appearance within or as part of a funeral service. Here, for the sake of emphasis, I will argue that traditional Christian funeral liturgies have not been 'memorial events' and I will explain why. Traditionally, funeral rites have been seen as marking the transition

---

[8] The phrase used in one edition of Peter Berger's (1969) study of religion in terms of the sociology of knowledge and the way meaning is generated in society.

of the deceased person from this earthly life into the future life of the world beyond. Beliefs varied as to just what that world would hold, whether a period of purgation or of a kind of spiritual sleep prior to a final entry into the fuller presence of God or whether an immediate transfer into the divine presence. Nevertheless, the rite would speak of the life, death and resurrection of Jesus and its consequences for the future resurrection of all the dead. God's status as a judge tended to predominate in the language of the rite that, inasmuch as it commented on the life of the dead person, it subsumed it into the ongoing lives of all people in 'the miseries of this sinful world'.[9] That phrase is taken from the Anglican *Book of Common Prayer* whose name for the service – 'The Order for the Burial of the Dead' or a rite 'At the Burial of the Dead' – was indicative of its perspective: the 'dead' is 'dead'. In that order two separate prayers mark a sharp difference struck between the body and soul. The body that is committed to the ground in one prayer whose stress is on its decay – 'earth to earth, ashes to ashes, dust to dust; in sure and certain hope of the Resurrection to eternal life', all through Jesus Christ who shall 'change our vile body, that it may be like unto his glorious body' through his 'mighty working'. Then, after an assertion of the blessedness of those 'which die in the Lord', another prayer addresses God – 'with whom do live the spirits of them that depart hence in the Lord'– and speaks of the 'souls of the faithful' as being 'delivered from the burden of the flesh' to be 'in joy and felicity'.

The element of thanksgiving in that prayer is grounded in the fact that it has pleased God 'to deliver this our brother out of the miseries of this sinful world'. Thanksgiving is more for delivery from a vale of tears than for any joy experienced during life. And this liturgical tradition flourished or at least continued in Britain until the closing decades of the twentieth century. Its rationale was, and for some remains, fine as long as the afterlife was postulated as a pleasure following pain, as long as it was reckoned to constitute life-fulfilment. But that is no longer the case for the vast majority of people in western Europe, and certainly not in Britain for whom this life is the focus of existence. To give a sense of the weight of this shift we return to the traditional Christian scheme underlying the 'life through death' section already dealt with earlier in order to develop and show it in contrast to changing trends. The way I present that scheme is through the notion of the eschatological fulfilment of identity.

Eschatological fulfilment

The phrase 'sure and certain hope of the Resurrection to eternal life through our Lord Jesus Christ' provides the matrix for an eschatological fulfilment of identity. Traditionally, eschatology has related to the four last things of death, judgement, heaven and hell. Here, I pursue the issue more in terms of identity, that of Jesus and of ordinary Christians. Speaking traditionally, there is a sense in which the identity of Jesus of Nazareth itself developed historically as the doctrinal formulation of ideas of the incarnation, passion, death, resurrection, ascension and

[9] As, for example, in the *Book of Common Prayer*, 1662. Burial Service.

heavenly session of Jesus suggest. As the Book of Revelation has it, for example, Jesus comes to share the divine throne as the glorified sacrificial Lamb of God who, with 'the Lord God the Almighty', is the focus of all, replacing any notion or need of either temple or even of sun or moon as sources of light.[10] Other biblical documents present this in terms of God's developing covenant relationship with Israel through a Messiah or a transformed High Priest.[11] The sense of divine purpose at work through history presses into a divine kingdom that is to come, whether on earth or in a heavenly form and in that context Jesus enters into a status that is an end in itself. Such a narrative approach of scripture, grounded in a variety of millenarian visions of world transformation, is very different in style from the doctrinal formulation of Christological ideas within the creedal formulations concerning the Trinity that are more abstract when accounting for the eternal relations of three divine persons within a single godhead.[12] Still, even the creeds present the abstract interrelations of Father, Son and Holy Spirit in a semi-narrative form. Liturgical readings are often, by nature, of a narrative type with, for example, I Corinthians 15 – long established in relation with funeral rites – providing one of the most apt and brief accounts moving from Adam, his sin and death, through to Jesus as the redeeming second Adam, his resurrection and the final consummation of all things in God who will be 'all in all'.

Believers are then brought into alignment with this developing identity of Jesus. They are redeemed by him, are associated with him through their baptism into his death, are sacramentally engaged with his redemptive body and blood in the Eucharist and die in him in order to rise as he was resurrected, thereafter to be transformed into his likeness. As the much used hymn expresses it: 'changed from glory into glory, till in heaven we take our place', until we become 'lost in wonder, love and praise'.[13] That doxological expression of destiny is what I feature in the notion of eschatological identity. Christians fully become themselves only in the vision of God. That eschatological identity embraces within itself both baptism and Eucharist and for the catholic tradition the other sacraments that also foster the life of faith in preparation for the glory that is to be revealed and into which believers enter now in sacramental forms.

Retrospective identity fulfilment

But not all live within that world-view, not even believers. And this is where the issue of memorials in funerals returns to centre stage in what I have called a 'retrospective fulfilment of identity'.[14] One of the most direct expressions of this retrospective form of identity fulfilment is to be found in late twentieth century shifts in practice concerning cremated remains and their use – a topic we retain for more detailed consideration in Chapter 8. Here we ponder other aspects of

---

[10] Rev 1. 17–18. 5. 6. 21. 22–23.

[11] As, respectively, in Romans and Hebrews.

[12] See Byron R. McCane (2003: 133) for differences between 'funerary' and 'apocalyptic' portraits of paradise', differences of context that reflect similar differences in images of Jesus.

[13] Charles Wesley's 'Love divine, all love excelling'.

[14] Douglas J. Davies (2002: 141).

what replaces the idea of a heavenly fulfilment of self, most especially the emphasis upon this life and what it meant to the dead and means to those remaining. Many are brought up with a strong outlook on the future as 'their future' and possessing a strong 'prospective' sense of identity. Plans for education, training, employment and developing relationships, partnerships, marriage and children and the hope that the future may be better than the past occupy many people. As life-expectation lengthens the issue of retirement comes to occupy another prospective phase. The idea of really old age, of potential disability and a phase of decline is not given pride of place and sits uneasily within our 'prospects'.

Once more, the key to interpreting changing attitudes to death lies in these attitudes to life. The prospects for which people live become the focus on which memories are focused when they die: a true reflection of the gospel notion that where the treasure is there will the heart be also. And this is where memorial services in and of themselves, or as a developing core element of funeral services, come into their own. Once more the element of identity and its fulfilment are useful dynamics for understanding changing custom. Within such memorial clusters we find people talking about the family, work, interests, hobbies and other aspects of life of the deceased. Many look back though, perhaps, with some comment on the ongoing influence of the deceased in projects or through living family and friends. The point is that all of this is 'this-world' focused. Apart from any traditional words that a formal liturgy brings to the occasion or which may be present in hymns, the event sets the fulfilment of that person's life in and through what has been done and not in what might happen to him or her in an otherworldly destiny.

The choice of a deceased's person's favourite music or poetry, or the literary choices of the mourners all enhance their past relationships and the role memory will play in their future lives on earth. The use of a popular song such as Frank Sinatra singing 'My Way' typifies this view of a self and the life it led. Ideas of reunion in heaven, once so commonly reflected on grave-monuments, are relatively rare and where they do often occur as on floral tributes, they seem to serve as ciphers of fondness and expressions of a sense of loss than as any doctrinal expression of faith in a divine afterlife.

The rise in popularity of this kind of memorial content for commemorative events or within funerals not only heralds shifts in afterlife beliefs by replacing them, to all intents and purposes, by attitudes to this life, but also suggests the relative ease with which practically all may share in such an event. Irrespective of religious belief, most present can look back at a person's life and find something worth recalling. It is a shared act that induces a sense of singleness of purpose without introducing divisive beliefs. In a post-modern context of mixed religious beliefs and secular outlook this affords a safe ritual space. It is significant that the Church of England made provision for such a service in its *Common Worship* book of 2000 with provision for entrusting and commending the deceased to God.

Eucharistic memory

Within the traditional patterns of Christian worship one form of memory of the dead relates to Eucharistic worship. Though traditions vary and are often contested there is a long practice of praying for the dead and in a ritual sense, engaging with them as part of ongoing liturgy. Though we can pinpoint this theme in the expression 'prayers for the dead' it extends much more widely than formal petitions as the use and presence of the relics of saints and martyrs have evidenced over many centuries, especially in Orthodox and Catholic contexts of the Divine Liturgy and the Mass. The presence of relics under altars from the fourth century marked a sharp divide between Christians and Jews over funeral practice.[15] This developed with customs such as kissing the altar before the Mass coming to symbolize the bond between the living and the dead. The decision of the Second Council of Nicea of AD 787 ensured that no church should be consecrated without possessing a relic and anathematized those who devalued them. The Reformation, however, found death a most fruitful arena for controversy and comprises an entire world of theological claim and counterclaim. The role of Masses for the dead was largely removed as were relics much devaluing the relation between the living and the dead Christian in the process.[16] The Protestant principle of individualism and personal faith in divine work of salvation transformed patterns of popular piety. Anglicanism, as a key example, entertains a history of these issues in liturgical debates and disputes over prayers for the dead. This is evident in contemporary church life and the specific issue of the relation between the living and the dead that may be fostered by liturgical contexts beyond those of the funeral, especially in the Eucharist. Here I draw from the 1990s research of the Rural Church Project[17] which addressed the issue by asking Anglican churchgoers in five English dioceses whether, for example, they gained a sense of the presence of dead loved ones during the Eucharist. The following table shows the percentages of people in different age groups who said they did so experience their dead.

Sense of dead loved one at Eucharist

Age	18–34	35–44	45–54	55–64	65+
%	50	39	31	27	47

Source: Table from Douglas Davies (1990: 28)

If we simply presented the average response of 40 per cent to this question of experience it would, of course, give pause for thought as to the dynamics underlying the silences of many people during worship and the thoughts following the words of leaders as they speak of the dead and of the bereaved. But presenting them by age groups gives a more nuanced sense of those worshipping together. Certainly, it is noteworthy that the two age groups with higher profiles were young adults and those of standard retirement age. That the latter reflects a group that we might expect to have suffered the bereavement of a partner, sibling or

---

[15] Byron R. McCane (2003: 112).

[16] Eamon Duffy (1992).

[17] Douglas J. Davies, Charles Watkins and Michael Winter (1991).

peer in their mutual older age is to be expected but the younger group is, perhaps, surprising and poses important pastoral questions that church leaders might wish to ponder for themselves. The most usual situation is one of the loss of a grandparent, making a deep early impact on individuals that weakens over time and into their middle age until old age brings a new phase of loss of partners and peers. No matter how these results are interpreted for these age groups, together they reveal a large minority of active churchgoers reporting some experience related to their dead in and through their Eucharistic participation. This should not, of course, be surprising since the theme of death underlies the rite with numerous phrases affording opportune prompts to activate personal prayer and the memories that pervade prayer. The formal naming of the recently dead as well as for bereaved relatives in general all provide a potentially powerful trigger.

The sensed dead at large

Other survey questions have explored issues of people having a sense of the presence of their dead at some time after the death at a rate varying from approximately a third to just under half of the population.[18] This includes those who reckon to see the dead, to hear, smell or touch them as well as a more pervasive sense of their presence. The great majority of such experiences occur in the domestic environment and relate to family members rather than strangers. Taken together, domestic and church contexts offer experiences capable of influencing how a person thinks about life and death irrespective of the source of those sensations. In strictly theological terms and the kind of general discourse furnished by mainstream churches, and not only Protestant Churches, such experiences are left doctrinally unfashioned. This is probably one reason why a small but significant minority of people engage with Spiritualist Churches after the death of a relative, especially if the death was of a child or of some other unusual nature. The absence of pastoral talk of the dead leaves open a curiosity and, much more often, also a sense of need to fill a much grieved gap in life's relationships and that is precisely what spiritualist mediums reckon to do. In this connection we ought to stress the practical significance of the experience of people engaging with such mediums and the theoretical importance of the theme of embodiment when interpreting it. There is often an excitement in the air when people voluntarily go to a spiritualist meeting. There is a psychological emotion of need and a readiness not to be disappointed. The tension is a tension between living people into which is brought the 'absent' person whose memory is evoked. In this context it is obvious that people care about the dead and have a clear sense of the 'spirit-world' in which they dwell. The emotions of bereavement and the shared life leading up to it are not downplayed and the group is supportive.

There is wisdom in considering these issues, whether at the Eucharist or in a Spiritualist meeting, rather than leaving them theologically and pastorally blank. Some might wish to adopt an agnostic view and invoke the mysteries of life and human identity while others accept such experiences as psychological processes of memories triggered by customary place and activities but retain a

[18] Douglas J. Davies (1990: 28–29).

pastoral silence over their views. Some will believe in spiritual presences and influence and have their own rationale of the interplay of the living and the dead. Whichever is the case the language of liturgy continues to provide a complementary liturgical role to that of the funeral.

One potentially significant and related issue here picks up the theme of memorial services mentioned above, viz., that the mode of discourse of such memorial events tends to shift the grammar of discourse into the past tense as far as the dead is concerned as well as explicitly developing the theme of memory and ongoing remembrance. This is quite unlike the trend that began to emerge at some point in the 1980s and 1990s when eulogies or addresses at actual funeral services adopted a second person singular address to the deceased person, a practice that gained enormous publicity in the funeral address for Diana, Princess of Wales and the language used by her brother.

Whether in funeral or memorial service or indeed at Spiritualist services, the unifying feature is attention to the dead. Modes of address and the expression of thoughts and feelings hidden or unexpressed for much of life come to the fore. The often rehearsed embarrassed silence over death is broken, albeit for a moment. Since few find that silence creative or helpful in causing the bereaved to flourish it draws attention to the positive value of ongoing rituals like the Eucharist that contain an explicit embracing of the dead in the ongoing narrative of the living. The growth in annual memorial events at churches and at crematoria over the closing three decades of the twentieth century also bear witness to this need in contemporary society. To allow the memory of the dead a formal place in the worship and community life of the living is to grant a form of respect, one that has long been known in terms of filial-piety and the like in many traditional societies where ancestors have an ongoing role in the life of their society.

Reverence for life

That kind of respect for the dead is perhaps but one example of a much wider attitude that has a part to play in a Christian appreciation of human nature and its place in the world, that of 'reverence for life'. This we approach here through two sermons of Albert Schweitzer, one delivered in 1907 and the other in 1919. Between these dates, in 1915 to be precise, he gained an intellectual-emotion insight that some might describe as a revelation and others as a discovery: it is enshrined in the phrase 'reverence for life'. Here we take these sermons as representing two phases of a single engagement with life and death and the meaning of each.

I take Schweitzer as an instructive case not simply because he was amongst the greatest twentieth century theological intellectuals and activists but because of these sermons as a pastoral mode of engaging with Christian destiny.[19] Addressing his Strasbourg congregation almost exactly a century before this chapter was written he spoke familiarly to them of experiences they all had, of thoughts they

[19] Albert Schweitzer ([1907] 1974: 67–76).

all knew concerning an embarrassed silence over death. This silence he saw as a deep injustice wrought upon each other and as something quite wrong within a Christian community, the very place where death is to be conquered rather than allowed to conquer us through our fearful, embarrassed, silence. 'Death', he says, 'reigns outside. It reigns over you.' He becomes very direct and poses the question, 'Does death reign inside you or have you conquered it within and settled your account with it?' We used this question at the very beginning of this book and return to it now because there are few more important questions in the world. It concerns in the deepest fashion the themes of survival, fear and love that underpin this book. It also remains an important philosophical question as Geoffrey Scarre reminds us when contrasting Montaigne's advice to look for death everywhere so as to remove its power to surprise with La Rochefoucauld's direct stratagem of looking elsewhere and thinking of other things as a means of evading what is essentially problematic.[20] This pragmatic view of ignoring death in the hope it might go away is likely to be one increasingly favoured by younger generations in developed societies when not under the influence of formal religious influence to give death a place within their life-view.

Schweitzer describes how it had once been customary to foster a fear of death in order to hold out eternal life as the hopeful alternative. But this was not the victory over death of Christ's kingdom, indeed, its outcome was what Schweitzer so tellingly described as 'numbness, numbness'. A sensation that produced the 'conspiracy of silence' and the pretence that death does not exist. He speaks of relatives as they 'play a comedy' thinking that they benefit a dying person by not telling them of their terminal condition', '. . . they turn to other topics'. His response to this rather pathetic cultural scene of the very early twentieth century is an interesting one. He begins by saying that he 'would rather not speak here on the church's teaching about the death of Jesus or to what extent his death is the victory over death', but rather of 'the direct teaching which his spirit enacts in us . . . if we are serious about it and confident that there really is something of the spirit of Christ in us'. He then expresses his belief that 'in our age the spirit of Christ really overcomes death, the last enemy, by helping us take a calm and natural attitude towards it.'

For him that 'natural contemplation of death' was a comfort because it delivered us from a life that had no end and would simply go on forever, leaving us 'enmeshed in the desires and troubles of this life' with 'envy, hatred and malice' continuing to 'pile up undiminished'. So to contemplate death is necessary 'if we want to grow into really good people'. He goes further to say that 'thinking about death in this way produces true love for life'. It brings us to 'accept each week, each day, as a gift' and it 'creates true, inward freedom from material things'. For him, 'the man who looks death in the face' removes that 'ambition, greed, and love of power' that 'shackle us to this life'. This he takes as an 'inward freedom from life'. But even if all this is achieved he says there remains one fear: 'The fear of being torn from those who need him'. We have referred to this in the previous chapter, now we give Schweitzer's answer to how we should respond when we

[20] Geoffrey Scarre (2007: 79–80).

dare 'to look deeply at each other' and know that we will be 'torn from each other'. In this he answers the question of 'how can death be overcome?' in the words, 'by regarding , in moments of deepest concentration, our lives and those who are part of our lives as though we already had lost them in death, only to receive them back for a little while'.

All this, he fully acknowledges, is not 'the ordinary way of looking at death' but he believes it to be 'the first and foremost mystery of Christ's religion – that those who belong to the Lord in spirit have shared with him in spiritual experience his death and resurrection to a new life'. And it is just such who 'now live in this world as men who are inwardly free from the world by death'. It was just such a sense of freedom, a sense grounded in hope, that characterized one of the most direct discussions of death, faith and attitude to biblical ideas presented by Marxsen who showed how the interpretation of difficult texts could be both rooted in their historical background and appropriated by a twentieth century German New Testament scholar and Christian. He was direct about his own faith, one that varied in intensity from time to time yet echoed the experience of hope which he saw as the most basic theme of earliest Christians.[21]

As with Marxsen, so with Schweitzer whose closing remarks of his sermon turned to immortality. He had omitted to speak of it, he said, because it had been talked of 'too much and too superficially . . . in order to comfort people in the face of death . . . the word has been depreciated'. Immortality believed in for the sake of comfort 'was not immortality'. For him it is the sense of eternal life that rises within us in this life that is far more valuable for it emerges as we live life with death before our eyes and as we 'receive life back bit by bit' and live as though life does not belong to us 'by right' but as bestowed 'as a gift'. 'Such a man believes in eternal life because he already has it, it is his present experience and he already benefits from its peace and joy.' Then and this is an important point given that it is Schweitzer who speaks, he says that this awareness 'cannot be described in words'. That a person 'may not be able to conform his view with the traditional picture of it' but that he 'knows for certain' that 'something within us does not pass away, something goes on living and working wherever the kingdom of the spirit is present'. His parting desire is that the vanquishing of death, the last enemy, might 'come true in us' in the kingdom of Christ: that his hearers should remember that they are 'called upon to save someone or other from this bondage. When the opportunity arises to say a word that might show him the way, don't hesitate'.

Gift and reverence

At the core of Schweitzer's sermon lies the notion of life as gift. This was long before anthropology identified gift-theory as a way of considering human behaviour in relation to human identity and before such gift motifs fed into

---

[21] Willi Marxsen ([1968] 1970: 174–188). One of the most lucid accounts of a once influential textual critic speaking to a general audience on '*The Resurrection of Jesus of Nazareth*', and its import for faith.

more contemporary use of gift as a useful means of theological reflection. One formal expression of this lies in the Doctrine Commission of the Church of England's 1995 Report, *The Mystery of Salvation*, whose counterblast against 'post-modern secular self-fulfilment' lay in a spirituality expressed as being 'fully myself only in receiving myself from God and in giving myself utterly to God'.[22] Utilizing some of these later anthropological concepts[23] we can see in Schweitzer the power of what was, subsequently called the 'inalienable gift'. Unlike the 'alienable' gifts that we use as presents to mark our relationships and to which we are obliged to respond with a return gifts, gifts that all carry some market value, 'inalienable gifts' are those of deep sentimental value, cherished objects or even events or persons that not only bind us together but link us to the prime values and beliefs of our society. These are things we cannot sell or put a value on: but they are the 'gifts' that add or even constitute the depth of life and its significance. In this sense we can speak of the gift of love, of children, of friends and even of life. In this sense, for example, we can speak of blood for transfusion as an inalienable gift of life when given freely. It is not the same as that blood when the donor is paid by the pint. Within Christian life the most obvious and telling case is that of Jesus himself. He whom Christians believe to have been the gift of God's Son and who essentially embodied love is the ultimate 'inalienable' gift. Yet he who, on this way of thinking, lay quite beyond 'market value', was sold for an agreed sum of money. Here, betrayal becomes the most powerful of ideas when aligned with monetary exchange.

It is entirely in line with this approach to gifts that Schweitzer may best be understood. Life is this inalienable gift. It is the depth of our existence, it links us with others in the society that gives us history, language and culture and that bestows an identity upon us. It cannot be bought, which is why the 'purchase' of children, of organs for donation or of sex rings false the note of humanity. But how to participate in the fullness of 'life' when it has death as a termination and when ideas of it haunt our thoughts and intrude from the wings of awareness? That is the very issue Schweitzer addresses as he advocated the serious contemplation of what we are as mortals and of how we dwell with our mortality. To see life not as something we posses by right but as a gift enables us to appropriate it 'bit by bit' and day by day. The liturgical and worshipful alignment of life as gift and Christ as gift offers an incredibly powerful cluster of resource for developing such a Christian ethic of life.

This perspective on life as gift is both complemented and enhanced by Schweitzer's notion of 'reverence for life', a concept that 'came to' him, that dawned upon him as something for which he was seeking as part of his philosophical, theological and ethical engagement with Christian thought. But it did not come until 1915, some eight years after that sermon delivered in Germany.

---

[22] *The Mystery of Salvation*: The Doctrine Commission of the Church of England (1995: 28–36, 120–143).

[23] Marcel Mauss ([1925] 1954), Godbout, Jacques with Alain Caillé ([1992] 1998), Maurice Godelier ([1996] 1999).

Then, at a time when he was pondering the failure of war-ravaged Europe to have developed a truly effective ethic of progress that did not also split itself apart in conflict an idea came to him, it 'flashed upon my mind, unforeseen and unsought, the phrase, "Reverence for Life"'.[24] This was during a 'continual state of mental excitement' when he was also 'already exhausted and disheartened' and had been covering 'sheet after sheet . . . with disconnected sentences'. It was when, on a three-day boat trip up-river in Africa as he made his way to see the sick wife of a friend that 'at the very moment when, at sunset, we were making our way through a herd of hippopotamuses' that 'Reverence for Life' flashed upon his mind. He subsequently set about ordering this insight to explore its life-affirmation, the sense that we need to experience life other than our own and to gain a sense of the sacredness of all life: only then, he says, does man become 'ethical'. 'The ethic of Reverence for Life, therefore, comprehends within itself everything that can be described as love, devotion and sympathy whether in suffering, joy or sorrow'.[25] He added the comment on the 'great mercy' he felt it to be that he was able to work on these thoughts and to 'save life' at his African mission-hospital at this very time when 'others had to be killing'.

Some four years after his 'reverence' insight in Africa he was found preaching again at St Nicolai's Church, Strasbourg: preaching on 'Reverence for Life'. It is 16 February 1919 and Schweitzer has the War in mind, exclaiming that if only we are honest we must admit that 'the Christian ethic has never become a power in the world. It has not sunk deep into the minds of men'. It is as though 'the teaching of Jesus did not exist as if Christian behaviour had no ethical principles at all'.[26] He argues that people need to know and feel that ethics are 'a natural endowment' or part of our 'faculty of reason'. There needs to be a base or foundation on which an ethical life sits with motivating conviction. It must be an ethics that does not regard others as strangers and while love for them, even for enemies, lies at the heart of this ethics it is not that foundational base. That base is reverence for life: intrinsic to this reverence, however, is a 'mystery so inexplicable that the knowledge of the educated and the ignorant is purely relative when contemplating it', viz., life itself. For Schweitzer, 'all knowledge is, in the final analysis, the knowledge of life'.[27] The sheer amazement that the mystery of life provokes brings a sense of context to all apparent 'strangeness between us and other creatures' let alone between human beings. We are all 'awesomely related' and to have insight into this involves 'removal of the alienation, restoration of empathy, compassion, sympathy'. This brings Schweitzer to his own confession: 'I cannot but have reverence for all that is called life. I cannot avoid compassion for everything that is called life'. And central to this is the experience he has had and on which he has come to reflect.

[24] Albert Schweitzer ([1931] 1933: 185).
[25] Albert Schweitzer ([1931] 1933: 188).
[26] Albert Schweitzer ([1919] : 108–117).
[27] Albert Schweitzer ([1919]: 114).

Intensive living

Even this brief sketch of Schweitzer highlights how the sensed awareness of mortality and of life appropriated as a daily gift may combine with a reverence for life to yield a vision of an ethical life rooted within a developing spirituality. In Chapter 7 we will pursue this perspective within a context of ecology and death but now our attention is with its qualitative outcome in terms of life-attitude where many streams of thought combine. We are reminded, for example, of existential philosophers and theologians who have ensured that life-concerns are neither ignored nor swamped by abstract rationalization. Paul Tillich's work and appreciation of Feuerbach and Kierkegaard reflect this as when he pondered the notion of 'passion' in relation to love and life itself: 'The passionately living man knows the true nature of man and life'.[28] Tillich too was influenced by Schweitzer respecting the 'inviolability of life'.[29]

As far as teaching or communicating these attitudes to life are concerned such existentialist theologians know the need of 'special forms of expression' to foster an attitude rather than any simple pedagogic method for the teaching and learning of facts. Deep views of the world are acquired rather than learned, caught more than taught. Here we are reminded of Rowan Williams and 'active discipleship' discussed in Chapter 2 and with the whole impact of an embodied state of life and not simply of intellectual ratiocination. Exemplars are needed and, perhaps, it is no surprise to hear of the Dutch peasant paying to attend an organ recital by Schweitzer as he sought funding for his African mission-hospital: the peasant explained that he came to listen to the man who did something while everyone else 'talked'. The catching of a vision may also be why the sermon rather than seminar may be powerful as the preacher becomes exposed as a creature of God to speak of ultimate things beyond mere self-assertion. The weakness of the self and an acknowledged finitude serve to express the depths of life itself as lived before God, it reflects that aspect of Protestant theology which emphasises the 'Word of God' present in the words of the human preacher. And this has a direct bearing on our view of death, it is what Tillich describes when he says that 'in order to be aware of moving towards death, man must look out over his finite being as a whole; he must in some way be beyond it.'[30] It is in one of his sermons too that Tillich saw prayer as one such means of 'elevating oneself to the eternal' perspective.[31] All this is quite removed from the seminar discussion of death where the speaker is above or in control of his reflection: in such a context the sense of mastery overwhelms the inevitable vulnerability of the person sensing their finitude and mortality. Here again life-style and death-styles interplay.

However, now we are not dealing with mastery but with mortality, with the sense that life is an inalienable gift appropriated day by day within a growing reverence and passion for life. To this vision comes Tillich's notion of 'the time in

---

[28] Paul Tillich (1959: 90).
[29] Henry Clark (1962: 171) Citing a television interview with Tillich.
[30] Paul Tillich (1953: 211).
[31] Paul Tillich (1963: 103).

which we have presence'[32] or 'the eternal now'. It is by gaining it that we are able, he says, 'to enter into the divine rest' expressed in the Epistle to the Hebrews.[33]

These elements of philosophical theology are profoundly important for spirituality and for complementing our embodied experience when pondering hopes for life after death in relation to a quality of eternal life in the here and now. Some Christians will find the emphasis upon talking about faith as a quality of the 'eternal' in the present as a means of avoiding belief in a life after death. They will, perhaps, also want to emphasize the importance of faith and a sense of God's presence today. For these the whole issue of how Christianity may properly be interpreted in different ways is of immediate importance. As one such expressed it:

> 'Once the mighty cosmic drama of the New Testament has been demythologized in our heads, we can allow it to be remythologized in our hearts. We can appreciate the essential meaning of the creeds, the liturgies and the art of the church, through which men of other centuries expressed their hope and trust about the meaning of human existence because we participate in that same existence and may share essentially the same hope and trust'.[34]

That is a direct and intelligible course, it is the narrative path of traditional belief. But there are others for whom the notion of a life after death makes no sense yet are committed as Christians to live in the community of Christ's church and who understand God and the nature of Jesus not in the supernatural terms of time passing into eternity but of eternity as a quality brought to their own time in life. It is life transformation in the face and knowledge of death that is at stake for both of these perspectives.

In connection with this I think it valuable to indicate a strong complementarity between this existential theological view of reverence for life as gift and its sense of presence on the one hand and the social-psychological-medical notion of 'intensive living' on the other. 'Intensive living'[35] is a term with wide application that can apply, for example, to those who are told they have a terminal illness and who decide that, while energy and opportunity remain, they will focus their attention on doing things, meeting people and going places, that seem important and significant for them before they die. It can also apply, for example, to parents who suddenly lose a child, perhaps a teenager or young adult in the full energy of youth who has a sporting accident or a sudden illness. The image of a very successful and professional parent whose life energy has been focused on work and many things suddenly brought up short by a domestic tragedy is far from uncommon. Within a day or a week life seems to change. Its patterns of meaningfulness and significance are dulled or shattered. Then, the person comes to an appreciation of the 'things that matter' in life especially the place of other people,

---

[32] Paul Tillich (1963: 110).

[33] Heb 3. 18–19. 4. 1–11.

[34] Henry Clark (1962: 169). He sees in Schweitzer an 'ongoing Reformation of our day'.

[35] B. G. Glaser and A. L. Strauss (1965: 131).

of human relationships and the power of mutual emotional support. Such a person engages, albeit for only a limited period, in 'intensive living', a phrase to be radically distinguished from a frantic or hectic life-style. Death that has been very much an invisible or background item in other people's lives has now come to the fore and made its effects plain and it has prompted a reaction, one that helps transform the outlook of the bereaved parent.

In some respects such a shift into 'intensive living' is not unlike a religious conversion experience in that it involves a renewed energy and shift of focus of personal identity. In the religious context converts often speak of life taking on a new colour and vibrancy compared with a certain drab repetitiveness of previous existence. Here we are in the domain of creativity and stimulation of imagination and can see human beings experience a new quality of life, albeit one that has been born of grief, anguish and anxiety. Although it is, practically speaking, impossible to compare the quality of experience pursued by the theologians covered above and the social-psychological domain of bereavement I think we are dealing with cognate aspects of life. They involve a person 'coming to themselves' from an unthinking involvement in many things to a focused self-awareness in the light of the knowledge of death.

The ritual practices of many cultures have sought not simply to educate the young in rites of passage from youth to adulthood but to give an opportunity for them to 'sense' the realities of life in order that they may engage with them. Stanner, for example, pursued this interpretation in his work on traditional Australian groups. He spoke of the 'covenant of duality', that sense of the 'refuge and rottenness' that comprises life amidst which we need the succour of others.[36] It is just such a depth of personal insight complemented by communal support that makes life possible and brings to it an insight that lifts us beyond the mundane perception of the everydayness of things. This is precisely where the communal nature of faith provides a resource for individuals.

---

[36] W. E. H. Stanner (1959–60: 264).

Chapter 5

Heaven and Hell

The history of Christian reflection on death has, for its greater part, often dwelt on the themes of heaven and hell as environments of the afterlife, often with deep interest in some transitional stage whether in 'soul sleep', a 'spirit prison', limbo or purgatory. This sense of destiny reflects the human drive to survive combined with a moral sense of human imperfection, the negative domain of Satan, and the moral perfection of the beatific vision of God. Pervading all these thoughts are the emotions of fear and love.

As with many doctrines, changing times shift perception. Geoffrey Rowell[1] explored this for hell in Victorian times and now, as the twenty-first century begins, parts of Christendom still adhere to hell and heaven in ways that reflect earlier literal conceptions, including after-worlds as physical places. Others transform hell and heaven in theological language that either leaves a considerable degree of uncertainty over hell and heaven as 'places' with medieval formats whilst still referring them to a post-mortem 'future' or else talk psychologically and philosophically of states of being present in this life. Indeed, the influential philosophical arguments of Martin Heidegger affirm death as frame and boundary marker that gives life an even more intense colour though, as Vernon White observed, there are feminist writers who see a pre-occupation with death as a male concern and who would prefer an emphasis upon 'birth, life and embodiment here and now'.[2] Certainly there is no uniformity of belief as Colleen McDannell and Bernhard Lang documented in their broad ranging history of heaven.[3]

Here, as much as anywhere within theology, what counts as wisdom is problematic. Certainly, as one world-shaping theologian taught us centuries ago, 'true and substantial wisdom principally consists of two parts, the knowledge of God, and the knowledge of ourselves', though, as he sensible added, it is 'not easy to discover' which precedes and produces the other'.[4] Though we might not agree with Calvin as he went on to rehearse the depressing depravity of our vision of ourselves and therefore of the necessity of pursuing the vision of God, we cannot but be encouraged by his commitment to the intimate connection of the two forms of knowledge and reflect upon the enormous growth in the knowledge of

---

[1] Geoffrey Rowell (1974).
[2] Vernon White (2006: 34).
[3] Colleen McDannell & Bernard Lang ([1988] 2001).
[4] John Calvin, Institutes I.I.I.

ourselves that recent centuries have yielded, knowledge that inevitably influences not only our knowledge of God but also of hell and heaven. The interplay between traditional theological resources and many contemporary insights presents opportunity for 'wisdom' of a profound kind, one that renders redundant any simple conflict between conservative and liberal interpretations that, themselves, often betoken the folly of using doctrinal flags as cover for ecclesiastical politics. For, whichever our preferred interpretation, issues of survival, fear and love are seldom distant from our theological ideas grounded in the lived experience of good and evil howsoever categorized in different traditions. Whatever may be said about the concept of hell it is grounded in the conflict between good and evil experienced by all save, perhaps, sociopaths. Heaven, too, reflects the moral victory of love as experienced in some degree, however small, in people. Unless goodness personified had some impact on us the very idea of it as an ultimate goal would be senseless.

The more we understand the influences upon our ways of thought related to issues of power, authority, gender, sexuality and certainly not forgetting age and the impact of biographical life-experience, the greater our potential for wisdom. We certainly cannot ignore the way ideas of hell and heaven have served many purposes, not least in terms of social control and moral coercion. The very fact that someone could write the following hymn shows that some can be motivated by the opposite sentiments to those expressed.

> My God, I love Thee, not because
> I hope for heaven thereby,
> Nor yet because who love Thee not
> Are lost eternally.[5]

Its expressed reason for loving God was, 'Not from the hope of gaining aught, Not seeking a reward', nor was it 'for the sake of winning heaven, Nor of escaping hell', but simply in response to the divine love manifest in and through the passion of Jesus Christ as he had experienced it. Historically, however, millions were probably motivated more by fear than love, with those claiming sanctions over behaviour that controlled the state of a person in an afterlife standing to gain considerable authority in this world too. Yet, ultimately, ideas of heaven and hell are grounded in the doctrine of salvation driven by belief in divine grace and goodwill. In practical terms Christian piety often appears happier with specific cases than with idealized versions of values, with saints and sinners, Jesus and Satan, rather than with abstract theologized notions of good and evil. And those perceptions have taken very easily to spatial images that appeal to the imagination, creating and answering the language of worship and scripture in the process. To see Satan, for example, not simply as having committed high treason against his Lord and Governor but as being 'in this World like a transported Felon never to return' made great sense in early eighteenth century England.[6]

---

[5] Francis Xavier *Hymns Ancient and Modern*, Translated by E. Caswall, Standard Edition, (1916) No. 106.
[6] *The Political History of the Devil* (no author) (1739: 23), fourth edn, London: Cornhill, Printed for Joseph Fisher .

Such spatial awareness touches our sensory life and our inner grasp of feeling and brings theology into life experience. Spatiality and sensation cohere for, normally, we have experiences in places, contexts embed them in our memory: place and experience cohere in our recall. The existence of Jerusalem as a site of divine promise and of the Kingdom of God excited Jews in the centuries immediately framing the earthly life of Jesus and prompted early and later Christianity to see it as destined for a future transformation. Contemporary Christian Zionism, for example, awaits the Second Coming of Christ and Jerusalem's role in a new world order. More 'heavenly' forms of Jerusalem have also played their part in Christian spirituality of the afterlife as a kingdom into which the dead pass rather than as a kingdom to be revealed in and through the places of the earth. Yet, there is an existential dimension to our knowledge of life that can go beyond any 'place': there is a sense in which 'experience of life' is not like an image. Severe pain, anguish, or grief, for example, provide a world of their own and furnish a sense of disaster befalling individuals such that to describe it as 'hell' seems entirely appropriate, albeit a 'placeless' hell. So, too, with some religious experience that seems as though heaven has been found, albeit for a moment.

For much of Christendom's history both heaven and hell have, together, furnished an alternative domain to that of earth, with human beings often wanting to be other than they are or where they are. But, as moral beings, the sense of good and evil is so great that it has seemed natural to posit a domain in which those qualities, so mixed in earthly life, can appear in their fullness. This is one reason why those perceived as really good or really evil seem out of place on earth. It is no accident that popular thought periodically speaks of dying infants as 'too good for this world' or of wishing wicked people to 'rot in hell'. Indeed, this last phrase now holds something of a particular venom in an age when expletives of a sexual nature or of the divine names are commonplace.

If the Jewish world set God in a heavenly domain, albeit one that might manifest itself in an earth transformed, Christianity as Judaism's offspring reinforced that vision and helped populate it with a risen Messiah, Patriarchs, Saints and the Christian dead. Hymns, creeds and liturgies elaborated that heavenly city and Kingdom of God where righteousness dwells. Believers could aspire to it, glimpsed afar in worship and sought as an afterlife domain. Yet, in twenty-first century Britain the idea of heaven is paradoxical for, while it hardly ever impinges upon life except at times of bereavement it furnishes the frame for a great deal of Christian worship and the doctrine of God. The longing for heaven, typical of periods of earlier Christian spirituality, now seems to hold a low profile and mainstream British churchgoers are hardly ever likely to hear a sermon on heaven: still less one on hell. By sharp contrast, ideas of heaven are dramatically profiled in contemporary eschatological ideas of 'rapture' and 'tribulation', especially in the USA, which argue that some Christians will not die at all but be caught up into the air to meet the returning Christ. This faith perspective, to be explored in Chapter 7, is mentioned here as a sharp contrast to a case from the English Reformation to show how the twenty-first and sixteenth centuries reveal stark differences in their theology of death, perspectives much influenced by social contexts.

Decension

This historical example highlights the theological importance of the afterlife framed by the religious politics pervading the Reformation period in England against a background of intense medieval interest in the dead and their wellbeing in the afterlife. The Protestant onslaught upon the Catholic commitment to ongoing relationships between the living and the dead, evident in many forms of popular piety and ecclesial ritual, did not and perhaps could not ignore the realm of the dead and the afterlife. In a classically Protestant theological turn the issue took an overt Christological rather than ecclesiological direction. If Protestants would not and could not speak of the dead in relation to the church they would speak of them in relation to Jesus. The meaning of Jesus Christ's life, death and resurrection was distinctively crucial for the Protestant understanding of salvation and this came to the fore in relation to 'the dead'. Just as the living needed some faith-grounded encounter with Christ as Saviour, so too with the dead. The form in which this complex issue took shape was in ideas on the creedal assertion that Jesus 'descended into Hell', itself a notion related to a very few biblical texts,[7] but not bypassed on that account nor left without its own complexity of biblical interpretation.[8] One example will suffice, and comes from a public disputation in Cambridge in 1552 between one Richard Carlil and Dr Smith on what was then readily described as the 'Decension' of Christ.[9]

Their debate asked whether 'the souls of the faithful fathers deceased before Christ went immediately to heaven' or had some previous status, and also argued the meaning of 'the Decension of our Saviour Christ into Hell'. Carlil's position was that, at death, faith ensured an immediate ascent into heaven. Even 'Adam. ascended into heaven immediately after his death: for the death of the faithful is the highway to felicity, and faith is the salvation of our souls. (1. Pet. 1.9) . . . His faith made Christ's death as present to him, as though it had been done in deed: for faith apprehendeth things absent (Heb. 11.1).' He added the further biblical proof that there would be no point in names being written in the Lamb's book of life in heaven if actual souls don't get there. For him there was a 'church in heaven' with Christ as its head and, for example, with Abel present in it. Having been slain by his brother Cain, he was there as 'the first martyr'.[10]

Turning to the descent of Christ into some domain of the after-world Dr Smith furnished a vivid account of the way God the Father heard the cries of the souls in limbo and, in response, 'biddeth his Son to gird his sword to his thigh, and like a mighty man of war he went to hell and commanded the princes of hell to open their gates or else he would burst them up.' This Christ did when he

> gave a dangerous assault, entered with a white banner, displayed his red cross upon the walls, and towers, cast down the hell hounds, hunted them

---

[7] 1 Pet 3.19. Eph 4. 9.
[8] For summary see Jaime Clark-Soles (2006: 193–221).
[9] Richard Carlil , debated at 'a Commencement in Cambridge' in 1552, published in 1582.
[10] Richard Carlil (1582: 12).

from post to pillar, bound Satan or Pluto himself with yron fetters and chaynes, and threw him into a deep dungeon, saluted the patriarchs, and prophets, shaked them by their right hands: there was joy without heviness: light without darkness, there they weeped for joy, danced like damosels, there were sweet odours, there were perfumes, musick, symphonie, melody, harps, lutes, shalmes, drums, tabrets, fyfes, whittles, bagpipes, psalters. . . . There he tarried three days and three nights, there the devils romled and roared like lions.

Then a kind of court is set up to try Christ 'who had done a haynous robbery in hell' with Solomon as judge. Jesus is brought in and appoints for his proctor and lawyer Moses who calls twelve witnesses to prove that Jesus did very well in spoiling hell. These include the figures of Adam, Abraham, Isaac, Jacob, David, John Baptist, Aristotle, Virgil and Hippocrates. In opposition to this panorama Carlil sees in it the perverse and modern doctrine of limbo of the Council of Ferrara of 1439 and accuses Smith, 'Are you not ashamed to call free men bound? Patriarchs prisoners, Saints slaves to Satan, citizens of heaven captives? . . . defrauded of the contemplation of the trinity? It is against reason to deprive the faithful of felicity'.[11] For him hell is worth pondering but it is a place 'appointed for vice'. Smith turns on Carlil to argue that, 'If Christ had not suffered in his soul, when he was in hell as great pains as his body did upon the cross, he had not satisfied for the souls but only for the bodies, which he did upon the cross. For the souls, he suffered in hell, or else our souls since Christ should have gone to hell, as well as they before Christ, and have been there afflicted'.[12] This did not meet with Carlil's agreement at all, for him Christ had, in Gethsemane, been 'extremely afflicted when for fear of death he sweat drops in quantity as . . . drops of blood' as well as suffering the pains of crucifixion.

The two devote much more time and argument to their disagreement over the dynamics of the afterworld and Christ's operation within it during the period of his death and resurrection. The variety of belief expressed can also be seen as of wider interest in their day from another work, that of Richard Parkes of Oxford.[13] Addressing his Archbishop of Canterbury he outlined a variety of contemporary opinions that Jesus variously, 'descended into hell while he was yet living upon the cross, . . . descended into hell, and suffered the torments thereof in this world. . . . descended not in person but in power only, . . . descended into hell in body and soul and there suffered torments after his death'. For him, however,

that which Christ performed upon the cross he needed not afterward to go down to hell to perform. (Numbers 24:9). He couched as a young Lyon. He lay down like a Lyon, when hanging upon the cross, he put down principalities and powers and triumphed over them in the tree of his cross. The devil rejoiced when Christ was dead, but by his death he was

---

[11] p. 43.
[12] p. 45.
[13] Richard Parkes ([1604] 1607).

overcome: He took his bait as in a trap, the Cross was the trap, the bait that caught the devil was our Lord's death . . . in the very instant of our Lord's death the souls of the faithful were delivered.[14]

The message of a strong Protestant kind emerges, focused in and on the cross whatever repercussions there may have been in the devil's domain. What even these few theologians show is not only that that death and the after-world remained a significant issue during the English Reformation but that the debates of their day mean very little in ours.[15] Indeed, it is telling that a contemporary and influential scholar, Crossan, has argued that 'somewhere between the Apostles' Creed and the Nicene Creed we lost the harrowing or robbing of hell', and adds that for him that was 'one of the most serious losses from earliest Christian theology, because it clearly emphasized that Jesus' resurrection was about God's justification of the world and not just about the exaltation of Jesus.[16] Perhaps it was the immediate awareness of many kinds of political vindication of Reformation Europe, as well as any sense of loss of death-related ritual, that prompted an affinity with the Decension motif. Certainly it was not an interest that endured. Why such theological concerns rise and fall is always a complex issue as Stroumsa has shown in what he called 'a major paradigmatic shift' from early Christian interests in the descent motif to late antiquity's abandonment of the idea.[17] Amongst the possible factors he adduces for this shift are an 'increased negative attitude to this earth' or 'demonization of the cosmos' matched by a desire for the soul to seek to ascend in escape from it. Or, again, the growing sense that hell was an underground location and thus to be avoided.

Times and seasons

From these various cases, whether of Christ breaking into the spirit-realm or the 'rapture' breaking into this life, we now turn to a current mainstream Christian perspective in Jerry Walls and his extensive discussion of 'Heaven', subtitled, 'The Logic of Eternal Joy.' Following numerous philosophical and ethical debates he argues for a firm Christian belief in heaven as part of a divinely ordered universe within which human life makes sense. Unsurprisingly, he sees 'moral faith' as 'best sustained by a worldview that includes a doctrine of heaven', itself the 'irreplaceable resource in our efforts to give our lives the meaning we crave', and offsetting a 'widespread doubt and anxiety about the very meaning of life' that is 'a distinctly modern and post-modern phenomenon'.[18] Yet, his passing reference to Ecclesiastes and his minor qualification that the ancient world might have had

---

[14] Richard Parkes ([1604] 1607: 185–86).

[15] One exception would be in Mormonism where Christ's work amongst the 'spirits in prison' holds a significant theological position.

[16] John Dominic Crossan (2006: 181).

[17] Guy G. Stroumsa (1997: 147).

[18] Jerry Walls (2002: 167, 185, 174 respectively).

some intimation that what we do may be 'finally meaningless', is hardly adequate to major shifts of human self-understanding whether in the Babylonian Epic of Gilgamesh, in the root and some branches of Buddhism or in Classical thought.[19] He rehearses a variety of current, naturalistic, views that ascribe some purpose and virtue to human life apart from eternity but regards them as inadequate. After fairly extensive engagement with death as a limitation to life's happiness he concludes with the simple question of traditional Christianity as –'to whether we can believe in God'– a Trinitarian deity who makes a meaningful world, inhabits it with creatures made in his own image and whose moral life is made plausible through an image of love as sacrificial reciprocity. All our life's strivings are given ultimate validation in heaven in which we contemplate God forever and with an ever new capacity for happiness: 'To believe in God is to believe happiness is stronger than boredom'.[20] Despite his sharp opposition between belief and unbelief, between traditional Christianity and post-modern fragmentation his pivot of 'happiness' versus 'boredom' strikes a strong post-modern note of self-concern. All it lacks is some reference to 'irony'.

Within western society at large, and in many parts of its Christian leadership, such ideas of heaven are strongly attenuated if not absent. From the seventeenth century onwards belief in heaven as a physical afterlife location declined. Growth in rational forms of engagement with knowledge and religious texts, as well as in a reconfiguration of the history of the earth and human populations saw an end to medieval visions of heaven and hell even if they were transformed into psychological, political and literary visions of more earthly realization. Christian theology not only felt the impact of these changes and contributed to them but did so within religious organizations that now had to negotiate the existence of quite different beliefs within themselves. Many contemporary churches have members who both do and do not hold what might be conceived as traditional beliefs over heaven and hell. This dynamic complexity sometimes becomes problematic when fundamentalists, conservatives, and liberals of various kinds engage in theological politics. The single most complex fact of contemporary Christianity is that it serves at one and the same time as a repository of traditional belief, with myths of ancient Israel combining with Hellenistic thought forms and early Christian sectarian hope of a millennium, all subjected to relatively new critical philosophy, psychology, sociology and natural science. In the light of that the miracle of Christian churches is that they exist at all and not that they lack a unified theology.

Theme of evil

One reason why differences of theological interpretation do not destroy Christianity is because each one seeks to deal with the experienced reality of life including

---

[19] Cicero, *The Nature of the Gods*, (H. C. P. McGregor, ed. 1972: 206–207). 'So no living creature is eternal . . . whatever knows pain must in the end know death'.
[20] Jerry Walls (2002: 197).

the emotional facts of grief, pain, fear and of joy. Here, for a moment, we ponder only the issue of evil and remain with Walls as a traditionalist. Certainly, he and others are correct in acknowledging that no theology of death can possibly ignore the topic of evil, though just how it is dealt with remains crucial. Here, for example, I prefer to speak, quite intentionally, of the 'theme of evil' in preference to the 'problem of evil', precisely because that 'problem' phrase sits too easily within many a Christian theological discussion whose assumptions of an essentially good God have to be reconciled with what certainly appears to humanity to be evil events and circumstances. Most certainly, evil is a problem to millions whose lives are marked by severe pain, suffering and loss of many kinds. This is not to say, however, that the grief of bereavement should be directly and immediately seen as the outcome of evil. Some discrimination is required here as also, for example, in the popular use of 'disaster' or 'tragedy'. To speak of any particular death as the effect of evil or as a tragedy is, obviously, to court ridicule for, sometimes, people find it easy to speak of a particular death as a 'blessing' or as a 'deliverance' from some situation that, itself, might more appropriately be regarded as evil.

While all enduring religions have their own explanation for 'evil' at large, Christian theology makes its way through the maze of pain, trials of life and hazards of existence with an explanation of evil that is far from systematic and, often, far from satisfactory. So much so that the often invoked expression, the 'problem of evil', seems to reflect the dilemmas of the theologian as much as the life-situation of those who suffer.

This phrase, 'the problem of evil' is, I suggest, best viewed as an example of what has been called a 'deutero-truth'.[21] This describes some widely shared notion that gives its community of users a sense that they are all talking about the 'same thing', that a problematic area has been identified and, in a sense, brought under control. In reality, no such ultimate control has been effected only a general working level of agreed reference. It is like the man in the street saying about some great issue, 'they say', when referring to some purported expert opinion. If consulted, that expert is quite likely to express uncertainty or a variety of options: indeed, expertise often lies precisely in the knowledge that opinions vary and that judgement takes precedence over certainty.

Hell

One of the easiest ways of dealing with the theme of evil was in the idea of hell, an ancient concept of a place or state of pained suffering for wrongs committed during life. But that avenue has not remained as traversable as once it was despite the fact that, as it were, in November 2006 the 'Gates of Hell' appeared in London's West End, in the splendid square that serves as an entrance to the British Academy. These 'Gates of Hell' – erected as an architectural exhibit – were artistically conceived by Auguste Rodin for the entrance to a museum that was

---

[21] Roy Rappaport (1999: 304).

never built and which were not actually cast in metal until after his death. As a public introduction to The Academy's Rodin Exhibition few objects could be as forceful: though the gates were firmly shut people could walk around them. Perhaps, no better symbol could express popular attitudes to hell in contemporary western Europe: they are of historical significance, worth noting, but easily bypassed. The gates of hell represent a historical memory and while Dante, on whose infernal regions Rodin creatively drew for this work, may have summoned images that warned a previous millennium they now furnish an exhibit and not a lesson warning of a pained afterlife. Two of the many details of this impressive work merit comment: the obvious figure is that of 'The Thinker'. Though Rodin did produce that familiar image as a separate sculpture there can hardly be a better example of where the full context adds dramatically to its significance, for The Thinker sits centrally above the main lintel of The Gates of Heaven. He looks down upon the many embodied forms and wraiths melting into the bronze doors as they pass from this world to the next. Dante would have approved of such a pondering. If The Thinker is unavoidable the second detail is quite the opposite despite its singularity. To the left of the gates, as viewed from the front, at the very edge of the sculpture, lies a neo-natally dead baby boy whose face is only partially formed and the sadness of whose bearing is telling. In both The Thinker and the baby Rodin's power to capture emotion is equally masterful: the one so knowing the other so unknowing and unknown and yet both, literally liminal, being fixed at thresholds.

Perhaps no sharper contrast of social context and intent than these gates of hell embraced by London's Royal Academy courtyard could be found than the dramatic performances of 'Hell House' religious presentations in some American Fundamentalist-Evangelical churches, as with Trinity Assembly of God Church outside Dallas, Texas, at Cedar hill where for some ten years some 13,000 to 15,000 people have queued to experience 'Hell House' events.[22] Brian Jackson has described the spatial surroundings, use of lighting and acting in performances through which the 'audience' is walked. Scenes of death and suffering, replete with blood and gore, show angels and demons contesting for human souls. The performance ending by passing into a room where numerous believers are already kneeling waiting to pray for any who now wish to convert before it is too late. He evaluated all this as an 'unfortunate strategy that relies on terror-and not only that, but the terror of young people in an unreflective moment of spatial horror – as the primary motivation for changing one's life.' He cited the historian Ethan Blue's opinion that a general sense of dread and fear following the terrorist attack on New York's Twin Towers intensified the 'cultural politics of Christian fear', making such Hell House performances all the more culturally acceptable.[23]

Though it is the case that such examples, along with social surveys, may register belief in hell that notion has largely disappeared within the general public for all practical purposes. The fact that a belief which played a significant role in the moral constitution of Europe for much of its history has been radically forgotten

---

[22] Brian Jackson (2007: 52–57).
[23] Brian Jackson (2007: 52).

or transformed into more psychological dynamics within the space of a century is a fact worth pondering. The decline of hell is a tale that has been told by several historians and theologians and draws from changing interpretations of scripture, of the cosmos and of the empirical fact that recent world wars inflicted horrors as great as Dante could conceive, and all in this world – no other was required in which to make people suffer for their sins. The subtlety of C. S. Lewis's popular theology could, in its way, broach the whole issue of the personal encounter with imperfection and malevolence and the need for a divine love that would win evil and self-centred hearts into a fuller realization of themselves in the incisive company of God. So, too, in other literary forms from Dante's infernal domains to Dostoevsky. It is telling that Yves Congar ends his theological reflection on hell with a passage from Dostoevsky's *The Brothers Karamazov*, where Father Zossima ponders the nature of hell as 'the suffering that comes from being unable to love'.[24] This rehearses the parable of the rich man[25] whose life of uncaring luxury leads him to Hades from where he longs that Abraham might come with a 'drop of living water' to quench 'the burning thirst . . . for spiritual love', a love he had rejected in life. Congar accounts for hell in an essentially orthodox fashion as 'the harvest of sin' but approached through the idea of meaning making and meaning loss. 'Salvation is essentially the giving of meaning to life – its real meaning, its meaning in God's eyes', and damnation is an 'abyss' of 'dreadful emptiness' of meaning, an emptiness rooted in a lovelessness. Congar, in seeing the power of narrative illustration to evoke a sense of his theological vision, furnishes his own parable of hell. It is like a child who has so 'provoked his parents' anger' that his own home has come to feel a hostile place, all is 'unsettled, hostile, with no way out'. That child 'has no other roof, no other table', no longer does he feel part of the only household he has: the 'ties of affection and dependence on which his happiness depends is no longer there'. So it is, he says, that 'the world of the man who is damned is rather like that'. As his parable suggests, Congar's description of hell as meaninglessness evokes the language of loss as a kind of grief. The damned 'is not alone', his existence is ongoing and he cannot cease to exist, and will continue in that state until he comes to 'love God', for 'to love God would be to come out of hell'. He even schematizes the differing moods of human spiritual existence, what he calls 'the stuff of things', with hell marked by 'an unchanging, unending existence without meaning and without hope', while earth is marked by 'faith and hope', and heaven by 'love, fellowship and the effects of grace'.[26]

Despite his desire to avoid the 'two extremes' of that sort of 'fundamentalism' or 'heavy handed literalism' that makes hell into a 'furnace that is as shocking as it is unthinkable', and a 'symbolic interpretation' that is 'far too "spiritualizing,"' Congar's Hell is as emotionally painful as the medieval portrayals of Hell-fire. His committed concern is not to 'whittle down' ideas 'to make them fit only what is clear to human reason'. Indeed, he notes the tendency of 'demythologizing'

---

[25] Yves Congar ([1959] 1961: 81–83).

[26] Lk 16. 19–31.

[27] Yves Congar ([1959] 1961: 78–79).

interpretation of his day, the late 1950s, and its desire to render doctrines 'acceptable to the scientifically-minded'. Here we encounter a profound and often intractable problem of theology as pursued by intellectual people viz., a sense of what reason yields within a mind familiar with modern world-views confronted by traditional ideas born in previous ages but validated in our own by powerful religious institutions within which we have gained and maintain a deep sense of identity. It is the kind of issue thinking novelists, including Mark Twain, have often pursued when pondering the afterlife and not finding the notion of 'Eternal rest . . . as comfortable as it sounds in the pulpit'.[27]

Basically, the idea of hell can resonate with our experiences of profound negativity, and with our knowledge of the existence of wicked people and the horror of much twentieth century torturous destruction, as long as it is not pressed too far: questions on the heat of hell-fire or what prevents the damned from being consumed by it whilst suffering constantly within its flames are redundant. In our more psychological age, however, the inner torment and sense of abandonment or alienation allows 'hell' to resonate with experience without the need for an afterlife underworld.

Political, economic and psychological realities all have the capacity and the dreadful reality of making life hell in the here and now for many. Rodin's Thinker and baby are but two expressions of this potential: the first opening the capacity for the meaningless of life that reflective solitude upon the ills of mankind may engender, the second marking the dashed hopes of parental fulfilment quashed in loss, and repeated millions of times in the genocides of most continents in recent centuries. Secular existentialists as well as modern historians do not find it difficult to reveal sufferings in the flesh that were no less great than traditional Christianity posited of the hellish afterlife. The one 'benefit' of the earthly 'hell' was that death finally came, the theological imagination, by contrast, posited an everlastingness to its terror. While it may be that some contemporary liberal Christians have been so conditioned by acceptable niceness as to reject beliefs in an eternal hell, there is no lack of hells of earth that demand to be rejected in and through social and political action that are expressive of a sense of Christian concern for justice and a commitment to the belief in divine love. This is one context in which what is seen must take precedence over what is not seen and what cannot be seen.[28] Membership in the Christian Church involves a complex commitment. To be amongst 'the faithful' is a dangerous status for, on the one hand there is a felt obligation to accept the truth expressed in the tradition handed to us yet, on the other, lies an obligation to pursue the truth in ways that bring the insights of our own day to interrogate the past.

Good, evil and hell

Though hell is one of the concepts whose traditional lineaments have been re-forged by broad Christian views over the last century its radical truth remains

---

[27] Archibald Henderson (1911: 195–200).
[28] 1 Jn 4. 20.

rooted in the human moral sense of good and evil and of the divide between the two. Life shows us that most people are a mixture of selfishness and generosity, with society encouraging a collaborative spirit for its survival. But experience also marks out some disastrously wicked individuals, as rare as great Saints, but as noteworthy. And it is in and through these people that we appreciate the embodiment of prime values.

To demythologize hell is wise, as is the demythologizing of its denizens, Satan, his fallen angelic companions and evil spirits of all sorts. And the reason for so doing lies in the need to deal with fear, and the fear of death. If it is true that many were restrained from wicked ways because of the fear of hell then, whilst that may have benefited society, it was a policing method doomed to failure as the human appreciation of life and the world expanded. The loss of hell was, in reality, no loss at all: it was the elimination of an unnecessary category whose real life arena of misery is, itself, all too real. What is more, to abandon an afterlife hell is to focus attention on the hells on earth, itself a far more pressing and salvation orientated mission.

But, before leaving hell in such an easy way it is important to note that in some societies vigorous notions of hell, highly reminiscent of medieval Christendom, but recharged by a biblical literalism and mood of fundamentalism, still exist. What is more its advocacy has been documented in highly critical ways. Boyd Purcell, for example, goes so far as to use the term 'spiritual terrorism' to describe how some church leaders impose an idea of hellish punishment on those who do not subscribe to a particular form of Protestant biblical theology on sin and hell. He describes this as one form of abuse of followers on the part of leaders, indeed, he reckons that this form of abuse also sometimes accompanies other forms of abuse. As a chaplain within a hospice care system in the Bible Belt of West Virginia he talks of 'typical' patients of between seventy and eighty years of age speaking of having tried to be a Christian for 60 or 70 years but now 'being afraid to die for fear of not being good enough for God to accept into heaven'.[29] He writes with a sense of deep regret, even of anger, at the kind of biblical interpretation that produces the kind of negative response of fear that overwhelms notions of divine love and grace.

Joyous surprise: pain or pleasure

But what of those sincere persons who, in this life, know that corruption of the heart whose imaginations are continually evil, and who also have a sense of God as the pure one? Certainly, the sense of conflict of good and evil within the self is common and little is gained from it being projected to a future time and place for its resolution. To cite Congar once more, it is not sufficient to rehearse the notion that, 'In Purgatory we shall all be mystics'.[30] If someone is not drawn to an awareness of the depth of crisis of encounter of lies and truth, the bad and the good, in the here and now, then any postulating such a dynamic

---

[29] Boyd C. Purcell (1998: 170).
[30] Yves Congar ([1959] 1961: 69).

somewhere else is redundant. While it is potentially admirable to see the self as requiring a purgation before the vision of God is possible that sense of self's future is also weakened through its romantically sad optimism. And here I wish to disagree with that broad Christian view of this transformation, whether aligned with a doctrine of purgatory or not, that roots it in a form of pain. A constant problem of and constraint upon all theological thought is the imposition of our human experience upon conceptions of the divine and divine operations. The fact of such 'projection' of human ideas in such a way that all theology is really 'anthropology' has been well known at least since Feuerbach argued that 'religion is man's earliest and most indirect form of self-knowledge', with the divine as 'nothing less than the human being freed from the limits of the individual': indeed, the divine as the human 'made objective'.[31] Yet, the theological imagination is such as to feel prompted by insights that amount to revelation, and to be able to engage in the critical judgement of human cultural ideas as part of its mission.

The doctrinal field of human self-development and moral transformation is a highly fertile ground for an engagement between projection and revelation and demands some comment. I approach this through a theological essay by my former Durham colleague David Brown, someone alert to the need of saying something that makes 'life in heaven conceivable' whilst not becoming 'a mere projection of what our own society happens to value'.[32] In his thoughtful reflection on, 'The Christian Heaven', more specifically on the issue of 'the purifying of ourselves for heaven', he observes that 'it takes but a moment's reflection to realize what a painful process that must be'. But does it, and why should it? Certainly, his reference to our self-deception and pretended goodness, to the hurt we impose on others, is well made. But then, as he ponders how we should come to terms 'with all such lumber from the past' he assumes that this will be a 'painful process,' later he also speaks of the 'newly dead (the church expectant) as they embark upon their slow and painful process of self-discovery'.[33] David Edwards makes practically the same point in his personal faith-intuition of heaven as being 'embraced by What and Who is reality more real than anything or anyone known by us previously'. For those willing to be so embraced, 'the change made when time is replaced by eternity, and space by the glory of God, will be "purgatory" in the sense that it will purge us. It will liberate us from everything which is unfit to share that final glory. We shall be changed'.[34] These would, I imagine, be good examples of what Wright describes as 'the revival of a quasi-purgatory in our own day'.[35]

Here our normal understanding of human processes seem to be projected onto an afterlife situation as the best judgement people are able to make and this, it seems to me, is questionable. Here Tom Wright's little reflective book is also

[31] Ludwig Feuerbach (1976: 14).
[32] David Brown (1995: 46).
[33] David Brown (1995: 48, 52).
[34] David L. Edwards (1999: 160).
[35] Tom Wright (2003b: 35).

useful as long as we expand the 'theological' and 'liturgical' reasons for holding purgatory to include the psychological issues of being self-aware about sin and personal imperfection. It is in this context that he set the 'revival of a quasi-purgatory in our own day' as a 'return to mythology' and that just at the point when influential Catholic theologians, especially Rahner and Ratzinger, 'have been transforming the doctrine . . . into something else.' He is especially keen to note Ratzinger's transformation of purgatory ideas through a Christological turn of thought making 'the Lord Himself . . . The fire of judgement which transforms us as he conforms us to his glorious resurrected body'.[36] This is a sentiment we will encounter in Chapter 8 in the earlier Catholic author Teilhard de Chardin. In this Christological shift Ratzinger does for purgatory what, for example, Karl Barth did when reinterpreting the Calvinist doctrine of double predestination as realized in Christ. God's predestining of one group to heaven and another to hell is transformed into Christ as the one who was destined both to suffer and enter into glory.[37]

But Wright's most crucial point is something other than these. It is focused in the assertion that 'bodily death itself actually puts sin to an end'. This emphasizes the embodied nature of Christian life and his sense that biblical authors are so concerned to see any future life as grounded in the destiny of that body and its transformation that it is 'actually quite difficult to give a clear biblical account of the disembodied state in between bodily death and bodily resurrection'. For him death itself acts as a kind of cleansing for 'all kinds of sins still lingering on within us, infecting and dragging us down'.[38] Between Wright and the Edwards-Brown type of interpretation lies a different sense of theological anthropology, a different conviction over what constitutes a believer's current and ultimate identity. For the former there is a more ultimate and miraculous transformative discontinuity, for the latter a stronger emphasis on a continuity of what is changed. The task and goal of the afterlife differs too, and Wright has no place for the purgatorial rhetoric of whatever kind.

The purgatory-analogue version, by contrast, is intelligible, however, in a world where we have to come to terms with what we have done, whether in psychological therapy or after the fashion of recent processes of reconciliation as in post apartheid South Africa or post-sectarian Northern Ireland. Certainly, one can see the logic driving both possibilities and if, as with David Brown, one can see but little point in formal ideas of purgatory it is also understandable why the 'painful' psychological model of personal reassessment emerges as a viable option.

Here, of course, I admit, that we are engaged in speculative ventures and since we are I would raise the quite different option of joyous surprise. For here we are thinking about God and the divine intention of humanity's salvation achieved through love, through the sacrifice pursued through love, and through the unity of those so redeemed. Once we admit that all of this language is radically human,

---

[36] Tom Wright (2003b: 10). This is a strong echo of Teilhard de Chardin.
[37] T. H. L. Parker (1969: 264–272). A magisterial essay on this theme.
[38] Tom Wright (2003b: 5, 31).

and all the relationships entailed in it forged on human models, we immediately acknowledge the limitations of our thought but also seek to leave an open-ended possibility generated by divine creativity. And that is where the option of joyous surprise may, perhaps, be entertained.

Transformed by surprise

Thomas Binney's hymn 'Eternal Light' is useful as one way into this perspective for he asks how we, whose 'native sphere is dark, whose mind is dim', may appear before the eternal light of God and bear upon us the 'uncreated beam'.[39] His soundly Protestant and Trinitarian answer embraces, 'An offering and a sacrifice, A Holy Spirit's energies, An advocate with God'. These are what 'prepare us for the sight, Of holiness above', as 'The sons of ignorance and night' may come to dwell 'in the eternal light, Through the eternal love'. Here there is no purgation but only preparation for the beatific vision, a preparation for seeing pervaded by a conviction of the eternity of light.[40] The key elements I take from Binney are those of the Holy Spirit's energies and 'the eternal love', both subject to the possibility of the model of, as C. S. Lewis might put it, being 'surprised by joy'. Surprise is the key. Surprise as judgement and surprise as the basis for self-understanding need not be a prompt for personal pain, anguish and regret, they are the moods triggered by a mind not yet surprised by the object of its vision. There is a sense in which worship is powerful when it takes us out of ourselves and brings to mind things other than ourselves, albeit transforming us in the process. To speak the language of transformed selves should allow us to entertain the potential of joyous surprise in glimpsing the sense of futility of pride that prompts those negative human traits that David Brown described.

Were we to think of surprise in alliance with humour then, perhaps, it might not be inappropriate to speak of seeing the 'funny' side of sin. Though, doubtless, one needs care here lest 'funny' be deemed foolish, yet it need not be taken as a weak response, despite the apparent weakness of the very word 'funny'. Just as some see it as a proper theological response to laugh at the devil, since radical pride cannot brook ridicule, so to be given to laugh at our sinful selves with creative laughter, granted by the Lord and Giver of Life as we are taken into the 'eternal love', would be salvific. On this basis, insight into folly while embraced by grace would be salvific and removed from any pain of deep regret. And this need not be a vision only of some afterlife. Perhaps it was no accident that some late medieval Christians engaged in 'Easter laughter', *risus paschalis* as a worshipful response to the resurrection.[41] Certainly, most early Christians sought to control laughter as they did many other bodily activities. Laughter did come to play a significant role in medieval festivals and has witnessed a significant resurgence as part of Christian reflection on life, so much so that the twentieth

---

[39] Thomas Binney (1798–1874). *Hymns of Faith*, (1964: No. 66) Scripture Union, London.
[40] Norman Mable (1945: 38–39).
[41] Peter L. Berger (1997: 199).

century has been identified as a period of dramatic change in appreciation of the phenomenon. Intrinsic to this is the sense that laughter and the humour motivating it is rooted in the 'perception of incongruity'.[42] And it may just be that sense of incongruity of sin that brings the mind to see its new world. These, however, are but speculations, though no less valuable for that and not essentially different from the speculation of a purgative process.

In all such ventures images predominate, whether of surprise or of regret. One image often at the heart of afterlife identity is that of fire, itself a powerful phenomenon open to strong positive or negative application. On the one hand it appears as the punishing flames of hellish torment and the cleansing flame of purgatory, on the other it is the creative fire of love, a divine hearth of cheer and welcome. In connection with the moods of faith the spirituality of festivals is instructive as when we compare the mood of the Passion and Good Friday with that of Easter and, perhaps, even more tellingly of Christmas. For there is in the folk-faith of many a Christmas Carol just that sense of mirth that underlies the joyous surprise of sin transformed that I have in mind. 'Good Christian men rejoice', catches something of this mood: 'Now you need not fear the grave: Peace! Peace! Jesus Christ was born to save; calls you one and calls you all, To gain His everlasting hall. Christ was born to save, Christ was born to save'.

The element of eschatological surprise offers a joyous transformation that is revelatory, a sense of insight gained under the influence of love, devoid of regret. Doubtless this is a model that, curiously, may find little appeal despite being intrinsically appealing. The constraint upon its acceptance is rooted in the lingering human desire of masochism, the sense of needing pain. And this itself is rooted in the fundamental human process of reciprocity, of that give and take that underpins all social and religious life. In religious people it is often a hindrance to understanding the nature of grace, of unmerited love, and of Christian fellowship. Purgatory and allied psychologies of purgative regret remain rooted in it. Yet, such striving is funny, it is risible. And that is why one aspect of the divine judgement allows us to see the folly of our life and to be graced to laugh at it and to turn to a future motivated by the joy of the spectacle and not haunted by its sinful shadow.

One strong theological view similar to this perspective is that of Boros, cited quite broadly in Chapter 2 but now focused on the role he gives to joy – 'the attitude which underlies all other attitudes of the Christian believer and which dominates his entire existence is a fundamental orientation towards joy'.[43] His theological approach offers a parallel account, at once both an eschatological and existential format, so that 'every man experiences heaven in his inmost being' when he knows joy, while the Christian 'bears witness to his faith in the world by experiencing heaven as the most real of all realities'. Boros is aware, and indeed, he makes it clear that, perhaps, he has 'overlooked the sadder aspects' of these topics and admits that they can all be interpreted more 'negatively'. But, then,

---

[42] Ingvild Saelid Gilhus (1997: 101).
[43] Ladislaus Boros ([1973] 1976: 62–63).

he says, that everyone has their own form of interpretation and his is 'more positive'.

For those who believe that Christian judgement comes in this life, indeed, comes daily, and for whom any 'purgation' comes in like timeliness, it is worth pondering the joyous surprise and the impact it can make upon our living. One of its consequences can be to turn the painful fire into the uprising passion for God's Kingdom in the here and now.

Today's surprise

To live in relation to such a surprise in the present moment is an encouragement to foster a spiritual life on earth that seeks to embody the Christian Gospel of salvation from sin, delivery from death and hell and to encourage a creative participation in life, albeit beset by many problems and marred by evil. The gift of love through the Lord and Giver of Life exists for a creative moving into the future with a creative revision of the past rather than any morbid circling in the vortex of negative memory.

In all of this the role of the imagination is crucial as it is in much of Christian thought as David Brown's wider work has done much to demonstrate and foster. On the issue of heaven, his view that the plausibility of a doctrine depends upon[44] whether it makes sense 'as an already present reality' is valuable, as is his stress on visionary ideas to excite the human imagination and thereby provoke it to faith. There is, however, a serious difficulty at the heart of his essay and it concerns slippage over symbolism. Certainly he wants to get away from ideas of 'heaven above us' by resort to the scientific notion of 'parallel universes', and to thinking of angels as part of the teeming hosts surrounding God as paralleling the teeming creation of earth: but the slippage here is great. To recall that angels' wings are symbolic of lightness of being contrasted with our heavy footedness as humans furnishes an excellent symbolic aside, but would become seriously problematic if the poetic and metaphorical allusion is read as an account of actual angelic beings.

It is worth pondering this because what is said of doctrine in relation to angels can also be applied to doctrines of heaven. In his spirited defence of angels he expresses his suspicion that the two causes of disbelief in them are 'twentieth-century arrogance and lack of imagination'.[45] Arrogance, because humanity has placed itself more at the centre of the universe than was the case in the Middle Ages, and lack of imagination because 'previous generations had an imaginative grasp of symbolic language which seems to have been lost by our own generation'. These important yet problematic points merit comment. While science has done much to bring our sense of being human to centre stage it has had little option of doing anything else, unless it would engage in radical confessional religion and begin any statement with a creedal note on God's existence. But, our very grounding of ourselves as the observing 'centre' of things is inevitable since

---

[44] David Brown (1999).
[45] David Brown (1995: 49).

we are not aware of any other 'centre', though not for the want of trying to find other intelligent life in the cosmos. Furthermore, astronomy and physics, in their view of what is about us have done much to contextualize us as infinitesimally small on the cosmic scale. We are more aware than ever of being very small fish in a droplet of very large oceans of oceans, and this, itself, demands considerable leaps of imagination.

Yet, at the same time as science has expanded the universe, increasing numbers of people report belief in angels just as many have reported being abducted by aliens. The shelves of new-age style bookshops are full of accounts of angelic interaction and encounter. Even at a popular and mass market end of film-making angels have an extensive following. To listen to someone speak today of their own encounter with angels is not to think that the Middle Ages are over. It is not the lack of symbolic playfulness in contemporary society that is a problem but the lack of it within some church circles where a great divide exists between the textual literalists, with their growth in number and ecclesiastical influence, and the post-modern, post-evangelicals and alternative-church devotees applying themselves to liturgical gigs. With that in mind, my problem with David Brown's reasons over change in outlook on heaven or angels is not that humanity is increasingly pompous or unimaginative but that comparative study demonstrates humanity's longstanding and enduring capacity to displace itself from centre stage through belief in ancestors, angels or even spirits, often because of fear and the desire to placate and seek survival.

It is despite those creative tendencies than many in western Europe have come to a change of mind over traditional religious beliefs. A certain pragmatism and a sense of the way things are has extended itself within this increasingly secular realm, and to it we could add the English speaking worlds of Australia and New Zealand. That these differ from much of contemporary eastern Europe and parts of North and South America, Africa and beyond cannot be doubted. But to describe this as 'European exceptionalism' is misguided, because Europe is internally divided at least between east and west as the twenty-first century begins. What we see here are ongoing shifts in ancient urban-centred and traditionally Christian cultures that are being secularized not simply in the sense of low church attendance and involvement but also of personal appropriation of traditional belief in the private domain. This does not mean that a sense of the depth of life is absent but that its expression changes as often attested by the growing terminology of 'spirituality' or 'the spiritual'.

The problem of Christian theology in this context, and nowhere is it better manifest than over ideas of death, hell and heaven, is to know what to do with traditional expressions of belief. The fact of this problem is evident in strident groups of conservatives and fundamentalists who advocate adherence to doctrines and to the bible-truths 'once committed to the Saints', as also in the smaller response of radical liberals seeking to retain a life of faith but framed by doctrinal interpretation that makes sense to them.

This crisis of tradition and post-modernity amidst the need of and for humanity is stark. Following the theme of this book, the issue as I see it is one of survival, fear and love. Churches seek survival as institutions at the same time as they hold a message of eternal survival for their members, at the same time they fear for their own future while seeking to foster love. As institutions churches have a life of their own in terms of administration, recruiting leaders and maintaining economic viability to achieve their perceived goal. That goal is, itself, complex in the sense that it is nothing less than the salvation of humanity, a goal whose achievement is difficult to assess and may even be recognised to be unassessible. The message enshrining that goal, the Gospel, comes in a traditional, creedal, form that involves belief in the resurrection of the dead and the life everlasting. But as times change, and they have never changed as significantly as over the last hundred and fifty years, the format of these doctrines has come to lie beyond the circle of life's meaning for large numbers of people in developed societies though, certainly, small numbers adhere to the tradition and seek to enhance and protect it through vigorous assertion and reassertion. In so doing segments of large denominations become more like sectarian movements in the defence of a theological territory and a saved personal identity. But while the large denominations of the Church of England or Roman Catholic Church contain such smaller groupings they exist to serve very large numbers of the general population a significant minority, or perhaps even a growing majority of whose thinking is no longer, at its core, attuned to traditional belief. It is in and through the funeral rites conducted by officiants of these churches that a key interface emerges between tradition and non-traditional belief. There are relatively few other social contexts in which major differences of belief and attitude encounter each other.

There is no easy solution to this practical fact of social life. Certainly, it needs to be borne in mind as far as pastoral theological issues are concerned and, in particular, it prompts the question of the possibility of having a this-worldly Christian theology of life and death. To return to David Brown, whilst sketching the vision of traditional Christianity as the unity of the church militant here in earth, the church triumphant in the heavenly domains replete with the angels, and the church expectant, that great company of those just dead, he then ignores 'that larger vision', one he knows holds potential as an inspirational vision for some, in order to stress 'heaven with us'. He hopes he is not unjust in stressing the one above the other but does so because of the need for doctrine that makes sense to people here and now. To make sense of heaven 'as an already existing yet present reality' is his practical desire, and one with which I entirely concur. What is interesting about the close of his essay is a final conundrum, presumably intentional and consonant with a style of evocative thought, as to whether 'the entire company of the redeemed, living and dead, worshipping together the God to whom we owe everything' is itself a symbolic expression for the vivid imagination of the living as they entertain notions of the great company of past and present believers, or whether it denotes an actual reality of domains of their existence. Here we are left to wonder whether what is given in one hand is taken away in the other, for his final sentence has all of us 'living of course in a shared expectation of the completion of all things at the end of the world'.

Words are important and, perhaps, must be allowed to bear diverse significance for those with ears to hear. But when they are on the point of passing from the imaginatively suggestive, inspiring our living, to the pragmatic assertion of the factual way things are, caution is valuable. This is especially true since contemporary Christian thinking in the west possesses three target populations.

A small elite of theologians including a penumbra of clergy, the worshipping faithful, and the wider public of mixed views. Theologians often simply speak to each other, though even the formal theology clergy may learn in training does not necessarily endure in their subsequent teaching, while both theologians and clergy seldom engage with the public at large, leaving the domain of the worshipping faithful as the major arena of teaching. As indicated above, one exception to this profile concerns funerals at which the clergy have, for generations, met with the great majority of the population. But, in Britain at least, this relationship is on the brink of a potentially major shift. For, with the growth of ideas of freedom of choice and consumerist options, and with secular and other ritual celebrants now increasingly available, those who no longer empathise with the traditional Christian language of heavenly afterlives are not guaranteed to use church rites for very much longer.

Chapter 6

Longings

'Like as the hart desireth the water brooks, so longeth my soul after thee, O God.'
So begins Psalm 42 in the *Book of Common Prayer* Psalter: it continues, 'My soul
is athirst for God, yea, even for the living God.' In this image of the thirsting
deer, pursued perhaps in life's hunt, the thirsting soul occupies a momentary self-
reflective spot-light, not at static pools for sated narcissism but flowing waters to
assuage the driving thirst of the parched. Today this longing for God is not voiced
as often as it is probably felt, nor as expressively as by the Psalmist yet it remains
a driving force in the spiritual life of many. In those for whom it is of fundamental importance for life it will, almost certainly, also play an important part in their
view of death.

It is just such a pattern of relationship between ideas of life and the longing for
God that this chapter describes as both a strong motivation for belief in life after
death and as the rationale for its possibility. To long for God and to have it
framed by some sense of relationship with the divine, is to possess a basis for an
intuition that this life is part of a life beyond death because God is sensed as being
'beyond death'. But just how to ponder this property of being 'beyond' everyday
life is the very question at the heart of this chapter as we consider the immediately
apparent route of an afterlife transcendence and the rather different route of a
this-worldly inner-life transcendence. Each needs to be set within the wider issue
of the resurrection of Jesus and the way it is interpreted.

Longing for God

One of the profoundest Christian roots of belief in an afterlife lies in a sense of a
longing for God. It is a longing related to the concern of the previous chapter
over the conflict between good and evil experienced as an interior dynamic of the
life of faith. It is also grounded in a human desire for completeness and not for
the partial.

To long for God is to yearn for some sense of the divine presence and if fortu-
nate enough to gain it, to sustain and develop it and to live by it. In this particular
style of spirituality the language of personal relationships expresses the need of
the believer not only to be recognised, acknowledged and approached by the
divine but also, in still more intimate terms of desire, to be accepted, embraced
and loved. This emotional need of life is itself pervaded by an intellectual need to
understand and own some insight into the nature of our existence, of our daily
and of our life-long endeavours. Here we find the sense of God as one who is
both near to us yet beyond us, both supporting and calling to new challenges.

The theological basis for this desire is forcefully voiced in many Christians, be they well-known to the world at large or unknown. St. Augustine famously framed it in his *Confessions* when acknowledging that God had made us for Himself and that our hearts would necessarily be restless until they found their rest in Him. In that context it is the very idea of God as Creator that motivates his reflection and which anticipates the condition of salvation as creation's consummation. Being aware of oneself as part of creation is seldom a sufficient reflection for Christian spirituality, neither is the friendship or even the love of other people always sufficient, since many move on, die, to leave us alone. Even the happy worlds that families create and consumerism fosters may become so fragile when they leave the scars of divorce on all concerned. Fragile too are the couple-focused informalities of contemporary life. Even a welfare state leaves gaps in the provision of care and large areas of shallowness even where care exists. It is no wonder that the human heart cries under its sense of need. Were Karl Marx still alive he might still have reason to witness to the human cry amidst a world perceived as heartless. Whether in his industrial world of physical hardship or our post-industrial domain of potential psycho-social hardship individual needs continue. And that, all without the needs that poverty still causes.

Here the Christian faith makes its own provision both in an offer of fellowship amongst believers and in the assuaging of the individual thirst for God. These are high ideals but even when individual churches, friends or partners fail, some still reach out for God: the longing is not abandoned. Part of the glory, even of failed or failing churches, is that they carry the scriptures and rites, and individual examples, that give voice to this desire and indicate the possibility of its achievement. And there are many, millions across the face of the earth, who feel their need answered. The very reason why such a scripture as Psalm 42, with its downcast self resurging in hope, can be read, owned and read again is because it reflects experience. Its truth to life lies in its not being simply an expression of need but of need met. That psalm recalls how the believer had known what it was like to be part of a great day of worship, of experience uttered as 'praise and thanksgiving', even though, just now, the spirit of praise and of the divine presence had given way to a heaviness of soul, yet a heaviness awaiting future praise.

While religious experiences at large pervade many people and places their significance here touches their intimacies and absences within the theology of death. For the moment, I wish to dwell upon the positive dimension of the longing for God and upon something of its satisfaction in relation to death. For many believers the sense of the presence of God, whether for brief moments or sustained periods in life, becomes intimately involved with their belief in an afterlife. The inner-life of faith is not always and perhaps seldom, revealed to others and even within churches or groups that do foster some form of testimony to it, albeit as a means of authenticating religious belonging, its stylised presentation can still cover a multitude of actual apprehensions.

For persons who do gain what they understand to be the presence of God the experience is one that demonstrates to them the existence and reality of the divine. At the same time, it furnishes an inner validation of their own life and faith. Such experiences bring beliefs in a wider and higher purpose of existence to that of the mundane world, and understands that purpose to be grounded in a 'personal God'.[1] It was the importance of the sense of God in this life that led Calvin, for example, in the earliest of his theological writings, to argue that the soul neither sleeps nor dies but passes straight to God at death.[2] The desire of the faithful was also used by Calvin in a most interesting way in relation to existence itself. Referring to the Patriarchs described in the Epistle to the Hebrews as desiring a better and heavenly country[3] he linked desire and being-itself in a way that George Tavard likened to Descartes' famous saying of a century later 'I think therefore I am.'[4] There is something in the humanism of Calvin and Descartes that is certainly not dissimilar, albeit set within different ultimate frames of reference.

For Calvin, identity was grounded in a desire aligned with a relation with God and was fostered by worship. On a wider Christian front, the power of settings for worship can by their very nature activate the emotional life of individuals as together they sing and pray of their mutual sense that God is with them. When, as has often been the case, the ideas engendered in worship involve deep emotional foundations embracing issues not only of sin, guilt, shame and regret but also of forgiveness, acceptance and mutual support, it is easy for other considerations to be overshadowed. The reality of present concerns makes others unreal, not least that of death. It is as though the intensity of group worship prevents that kind of engagement with notions of death that are fostered by solitude. Certain ideas and their associated moods, are mutually exclusive. The sense of the presence of God banishes both a sense of time and of decease.

These contexts of faith are instructive in showing human beings seeking meaning of both emotional and intellectual kinds. More specifically still, both these elements of emotion and reason combine in the process of seeking moral meaning in the world and it is precisely that moral meaning that enhances personal and communal life, allowing society a degree of integrity as it interprets its history and moves into the future. And that 'moral meaning' gains added power from a sense that death will not terminate the outcome of today's moral endeavours. More than that, the afterlife is anticipated as the arena in which earthly wrongs will be put right.

When individuals enter into a community of faith and gain their own experiential affirmation of what that community teaches about God they become strong, they flourish. Their sense of identity is enhanced and they sense that they belong not only to their church or to the world but to God's very self. As God is taught to be creator and redeemer of the world, and because people gain a personal validation of this their whole sense of self expands. Their identity is not simply one relating to the daily life lived but to the widest possible framework of life, one extending beyond death. To have a sense of the presence of God in this

---

[1] Paul Tillich (1959: 131–32) argues forcefully for the idea of a 'Personal God' as 'indispensable for living religion', and for its full status as a 'symbol'.

[2] George H. Tavard (2000: 80). An issue we pursue in Chapter 8.

[3] Heb. 11. 16.

[4] George H. Tavard (2000: 103). Compare Calvin's, *Si appetent, sunt* (If they desire, they are), and Descartes', *Cogito ergo sum* (I think, therefore I am).

life becomes the guarantee of and for a sense of that presence after death. All in all, the sense of identity of a God-related person is as eternal as God is believed to be eternal. To think in terms of this life only as the context for an experience with God would throw into question both that experience and the idea of a transcendent God.

Of the many ways we might ponder this core of religious life one of the most fruitful is through a hymn. This is because a hymn is in itself a symbol of unity in which words and music creatively fuse to yield more than the sum of their parts. Not only does it bring aspects of the rational and emotional domains of our being together but it allows us a sense of transcendence over the normal verbal realm of reflection. When sung with others hymns create community and it is precisely these integrating, transcending and community-building properties of hymns that make them such an appropriate medium for considering our sense of identity in relation to God.

Here I take but one example, George Matheson's hymn 'O Love that will not let me go' as a fine description of a believer who, amidst weariness feels held by the divine love, and whose sense of life is of a gift that now can be returned to the divine giver. The longing for depth, richness and fullness is seen to be part of the divine ocean. From these images of human weakness and divine strength the blind Scottish minister, Matheson, takes up the image of degrees of light as fire, comparing the flickering torch of weak faith with God's sunshine blaze in which there is a return as 'My heart restores its borrowed ray'. Then we move both to pain and to the divine joy that seeks me through it, a joy to which I cannot close my heart but rather turn to see amidst the rain of my life the rainbow of God's covenant, a promise 'That morn shall tearless be'. From the second and third verses with their strong Old Testament motifs of the divine light leading the exodus from Egypt into the wilderness and the rainbow covenant with Noah, the hymn writer moves to the New Covenant and to its sky-profiling cross of Christ. Here the symbolism is all the more powerful for not being direct. This too reflects something of the believer's bonding with God in life experiences that are, themselves, seldom simple and direct. He identifies with Christ both in terms of Calvary and Gethsemane, of the Cross – 'that liftest up my head'– and of the passion-filled obedience of the one who asked that perhaps the cup of trial might pass him by but whose final prayer is that God's will be done. It is to the biblical account of the agony of Christ witnessed in his sweating as though he sweated blood, as though great clots fell to the ground, that Matheson turns:

'I lay in dust life's glory dead,
And from the ground there blossomed red
Life that shall endless be'

In this hymn, experience of God is a vital dimension of the identity of the person deeply engaged with the divine through experience, thought and belief. And this complexity is of considerable importance as far as attitudes to death are concerned for, what I have been arguing here is that when the longing for God is realized, in some measure, in this life, it becomes integrally related to a belief in an afterlife. The sense of knowing God does not appear as 'temporary', even though such experience may be gained periodically, rarely or perhaps only once. An afterlife follows emotionally, logically and theologically from contemporary experience. For Matheson that contemporary experience has, variously, been linked with a broken engagement, a bereavement and such doubts prompted by Darwin and other scientific thinkers that he was on the brink of 'giving up the ministry and leaving the church'.[5] Whichever the factors might have been, it is said that when on the brink of giving up he felt that there was one who would not let him go. Such are the life experiences that drive the embodiment of faith.

Experience and Christology

I have dwelt upon such experiences before raising the theme of Jesus and his resurrection even though any theology of death might be expected to begin with the resurrection and move to reflections upon it. My intention in this ordering of issues aims to differentiate between the theme of a personal cluster of religious experience of God on the one hand and of the resurrection of Jesus on the other. While appreciating the practical fact that these two domains run together in Christian life there remains some advantage in being aware of the different dynamics at work in the ways in which they relate to the theology of death and particularly, of life after death. The point at emphasis is that attitudes towards an afterlife may be fired in differing ways even though, in formal doctrinal and creedal ways, they may be formally defined in a single expression. Ordinary theological convention tends to relate 'the life of the world to come' with the resurrection and encourages us to pursue ideas of an afterlife directly in relation to 'the resurrection of the dead'. That is, certainly, the prime traditional path but it is not the only way of pursuing the argument.

These expressions of resurrection and future life, taken from the Apostles' Creed, tend to convey a sense of time and eternity as sequential and speak of duration as a kind of salvation history. The Athanasian Creed moves even more directly from a statement about belief in God the creator, through aspects of divine communication through prophets, to the life, death and resurrection of Jesus, to the life-giving power of the Holy Spirit and on to final judgement, the resurrection of the dead and the ultimate 'life of the world to come'. Scripture and traditional liturgy combine to frame existence as one in which this life takes us on to another. The language of heaven seems perfectly natural. It also seems perfectly appropriate as a development of the idea of a longing for God and an imperfect experience of God in this life. But this conceptual literalism, as familiar and motivating as it is, is not the only way of framing life and death.

There are theologians who seek to maintain a traditional Christian belief in an afterlife who do so in language and terms that seek, by their very nature, to free us from overly literal notions in order to open mental possibilities for unimaginably positive futures. Here I simply choose David Edwards, an Anglican priest

---

[5] Norman Mable (1945: 130–131).

with intellectual depth of vision whose position epitomizes the view that belief in eternal life is grounded in the very nature of God in a way that takes the argument beyond that of Jewish or Hellenistic or biblicist roots. He represents a view that likens 'resurrection by God with remembrance by God'.[6] Here love is the key. The sense of love known on earth amongst people is seen as the model that gives the clue to eternal identity. We are always loved by the eternal God and remembered by that God. In that sense we are eternal. Edwards does not think that death is the end on the basis of resurrection or because we have eternal souls but because God never ends and because God 'continues to love the personality of the human to the extent of replacing the body which was its basis with a new basis: himself in his eternal life': all this is a direct expression of faith, 'no more and no less' in 'the immortal power of God'.[7] Edwards is clear, direct and in his terms properly simple and quite correct, too, when he comments on the various scientific interpretations of eternal life offered by thinkers like John Polkinghorne.[8] For no scientific rationale, not even one based on physics of a high order, bear much relevance to what is, essentially a statement of faith grounded in a sense of God. Whether in Polkinghorne or Edwards we are dealing here, quite basically, with personal intuitions, schooled by the Christian tradition, and expressed in the best concepts that contemporary believers have at their disposal: physics for the one and imaginative, loving, memory for the other. In either case, however, the direction and trend of belief finds its goal beyond and after this life. In the remainder of this chapter I want to turn to a different direction, and to ponder Christian eternity as an attribute of the life of faith in the here and now.

Tillich: courage and confidence

What I have in mind is exemplified by Paul Tillich's discussion of what he calls the 'courage to be' and, more particularly, the 'courage of confidence.'[9] Here, once more, we focus on a single scholar, one whose approach turns traditional theological ideas to an account of experiencing God that yields an attitude to death of a distinctive kind.

Once much better known and appreciated than at the start of the twenty first century, Paul Tillich (1886–1965) furnished a *Systematic Theology*[10] of particular value for any study of the theology of death. Publishing, as he was, largely in the 1950s, after experiencing both the First World War as an army chaplain and a cultural relocation from Germany because of political antagonism towards Nazism, he became a naturalized American in 1940. His intellectual roots were deeply European and drew from a rapidly changing past while his theological

[6] David L. Edwards (1999: 83).
[7] David L. Edwards (1999: 160–162).
[8] David L. Edwards (1999: 106).
[9] Paul Tillich ([1952] 1962: 156, 160).
[10] Paul Tillich ([1951] 1953). Here we also draw from his *Courage to Be* ([1952] 1962).

quest was to correlate the cultural questions of his day with Christian forms of understanding life. He viewed that world as one in deep anxiety over human life itself. Appropriately, his theological engagement took the form of an existential philosophy influenced by the growing stature of psychological views of life, not least in the USA. Accordingly, Tillich approached the fact of death through the joint themes of finitude and courage. Ironically or appropriately, depending upon one's perspective, his use of existentialism corresponded with the Catholic Church's objection to that philosophy in the 1950 encyclical *Humani Generis* of Pope Pius XII.

However, for those prepared to enter his pattern of theological reflection and accommodate to his existentialist rationale, there exists a satisfying realism over the human condition and over a Christian response to it that does not take easy refuge in a calming supernaturalism. He introduces the importance of the basic categories of thought by and through which we are able to think at all. Rather traditionally, he identifies the categories of 'time, space, causality and substance' and sets out to show how these very bases of our human self-reflection may participate in either 'being or non-being.'[11] This theme of being and non-being is of fundamental significance because its polarity of theological thought can also be taken as a frame for our life and the way in which we grasp our sense of it and set out to live it. The category of time is particularly important for it is in pondering the issue of time that we are aware both of its positive opening towards the future and its negative certainty that this future involves our death.

Thus arises the phenomenon of anxiety, a powerful notion in his theology, especially the anxiety resulting from the awareness of our 'having to die'. It is the impact of knowing that there is an insistence upon our having to die that is the root of anxiety. In that awareness we experience 'non-being . . . from the inside'.[12] Such anxious knowing would be overwhelming were it not for 'courage'. And it is this very notion of courage that resounds throughout Tillich's approach to death. Each of the categories of thought reflects a combination of anxiety and courage and furnishes an arena of and for human life providing an opportunity for the individual to exercise courage and face the recognized anxiety. One should not flee in the face of anxiety but find the courage to engage it, even when what lies before us is death itself. Here, for example, Tillich sees the human desire for 'the immortal substance of the soul'[13] as an understandable but unfortunate response.

Vitality

Into this train of thought Tillich introduces his idea of 'human vitality', a power driving human creativity and relating an individual to society and environment. Such vitality, aligned with our power of existence, is expressed in the cultural

---

[11] Paul Tillich ([1952] 1962: 214).
[12] Paul Tillich ([1952] 1962: 215).
[13] Paul Tillich ([1952] 1962: 219).

products of human creativity. Once we have been creative and allowed our vitality ample scope it may, as it were, become intimately associated with the things we have made. But those things pass away and as they pass so our sense of existence is depleted. This tends to mean that we are paradoxically centred in our world. We long to express ourselves, to manifest our courage and reveal our nature but, at the same time, we are aware of the vulnerability to which we expose ourselves through our action in the world. The possibility of having this courage amidst life's negativity is, for Tillich, grounded in the figure of Jesus as the Christ. This formulation of 'Jesus as the Christ' is, for Tillich, far more than a title –'Jesus Christ'– itself a designation of a personally named man identified as the Jewish Messiah: rather, it encapsulates the sense of one who participates in being-itself. As such, Jesus the Christ is one who has conquered the anxiety of fear of non-being and is the basis for our understanding of God as 'ground of being', as the very basis of all that can possibly relate to our 'ultimate concern'. In fact he describes the figure of Jesus the Christ as a 'life in which all forms of anxiety are present but from which all forms of despair are absent'.[14]

Much of his *Systematic Theology* concerns Jesus as the Christ and the way the believer's life may come to participate in the Christ's nature. In *The Courage to Be* many of these systematized themes are displayed in brief yet impressive compass, not least his exploration of both that emptiness that may beset human life and the despair that may be felt by many. 'Meaninglessness', as an ultimate state, is contrasted with the more relative condition of 'emptiness' and is depicted as forever lurking behind 'emptiness'. What is more, it is the sense of having to die or, indeed, of the knowledge of the death of an other, that is trigger enough both to cause an emptiness and to allow it to be engulfed by meaninglessness. It is precisely here that the 'courage to be' emerges as radically important and accounts for a state that is both profound and paradoxical.

As far as death is concerned Tillich describes two relatively traditional forms of religious belief that I take to be active resources for believers when they are bereaved. The first is that sense of 'divine-human encounter' when the believer is aware of a personal experience of God. This furnishes a strong undercurrent in most forms of Christianity though its particular fostering in Protestant Evangeli-calism's sense of a personal relationship with Christ is an obvious example. The second concerns mysticism: the sense of a state of union with the divine. This is not the place to argue how these two states resemble each other, though that is an important issue in the philosophy, phenomenology and psychology of religion, yet each certainly has to do with the self and its perceptive awareness of the divine. In the former the stress is on the two 'persons' who are related by faith, in the latter the stress falls upon the merger of the two identities into one. My interest, however, is on Tillich's concern with doubt and with the sense of mean-inglessness that may come to inhabit and pervade a person's religious state. The mystic may take doubt as a stage in the process of moving towards a sense of unity and regard its negativity as something to be transcended. That is fine for the

[14] Paul Tillich ([1952] 1962: 224).

mystic but few are mystical in that way so that doubt plays a different role for those given to the divine-human encounter. This more regular form of Christian piety tends to deplore doubt as some kind of weakness in faith and exhorts people towards a stronger or firmer faith: doubt may even be explained in terms of moral failure.

However, Tillich is concerned for those who know that their doubt is real and who cannot find it within their system of belief to reach for ever stronger beliefs to hold up a crumbling ideological edifice. Indeed, he speaks of 'the grip of doubt and meaninglessness.'[15] For such people a solution must come from amidst the perceived reality of their problematic condition, for it will come from nowhere else. Here he begins to construct a language of faith that includes doubt, in which the acceptance of despair is in itself 'faith and on the boundary line of the courage to be'. In the fullest of senses 'the meaning of life is reduced to despair about the meaning of life.'

Here we come to the crux of his argument, that when, or if, this sense of despair 'is an act of life it is positive in its negativity'. This kind of despair requires a courage, courage that expresses the power of being. 'The act of accepting meaninglessness is in itself a meaningful act. It is an act of faith.'[16] Even despair depends upon a certain power of being and it is that power of being that enables someone to embrace meaninglessness. When Tillich speaks both of the power of being and of a sense of courage he is using words that combine philosophical thought with human experience. He acknowledges that both the divine-human encounter and mystical forms of religious life may disclose some element of courage and some participation in the ground of being but, for him, the power of doubt and meaninglessness amidst religious life cannot be ignored as unworthy forms of religion. Rather, they become a means to a sense of 'God above God', of an encounter with or experience of the ground of being that affirms being over non-being, despite and because of radical doubt. In line with that he asserts that 'there are no valid arguments for the "existence" of God, but there are acts of courage in which we affirm the power of being, whether we know it or not'.[17] This assertion is valuable because it makes clear that we are dealing with philosophical issues embedded in life and not constrained by formal logic. To be part of a church that so sees and announces the nature of things is to 'receive courage to be'.

In terms of Tillich's existential theology, then, the key feature relating to death is that, 'The courage to be is rooted in the God who appears when God has disappeared in the anxiety of doubt.'[18] This depends upon 'absolute faith' with its concomitant 'courage to be', not least because of the 'anxiety of fate and death' and the fact that, for some, the time comes when 'the traditional symbols' by which we cope with such 'vicissitudes of fate and of the horror of death have lost their power'.[19]

[15] Paul Tillich ([1952] 1962: 170).
[16] Paul Tillich ([1952] 1962: 171).
[17] Paul Tillich ([1952] 1962: 176).
[18] Paul Tillich ([1952] 1962: 183).
[19] Paul Tillich ([1952] 1962: 182).

Here two points may be made that will appeal, in quite different and opposing ways, to two kinds of readers. The first concerns those who experience the kind of radical doubt that leaves but little sense within traditional religious patterns of belief. For these the apparent option is to abandon institutional Christianity as so much fabrication. Doubt has intruded, prompted perhaps by bereavement or the pain of death in the world at large, and while they may long for what they once believed to be true, they sense that it is not, and that there is no return to their prior belief. The second relates to those for whom this picture of radical faith will offer a significant appeal. Underlying their outlook is an emotional commitment to an ideal of truth alongside a deep relational motif of existence. They long for truth but have lost a particular content furnished by traditional religion. For them the sense of doubt and meaninglessness is profoundly real and cannot be sidestepped. Precisely because of this, Tillich's advocacy of doubt as integral to faith may come as a relief: certainly, this involves a depiction of ideas deeply motivated by an emotional sense. Here Tillich talks much about acceptance and plays with the concept before arriving at the formula of sensing and accepting that one is accepted. This strikes a strong Lutheran note of defiance against the negative dynamic of existence in order that a positive sense might emerge. It is as though a form of desire for truth is retained whilst its content is evacuated. Radical doubt becomes a labelling process of and for that negativity, but it is not left as the last word. In some way believers enter into doubt and meaninglessness and yet do not find themselves dismayed or lost. What emerges is a courage to take all this negativity into itself and to come out with a positive commitment to life. This courage – Tillich called it 'the Lutheran courage' echoing both the life-transformation in religious understanding associated both with Martin Luther and the tradition he began – furnishes 'the boundary line up to which the courage to be can go. Beyond it is mere non-being'. The very last sentence of *The Courage to Be* makes his point well: 'The courage to be is rooted in the God who appears when God has disappeared in the anxiety of doubt.'[20] A similar sense occurs in the conclusion of Marxsen's New Testament study of Jesus' resurrection where it takes the form of 'being safe', despite all odds.[21]

The courage of confidence

This theme of confidence, courage and death is important for Tillich, indeed, he develops it from the significance of anxiety over death and the fate of human life that pervades both the Renaissance and the Reformation. He links the anxiety bred of guilt with that of an uneasiness over one's fate and sets such conjoined anxieties against an interesting Lutheran theological idiom caught in the German word '*trotz*' –'in spite of'.[22] As a word can often capture a mood we often find particular idioms standing as watchwords for different churches, movements or

---

[20] Paul Tillich ([1952] 1962: 183).
[21] Willi Marxsen ([1968] 1970: 188).
[22] Paul Tillich ([1952] 1962: 157).

eras: 'in spite of' is one such, both within Lutheran thought and within a certain general Protestant presentation of biblical ideas. Its power lies in catching the nuanced paradox of contradiction that many come to feel within their religious life, especially if that life is played out amidst competing sets of authorities. It gives expression to those positive and negative aspects of life that are encountered as being at war with each other and yet – and this is the crucial feature of the overall experience – does not leave the individual dismayed. It reflects Paul's self-reflection upon his own religious condition in relation to God's saving action when, after rehearsing God's scheme of salvation, he spells out his own sense of wretchedness and speaks of a law of the will by which he actually finds himself doing what he does not want to do.[23] It is interesting to see him use the word 'law' not only to describe the principle that he does what he does not wish to do but also for the double observation that he 'delights in the law of God' in his 'inner man' yet finds that delight opposed by, or fought against by 'another law' within himself. He emerges from this turmoil from what he actually describes as 'this body of death', or 'the body of this death', by passing immediately, from 'this death' to 'thanks be to God through Jesus Christ our Lord'. But, even having said that, he continues by saying that he is still engaged with the 'law of God' and the 'law of sin'.

Even this brief reflection of Paul affords a good example of the 'in spite of' attitude that Tillich highlights within Lutheran thought. It marks, too, the conflict that would, nearly a millennium and a half later, come to be expressed in the Reformation notion of the Christian person as being at one and the same time both justified and yet a sinner before God.[24] These theological points, germane enough were we analysing ideas of salvation, are also directly relevant to a theology of death because of the significance of Paul's 'this body of death', and Tillich's 'in spite of'.

In spite of

Here we are faced with the paradox of our perception of death, with the idea that things are not as they seem. That 'in spite of' the evidence of the senses – that someone is dead with the corpse as the clear evidence of it – there remains a work of God. There is, underlying this '*trotz* paradox', what amounts to a recurring motif in other aspects of Protestant thinking as, for example, in Luther's theme of the 'two kingdoms' through which he interpreted life as lived both within the political kingdoms of the world and the divine kingdom of God. Such a two-foldness is also taken up by Tillich when, for example, he addresses himself to the nature of death in the case of Socrates. Tillich argues that Socrates approached his famous death, through drinking the state-prescribed poison, knowing 'that he belongs to two orders of reality and that the one is trans-temporal'.[25]

---

[23] Rom 7. 19–21.
[24] Regularly enshrined in the Latin *simul iustus et pecator*. – at once a justified person and a sinner.
[25] Paul Tillich ([1952] 1962: 164).

Here, Tillich's Protestant habit of thought and existential philosophical inclination are clearly spelled out as he argues that it was Socrates' courage that actually 'revealed to the ancient world that everyone belongs to two orders'. What is more, the 'two orders' were not – as we might expect from Greek philosophical debate involving Socrates and his pupil, Plato – those of this world and some world that the soul would pass into after death. Not at all. To speak of them as the 'temporal' and 'eternal' orders, as Tillich does, is also not to divide between this world and the next, rather, it is to distinguish between two attitudes towards life as lived now. One is the more ordinary form of living in which we share communal values and the other is a much more individually focused commitment to the nature of the integrity of the individual when set before the reality both of that community and of death. What happens to Socrates as he faces death is that he acknowledges that his own essential being is not compromised by death. At least this is Tillich's view. He goes on to argue that Socrates was not taking refuge in any idea of the immortality of the soul itself but in a mixture of 'courage and escape' that seeks to perpetuate 'self-affirmation even in the face of one's having to die'. The problem with the belief in immortality is that it maintains an illusion for the individual, it delays forever the fact of death. It delays that which cannot be delayed, death itself. For Tillich, then, death is a certainty. What is optional is how we, or Socrates, or anyone else, approach it. He staunchly argues that the idea of the immortality of the soul 'is a poor symbol for the courage to be in the face of one's having to die'. There is, as it were, a failure of integrity lying within the claim to an immortal soul. But, and here an important issue emerges, the Greek frame of reference did allow the individual to gain the integrity of a self knowing it was to die and facing death and taking death upon itself. Here is a form of nobility and wisdom, one that involves a kind of freedom from the fear of death. The Christian understanding of matters, however, does not accord that degree of freedom to an individual precisely because of the idea of the Fall or, in different theological terms, because of our estrangement from our 'essential being'. For the Christian death can only be approached in this more open and free way once we are freed from the sense of death as the 'wages of sin'. It is by being accepted by God and having a sense of having been accepted by God that a state of freedom emerges within which we can approach death as those no longer estranged. Here Tillich comes through his argument to the point at which he can say that 'he who participates in God participates in eternity'.[26] It is that condition that engenders the courage allowing believers to take upon themselves 'fate and death'. Though Tillich does not spell it out in these terms his argument leads to the position that the Christian believer becomes free to die.

While this may seem an odd way of talking about death, it indicates one kind of Christian spirituality whose dynamics have much to contribute to a theology of death. It is so important that it must not be passed over lightly. What makes this perspective a potentially powerful one is the way Christ is seen as freeing believers from sin and death in order that they may come to 'accept acceptance' in order that they may die in faith and die freely. Several deep and risky concepts

---

[26] Paul Tillich ([1952] 1962: 165).

cluster around this outlook. One concerns meaning and meaninglessness and Tillich is at pains to argue that even when set in the 'abyss of meaninglessness' or when encountering the 'destruction of meaning' the believer 'is aware of a hidden meaning.'[27] Here, again, we are with Tillich's use of Luther's 'in spite of' and with the Protestant 'two-foldness' in our experience of things. On the one hand there emerges the sense of meaninglessness yet on the other an awareness that 'the acceptance of despair is in itself faith and on the boundary line of the courage to be.'[28] This reference to the 'boundary line' reflects Tillich's distinctive theological method of correlation which seeks to align theological answers and the basic questions posed by our lives and which hallmarks the two-fold element in his thinking. Nowhere is it more appropriate than in a theology of death, but this approach will not find easy acceptance by all: each needs to decide whether these apparently philosophical arguments genuinely reflect their experience and enhance their reflection upon their life of faith. Words and apparently logical formulations are no guarantee of validity in life itself. Still, for some, Tillich's affirmation that –'the act of accepting meaninglessness is itself a meaningful act. It is an act of faith.'– will ring true. They, too, will see the point that, 'even in the despair about meaning being affirms itself through us.'[29] The form of Christian existential language in which this approach to life and death are couched is language with which few are now familiar, yet it possesses a power for those prepared to ponder it. Its particular efficacy lies in the point already made but which now needs expansion, viz., that we are set free to die. This is Tillich's version of the various more traditional Christian languages of atonement and Christ's victory over sin. It is grounded in an awareness of God, indeed in a form of personal acceptance by God, grounded in Christ and in the salvation achieved by Christ in and through his life and death, that leads individuals to accept themselves as acceptable. It is, then, the freedom found in the new Christian identity, in association with Christ as the source of the 'new being', that enables believers to venture into the deep waters of guilt, fate and destiny. It is no accident that Tillich uses words such as 'power' and 'vitality' when addressing themes such as 'meaninglessness' and seeking to describe what faith can be in that context. We have already encountered a similar outlook in Schweitzer's work and it is easy to see how such power and vitality can relate to the theme of intensive living that we considered there.

Power and symbol

Power and vitality aptly describe what we feel in those life circumstances that move us deeply, not least in grief. Tillich's theology aims to do justice to such experience even though his philosophical language can, ironically, easily appear quite remote from the realm of actual experience. It is, however worth plumbing his scheme because it is one that does have the ability to marshal ideas of life and death in a distinctive fashion. Central to it is the emphasis placed upon the idea

[27] Paul Tillich ([1952] 1962: 171).
[28] Paul Tillich ([1952] 1962: 170).
[29] Paul Tillich ([1952] 1962: 171).

of a 'symbol' and of the centrality of symbolic thought for, as he puts it, 'every assertion about being-itself is either metaphorical or symbolic.'[30] Symbolic talk becomes the medium of theological reflection about life and death and central to it is the way experience and expression of experience become one. He presses the point that the symbolic character of language 'does not diminish its truth; on the contrary, it is a condition of its truth'. Even more potently he affirms that, 'to speak unsymbolically about being-itself is untrue.'[31] Never is this more important than for a theology of death, for while death in the form of a corpse is as concrete an entity as our senses may wish to encounter our reflection upon that experience takes us well beyond the concrete. It is not that our 'emotional experience' is one thing and our 'philosophical reflection' is another, but rather that the one is taken up into the other allowing Tillich to say that 'the courage to be in all its forms has, by itself, revelatory character.'[32] As he puts it in a telling play on the prologue to John's Gospel, 'one could say that being includes non-being but non-being does not prevail against it.'[33] This is, for example, a quite different approach than is found in that other Protestant beacon of the twentieth century, Karl Barth, for whom negativity, the 'shadow-side' of creation, could not be so embraced by God. For example, Barth could never say, with Tillich, that, 'Non-being opens up the divine self-seclusion and reveals him as power and love. Non-being makes God a living God.'[34] But that contrast will not be pursued here, for we stay with Tillich's firm conviction that 'there would be no revelation of the ground of being, there would be no life', were it not for 'the No he has to overcome in himself and in his creature.'[35] In regarding 'the courage to be' as possessing, by itself, revelatory character' Tillich is presenting an account both of God and of the believer.[36] This emphasis upon the negative aspect of things underscores the nature of change and process, of the interaction and engagement by which a higher order grasp of things comes about. And it is here that Tillich's use of the existentialist relationship between existence and essence comes into play. For him it is within acts of courage that we participate in 'the ground of being'– the enigmatic phrase that is Tillich's most renowned means of referring of God. In more traditional theological terms it is because God has the property to engage with negativity and transcend it that the human being is able to do the same. Accordingly, he speaks of the person 'who receives this power in an act of mystical or personal or absolute faith' as the one 'aware of the source of his courage to be.'[37]

Absolute faith

Having already spoken of Tillich's description of different forms of faith it is now time to emphasize the issue of 'absolute faith' in terms of theology and death.

---

[30] Paul Tillich ([1952] 1962: 173).
[31] Paul Tillich ([1952] 1962: 175).
[32] Paul Tillich ([1952] 1962: 173).
[33] Jn 1. 5. 'The light shines in the darkness, and the darkness has not overcome it'.
[34] Paul Tillich ([1952] 1962: 174).
[35] Paul Tillich ([1952] 1962: 174).
[36] Paul Tillich ([1952] 1962: 173).
[37] Paul Tillich ([1952] 1962: 175).

This is quite crucial in Tillich's theology because it depends upon what we might call an analysed awareness. While, for him, there are 'no valid arguments for the "existence" of God', there are 'acts of courage in which we affirm the power of being' and such acts can be revelatory – indeed, 'the courage to be is the key to being–itself.'[38] While Tillich notes that such courage may or may not be consciously acknowledged when it is so recognised it moves the believer in a way that transcends theism. What comes about is an ability to take both doubt and meaninglessness 'into itself.'[39] The image that best expresses this is none other than that of the cross. But, rather than the general idiom of the theology of the cross that we might expect in Tillich's Lutheranism, what is fore-grounded is 'the Crucified who cried to God who remained his God after the God of confidence had left him in the darkness of doubt and meaninglessness.'[40] Finally, Tillich describes such 'absolute faith' as the state or condition that comes to underlie life, it is not a constituent part of life but a mode of living. He talks of it, once more, in terms of his favoured notion of the 'boundary'. Absolute faith and its courage to be '*is* this boundary . . . it is without the safety of words and concepts, it is without a name, church, a cult, a theology. But it is moving in the depths of all of them'.[41]

The signal importance of his argument here is that human awareness of such faith is identified with contexts of 'fate and death' when 'traditional symbols, which enable men to stand the vicissitudes of fate and horror of death have lost their power. When "providence" has become a superstition and "immortality" something imaginary.'[42] His concern is that it is precisely when familiar beliefs and their doctrinal and symbolic expressions are denuded of their traditional meaning that the 'power' that once inhabited them can be experienced in and through absolute faith. This is where he comes to affirm that 'the courage to be is rooted in the God who appears when God has disappeared in the anxiety of doubt.'[43]

One useful and more popular interpretation of Tillich and human experience in relation to death lies in Richard Grigg's notion of 'the phenomenon of empowerment'. This defines 'the experience of being enabled to overcome a conflict between a goal and a barrier within oneself to reaching that goal.' His approach works on the assumption that Tillich belongs to that same view of humanity reflected in William James' model of the divided person who senses himself as 'two deadly hostile selves'.[44] While many philosophical and psychological issues are embraced by this scheme, not least whether it is better to develop Tillich's thought either as a mode of transcendence or imminence[45], it raises the prime issue of an emergent attitude within life that is empowered by its own engagement with death and which is reflected in the notion of 'intensive living'.

[38] Paul Tillich ([1952] 1962: 176).
[39] Paul Tillich ([1952] 1962: 182).
[40] Paul Tillich ([1952] 1962: 182).
[41] Paul Tillich ([1952] 1962: 182). Original emphasis.
[42] Paul Tillich ([1952] 1962: 182).
[43] Paul Tillich ([1952] 1962: 183).
[44] Richard Grigg (1985: xi, xiii).
[45] Richard Grigg (1985: 130–131).

Today's eternity

In terms of Christian spirituality an interface opens up between the longing for God and the venture of intensive living. It is one to be pursued as much through worship and ethics as through rational reflection. One entry to it would be through a hymn like that of Bianco da Siena's fifteenth- century composition, 'Come down, O Love Divine, seek Thou this soul of mine'. It provides one telling element within the theological opportunity for discussion and encouragement, reflecting both the longing for God and the sense of knowing or being with God that lies at the heart of Christian thoughts of ultimate destiny. Moments of love appear timeless. Real relations of mutual bonding seem everlasting, it is the sensed quality of that context. Worship of God reflects the same sense. This is why the love-union traditions of mystical aspects of numerous religious traditions are so similar. It is the very experience of love that makes the idea of an ongoing relation after death so obvious and yet so problematic. Here the very categories of our thought and the emotions that pervade them make us giddy if once we look in a different direction and think the thought that our death is our end.

To know that we will die involves a pause for reflection. Modern life is characterized by a busy-ness that brooks no stop. But stop we must for stop we will, inevitably, when death overtakes us. It is one of the phenomena of contemporary life that restless people are dragged to a halt when someone close to them dies. For a moment at least they appreciate that they need to appreciate life. But often it is not long before they are back in their old habit, a potentially powerful lesson ignored. But we will die. My hands that work will be still, my teeming brain silent within itself. Here is my true kinship with nature, with its transient beauty and realistic hardness. If I look at the world and forget death then I am easily overtaken by a wishful thinking as charming as it is futile. For the beauty of the flower lies in its transience. To know this rationally is one thing, for it to become embedded in our knowing is quite another.

After its initial image of the panting deer and the human thirst for God this chapter has been largely devoid of further paradigmatic scenes due to its more abstract engagement with issues of philosophical theology and religious experience, a tradition that speaks more to some than others and one differing quite considerably from the often dramatically image-full topics to which we now turn in Chapter 7. The difference in these methods indicates something of the breadth of Christianity and the variety of resource available for theologies of death.

Chapter 7

Grave, Grove and Rapture

Though the expression, 'Earth to earth, ashes to ashes, dust to dust' has become established in the English language from its association with the burial service it is the argument of this chapter that not all earth, ashes and dust are the same. Their differences become particularly apparent in this chapter where we describe the concrete ritual variants of traditional burial, woodland burial,[1] and cremation and, paradoxically, the American case of 'the rapture' where there would be no remains. Complementing the attitudes to death inherent in these socially affirmed cases we conclude with a brief comment on suicide and its paradoxical nature in contemporary life.

Paradigmatic scenes and death

Unlike the strongly philosophical abstractions of the previous chapter, these four topics furnish imaginative reflections with certain key images that are valuably classified as paradigmatic scenes.[2] Such scenes depict the prime beliefs and capture those emotional moods of a group that not only move us in faith and prompt our living but also infuse our preferred theological outlook. Most Christian denominations live by their own choice of scene, by its underlying theological rationale and by the moods it engenders, fewer things can be more important in the formation of spirituality, not least in the face of death where the way Jesus and his death have been depicted are highly influential. Just how that Jesus-focused scene is related to the funerary rites of Christians is an important issue. The variety of rites pertinent to this chapter include coffin-burial in cemeteries, the crematorium oven with its resulting urn of ashes, the woodland glade with disposable body-container and finally, that of living Christians rising to meet Jesus on the clouds of heaven. While some of these are familiar to all with the last two being, perhaps, less so, each is related to what might best be called doctrinal-myths by which I mean creatively speculative interpretations of doctrine embedded in some kind of narrative form.

The Garden of Eden easily presents itself as a narrative myth describing the evil of death, while the image of Jesus as the divine father's incarnate son whose own suffering allows him to be sympathetically present to those who suffer today,

---

[1] We speak, variously, of 'ecological', 'woodland', and 'green' burial in this book. Usually using them synonymously unless the context demands an obvious emphasis.
[2] Rodney Needham (1981: 89).

say in bereavement, may often be presented more as a conviction of faith informed by doctrine despite its own symbolic nature. In 'the rapture' we have a stark case of what some believing Christians regard as clearly mythical even though its devotees would probably identify it as the truest of doctrine in a direct literal sense. In terms of mythical narratives that help direct human thought and life it is also worth noting the mythical nature of scientific models of the earth's survival or failure in relation to human behaviour and its destructive unbalancing of eco-systems.

As these doctrinal-myths indicate, contemporary Christians have a series of options on how to ponder death and approach funerals. As the twenty-first century begins, the great majority of just over 70 per cent of Britons, for example, will opt for cremation, the remaining minority will be buried in cemeteries or, space permitting, in local churchyards. Then, a small group opt for burial, not in either of those locations but in what is a growing number of woodland burial sites. This chapter considers theological aspects of these several modes of funeral and will, in passing, also consider the other options of body-composting (promession) and cryogenics. In framing this discussion in relation to paradigmatic scenes we recall the importance of the coherence of life-style and death-style raised in previous chapters and emphasize the theological ideas influencing them.

Grave

Christianity offers contemporary believers these and other images by which to ponder death. Graves make Christian sense because of the underlying motif of the Garden of Eden with its narrative myth of God forming the first man from the pre-moistened 'dust from the ground' into which the 'breath of life' is given and to which he is fated to return after disobeying the divine command not to eat of the tree of the knowledge of good and evil.[3] This Jewish myth is, then taken up in the birth, baptism and life of Jesus as it moves towards the Garden of Gethsemane, Calvary and the tree of the Cross where Jesus becomes the 'second Adam'. The events around the Cross constituted the major paradigmatic Christian scene of death and salvation yet it, too, is surrounded by the events of the passion that include the equally potent scene of the Last Supper, Christ's agony in Gethsemane and his betrayal. Depictions of the empty tomb, folded grave-clothes and the hopeful excitement of something about to happen or actually happening – as in Mary misidentifying the risen Jesus as a gardener or the walkers to Emmaus joined by a stranger revealed in the breaking of the bread – also play their part in an emergent Christian hope. Initially this was a hope of a Messianic Jewish Kingdom but with time, it became hope related to a wider Kingdom of God realized on this earth or in a heavenly domain. For some the kingdom motif narrowed down to personal survival in heaven.

---

[3] Gen 2. 7. 'The LORD God formed man of dust from the ground, and breathed into his nostrils the breath of life; and man became a living being'. Gen 3. 19. '. . . till you return to the ground, for out of it you were taken; you are dust, and to dust you shall return' (RSV).

When I was a boy the custom still existed in some Welsh families for a hymn to be sung outside the house when the corpse was brought out to be taken for burial. In effect, a local congregation was created at this point of departure, to sing of the heavenly Jerusalem as the earthly home stood hard and cold to rub shoulders with the heaven now awaiting the departed one. And the love and grace of God would ensure the transition safely made. That tradition involved a 'men only' funeral at the graveside, the women remained at home in a direct symbolism that they had already taken leave of the dead. Having kept the body in the house, within the domestic circle, they had done their family duty of grief within the home, where so much of their life-long endeavour had been experienced. Now it was the task of the men to go out and do men's work, of digging, carrying and burying. The 'funeral' was so very much more than the cemetery. The minister had already been in the house, the scriptures read and prayers said. The reality was of a community as the arena for the embodiment of death, the departure of the dead, but also ongoing life so soon symbolized in the food those women prepared for the post-interment gathering.

Urban tombs

A millennium before that, Christianity, following aspects of its Jewish social and urban culture also including tomb and catacomb disposal of the corpse located outside normal residence areas. Jewish practices of double-burial involved an initial phase of corpse decomposition and a secondary phase of bone collection in ossuaries. Though cremation was practised in the Mediterranean world of early Christian and some early Christians employed it, an emergent preference for burial became strong, not least in association with the change in status of Christianity as a state sanctioned faith within the Roman Empire whose Emperor Constantine came to ban cremation in parts of the classical and Mediterranean pagan world. Burial accorded well both with references to the dead contained in the Hebrew scriptures now owned by Christianity and in the new faith's own Epistles and Gospels. The death, burial and resurrection of Jesus was symbolically consonant with the death and burial of later generations of Christians. Burial was not incompatible, for example, with the exhumation of bones and their being placed in crypts or charnel houses. In later periods Greek Orthodoxy, a church whose theology of resurrection stands out in emphasis amongst all Christian denominations, folk-custom 'in the world' [4] engaged in frequent exhumation of bones paralleled by an evolving practical theology and popular belief in decay as a sign that the deceased's soul had well and truly departed.[5] Any who remained un-decayed posed the problem of deciding whether this was because of divine good-pleasure at their particular sanctity and should lead to a status of Saint, as with many in that tradition whose bodies became a form of relic, or whether they were particular sinners in need of further forgiveness in order that their soul

[4] Bert Groen (2001: 213).
[5] L. M. Danforth (1982).

should depart and allow the body to decay in the proper order both of nature and of grace. Appropriate liturgical action was available for that to occur. This general grammar of theological discourse has sustained orthodoxy in its general opposition to cremation. The Roman Catholic opposition was rather different as the next chapter shows.

Burial, whether in the unmarked graves of the poor or the elaborate tombs of the politically powerful, manifested the spectrum of Christian cultural influence across the world for two millennia and literature on it is extensive. Here, our limited intention is to consider one development of burial in Britain as the twentieth century ended and the twenty-first began, that of woodland burial, a practice not driven by the Christian doctrinal-myth of Adam-Christ but, economic factors apart, by ecological themes. Significantly, we propose here that the dust of death now becomes the dust of life. The opening of the first woodland burial site in Britain at Carlisle's civic cemetery under the visionary management of Mr Ken West was, itself more pragmatically driven by people's awareness of the cost of traditional burial with its coffins and headstones than by any ideological programme of ecological concern. Indeed, as with many social innovations that and later developments reveal a multiplicity of concerns and interests whose detail remains to be researched. But one emerging factor that cannot be ignored is the attitude to the body and its relation to the world as a single ecological system.

Grove: Spirituality and Ecology

Woodland burial is a complex theme with many motivations behind it. Here our concern is only with the link between human bodies and the theme of ecology. But we begin our discussion not in the philosophy and economics of ecology but by drawing again from a different philosophical-theological source, that of Albert Schweitzer. Already in Chapter 4 we saw his theology of life and death focused on a reverence for life accepted daily as a gift, a perspective grounded in a form of existentialism aligned with an intuitive experience of existence. As such it was not ecologically but philosophically driven as his sense of existence and the amazing mystery of life combined with an acknowledgement of a 'will-to-live'. Ecology as such was hardly an issue in his day. Schweitzer, in what was a dramatic criticism, said of Descartes' famed *cogito ergo sum* that to say, 'I think therefore I am,' was 'the stupidest primary assumption in all philosophy'.[6] From a lesser thinker such a comment is ignorable, but not from Schweitzer. His logic demanded that thought have an object, that when thinking one needs to think of something. It was not enough for some primary and momentary thought to know that it was thinking and then push out into meditation upon things in the world, as he saw in Descartes. Far from it; Schweitzer speaks of the 'will-to-live' as an entity that begins to think, and when it does so it finds life before it as a mystery to which we may come to cling out of reverence for it. This form of awakening to the capacity for thought, and the proactive response in coming to see life before it,

[6] Albert Schweitzer ([1936] 1962: 183).

brings with it a profound sense of choice: 'For, when it begins to think, the will-to-live realizes that it is free. It is free to leave life. It is free to choose whether or not to live.' In a most telling fashion he refers to suicide, though without using that word, for he sees this choice for life or for death as more easily achieved 'in this modern age, when there are abundant possibilities of abandoning life, painlessly and without agony'. And it is precisely this issue of whether life is worth living at all that is, he thinks, 'the question which haunts men and women today'. He highlights that difficult experience when one day we talk to someone and they seem 'in the full joy of life' and the next they have killed themselves. His insightful comment on this is that 'we are all closer to the possibility of this choice than we may guess of one another.' This is an important point because in contemporary Britain, for example, suicide is perhaps the one taboo point of conversation, since many other aspects of death, not to mention sex, have long come onto the social conversational agenda. Lest it be thought that the topics of assisted suicide and euthanasia contradict this observation, it is worth thinking twice about it. For those forms of death are always linked with topics of terminal illness or unbearable suffering and are quite unlike the cold-blooded decision of a person to kill themselves when not in such a situation and without subscribing to issues of mental imbalance. Schweitzer spoke of such a general context of whether life was worth living or not. And there must be few persons who have not dwelt on this theme when with a person who has attempted suicide and failed but who still has no sense of life's mystery, wonder and worthwhileness, who has, in other words, nothing of Schweitzer's reverence for life nor will to live. Indeed, it is fascinating to see the divide that exists today between those able to under-stand and empathize with the possibility of suicide and those unable to under-stand that outlook.[7] It is, perhaps, no accident that there is often a 'problem of obfuscation' associated with suicide 'in law . . . history and the analysis of suicide and its representation'[8] in art, for in it we have a true symbol of the possibilities of life and death in human hands.

To speak so much of suicide under the heading of woodland burial might seem odd. The intention, however, is to stress the importance of motivation in each case: one involves self-destruction against what life offers, the other seems to unite death with what the world's life means. And Schweitzer's reverence for life affords an apt perspective upon each. His reverence for life motif, driven by a 'conscientious rationalism . . . and individualism',[9] emphasized the mystery of life and took it into the ethical domain of how to live in and with this world, it was concerned with the world's moral future as a civilization. His was a post and pre-war modernist world of political, philosophical and religious concern within a relatively robust natural world. It was assumed that the world, battle-scarred as it was, would survive. The preoccupying question was whether thousands would die again in the cultural anarchy of war, an issue that is still of serious though

---

[7] Henry Clark (1962: 105) thinks this issue remains 'undecided' over whether suicide is admissible or not given Schweitzer's commitment to reverence for life.

[8] Ron M. Brown (2001: 217).

[9] Henry Clark (1962: 169).

often denied importance as twenty-first century political powers scan the available natural resources that will be needed to fuel their economies and feed their people.

Despite a difference in the feel of the rhetoric of his day and ours the deeper concerns are similar. From a wider humane perspective Schweitzer merits renewed consideration not only as 'one who did something while everyone else talked',[10] in his own day, but also because it is very easy for contemporary concerns over ecology – understood as a desire to 'save the world'– to become an utilitarian end in itself. For, from a Christian perspective, it could be argued that there is little point in 'saving the world' as such, if it is not part of a wider reason for living. Rehearsing the covenant-salvation theme of Chapter 1 we might see such an ecologically 'saved' world as a symbolic equivalent of the tower of Babel. There is no doubt that if humanity manages to destroy its own supportive environment and, thereby, is itself destroyed, it will not matter as far as grass and ants are concerned. The world without humans will evolve in its own way and many a beautiful flower will bloom unseen by human eye. But, it is precisely a world perceived as 'promised' or covenanted that provides a backdrop for a Christianly meaningful existence.[11] It is easy in the contemporary context for theological opinion to move away from a proper theological anthropocentrism in order not to be tarnished with previous accusations of a proud dominance over nature, but there is a proper anthropocentrism motivated by both a natural and divine reverence, indeed by a reverence for life.

In theological terms the 'dominion' motif of Genesis[12] needs setting alongside the complementary process of self-knowledge and self-will within the world over which humanity is to have dominion. My friend and former colleague, the Tillich scholar John Heywood Thomas, is valuable here when recalling the first of Tillich's sermons he heard, it was on the text that 'a man leaves his father and mother'.[13] Though cited by Jesus the text originates in Genesis and was used by Tillich to express his idea that, as Heywood Thomas put it, 'for a man to be man he must achieve individuality, he must distinguish himself from the ground of his being'. But, paradoxically and cautiously, this separation is both needful and dangerous since, 'estrangement from the ground of his being is what sin means. Finitude is not sin but the distinction between them is very subtle; only a hair's breadth divides them'. It is that hair's breadth between a responsible finitude of self-regard and care for the world and an irresponsible finitude of pride and disregard for the world that can be expressed in the flaming sword of Genesis whose angel bars the way to paradise.

So much hangs on the language of expression in theology for not only can it divide between the orthodox and heretic on the potential meaning of a word but

---

[10] Gerardus van der Leeuw ([1933] 1967: 664).

[11] In the sense of oikumene – an integrated world of habitation.

[12] Here I combine the myths of Adam in Gen 1. 28, and of Noah in Gen 9. 3. Though much could be said on the distinctive elements within these contexts.

[13] John Heywood Thomas (1961: 15). See also (1965: 22–28).

also, and sometimes this is even more important, the 'mood' that it catches and manages to express can assure its popularity or abandonment. John Heywood Thomas suggested that it was precisely the 'matter of mood' that caught the mid twentieth century's interest in Tillich rather than much of his philosophical theology that was, essentially, rooted in the German Idealism and Romanticism of Hegel and Schelling.[14] Our early twenty-first century mood over religion is fragmented. It includes a disciplined literalism reinforced with a collective sense of group power amongst several Evangelical groups, an imaginative and sensory spirituality of embodiment expressed both within charismatic churches and non-church therapeutic ventures and a socially-focused concern with justice and community development. Older-fashioned liberalism senses itself isolated. Behind all of these stand the bureaucratic structures of churches with their own rationales of continuity in organization and personnel. Yet people die in these movements as across the world and each has to furnish their own death response with moods to match and with theologies that can place death amidst the natural order of things.

Nature's order

As for that order with its animals and plants, the history of western thought in recent centuries has been the history of an enlarging vision of concern, the well-known initial abolition of the slave trade following 1808 brought human conditions into view, though the industrial revolution would hardly see the life and death of millions of coal, iron, and mill workers treated well, then for a century or more the case of animal welfare emerged. Certainly the emergence of evolutionary theory helped in this, though even before then moral concerns were not uncommon as this singular example will demonstrate.

On 5 March 1826, Thomas Chalmers, influential Professor of Moral Philosophy at St Andrews University, preached a sermon in Edinburgh 'Against Cruelty to Animals', following the unique provision for an annual sermon in Edinburgh on 'Cruelty to Animals'. He sought to relate the 'moral' aspect of life that involves our 'sympathy' and our 'heart' with the 'intellectual' aspect with its 'attention' to things rooted in our 'mind'.[15] These closely related forces ensured that what we might see as part of our intellectual attention to the world will prompt what we will feel in response to it. What we see matters for our moral response. On the basis of this generalization he argues that 'nature seems to have limited and circumscribed our power of noticing' so as to shield us 'from the pain of too pungent, or too incessant a sympathy' and to protect us from the attrition of character that such oppression would produce. Our heart would become ten-fold more rigid were we aware of the millions of small and invisible creatures we kill

---

[14] It is interesting to see Tillich taken as the one theologian much deployed by Roy Rappaport (1999) in his magisterial text on cultural anthropology and human religiosity.
[15] Thomas Chalmers (1826).

as we walk abroad and which only a microscope allows us to see. So it is that the 'law of emotion by which the sight of pain calls forth sympathy' is controlled and we 'palliate the atrociousness of cruelty', as in some experimental science we produce 'agonies of martyrdom' in animals' pain.[16] As for kindness, he even speaks of a 'decent funeral' for the aged dog, as part of his ultimate message which was the 'circulation of benevolence . . . from one species to another'.[17] This benevolence, sensitive as it is, remains far removed from Schweitzer's reverence for life, itself more touched by rationalism than romanticism. And, certainly, Chalmers had no worry over plants. Later, it took the twentieth century's rude awakening to atomic and nuclear power to open eyes to the potential for destroying life in moments. Later still, as the centuries changed, ecological and political awakenings to scientific analyses of changes in the world did bring plants into the frame of cultural survival. The clearest example of this concern emerged with The United Nations Environment Programme Report of 2007, popularly seen as an environmental audit it gained prime attention as an index of climatic and environmental changes with serious consequences for human as well as animal and plant populations.[18] In all this the element of fear is not far removed from the theme of survival, as the emergent life-styles of nations begins to resonate with consequence for their death-styles. Indeed, it is the very issue of coherence between the possibilities of life and of death that echoes in the apparently simple topic of woodland burial.

Tree of life

Woodland burial offers a new symbolic field within which to relate life-style and death-style and to provide opportunity for symbolic creativity. Certainly, there are strong pre-existing symbolic possibilities so that, for example, much could be said about the extensive theological iconography of the cross as the tree of life.[19] That would, however, focus on salvation from a fallen creation in the Christian tradition or, indeed, could elaborate upon trees in other religious symbolism. Richard Hutch, for example, having noted the way William James considered the 'completest religions' of the world to be those that best developed 'the pessimistic elements' of existence, took those negative elements and considered them through the 'sacrificed life' motif that he developed as a means of analysing the human engagement with death. There he aligns the cross, in its symbolic form as the tree of life, with the Bo tree under which Siddhartha Gautama surrendered his pursuit of enlightenment.[20] While our concern lies less with 'pessimistic elements' than with positive possibilities the background connection is important because of the underlying mythical power of arboreal imagery in human endeavour. Within the Christian tradition there is much that could be drawn upon of a positive kind as I have indicated elsewhere, whether from texts such as the second

---

[16] Thomas Chalmers (1826: 16, 18).

[17] Thomas Charlmers (1926: 36, 37).

[18] *The Times* of 26 October 2007 and many other major newspapers carried this as front page news along with extensive comment.

[19] Douglas J. Davies (1988: 32–42).

[20] Richard A. Hutch (1997: 121).

century *Shepherd of Hermas* with its powerful tree of the Lord's planting that grows to cover the earth, to the Apocalypse and its tree of life.[21]

Woodland burial

As the twenty-first century begins Britain is marked by the innovation of wood-land or green-burial much as the twentieth was by that of cremation. But, what of the 'dust of death' in this context? Here, some new possibilities run alongside the old. In the 'Eden-image' human dust is sin-infected, Adam's disobedience caused the ground to be cursed and resulted in a life of sweat-stained toil until he would return to that very earth.[22] That motif could, of course, be deployed in any burial and bears considerable potential for images of unity with the earth itself as well as of rest from labour. But it is not the only, and indeed, not the likely option within modern woodland burial where ecological values are more likely to dominate. Here the value of human 'dust' lies precisely in its unity with the earth itself. The return is one of like to like but, and this is a crucial factor, that dust is not likely to be viewed as sin-tainted. It is the 'naturalness' of matter that now comes to the fore in the human kinship with nature and its ongoing life. In the Genesis account of human creation a key motif lies in the dryness of the dust of death. Indeed, moisture lies at the heart of the Hebrew vision of life and it is seldom far removed from the breath or wind of the spirit of life. It was, in particular, from the moistened earth that Adam was formed and to which the breath of life came.[23] So, too, in the paradigmatic scene in Ezekiel's prophecy of the valley of bones whose hopeless dryness is reversed not simply by the addition of sinews, flesh and skin, but by the spirit that came from the four winds.[24] The Hebrew biblical picture is one in which life is intrinsically allied with a breath-spirit of wind-filled wetness framing notions of creative mists or fountains whilst death is grounded in dry and breathless barrenness. The Hebrew scriptures do not, however, speak a language of ecology, it would be anachronistic if it did. Rather, 'nature' is a creation of God and an environment for humanity in which divine covenants take their course.

Just how we may come to appreciate and emphasize these themes is what is important today. Some have argued, for example, that 'preoccupation with death and what is beyond' is 'typically a male preoccupation' and that a more Feminist theological stance would 'focus on birth, life and embodiment here and now' as Vernon White has written. A view he takes further under a form of sacrificial motif to see death as 'giving space for others' as we give ourselves 'back to the womb of the natural world, to nourish the new birth of others from our bodily decay' in what would be 'a sort of theology of recycling'.[25]

With that in mind, the corpse underlying ecological burial is unlikely to be viewed as the symbolically dry version of Genesis but as a fertile element

---

[21] Douglas J. Davies (1982: 38–39).
[22] Gen 3. 17–19.
[23] Gen 2. 5–7.
[24] Ezek 37. 7–14.
[25] Vernon White (2006: 35). He cites Rosemary Radford Ruether (1993).

returning to a fertile world. Here, as everywhere, everything hangs on the way the world is understood and classified.[26] And in this case it really is 'the world' at large that is reclassified, albeit still in a way that does not ignore the moral opposites of good and evil. Here we need some care in bringing moral opposites into alliance with the core theological doctrines of creation and salvation, a necessary development of our discussion since the interplay of creation and salvation provides the core dynamic of much theology. In this ecological context the 'good' relates to the ongoing existence and flourishing of the earth and of humanity upon it, while evil has to do with its discontinuity and potential destruction. Instead of any notion of a prior 'fall' of humanity with the Genesis myths as its charter it is possible to speak of the contemporary 'fall' of humanity in a wilful abuse of the earth. 'Eco-friendly' burial comes to share in what may then be viewed as salvation behaviour, in that it is reckoned to contribute to the welfare of the planet, as opposed to cremation whose output of gases from human combustion can be deemed unhealthy. Of course, such terminology gives the creation-salvation division a different set of meanings, but one of greater intelligibility to many contemporaries. The trees so often identified with eco-friendly burial, and giving their name to 'woodland burial' may, in a sense, be associated with those trees of Eden that were 'pleasant to the sight and good for food',[27] but whether they bear any relation to either the symbolic 'tree of life' or of the 'knowledge of good and evil' is another thing altogether and lies open for theological debate.

Finally, in ritual terms, to place earth upon an ecologically buried corpse is to deploy a perfect symbol of death and of life. A symbol, as has often been recognized, reveals whilst it yet conceals, and this is true of this 'earth' which reveals death by indicating that the body will now return to earth whilst also concealing the fact that such earth will, in due course, become the basis for a fertile soil. The theological meaning given to 'earth' is so differently nuanced in this woodland case from that of traditional cemetery burial.

Cremation

If anything, cremation brings the 'earth to earth, ashes to ashes, and dust to dust' idiom to even greater dramatic focus in the rapid reduction of the corpse to cremated remains. But here we find a complex situation emerging. On the one hand the ashes are a stark reminder of the Genesis affirmations of human destiny that it is from the earth we are made and to it we return; if anything, cremation highlights the Genesis idiom of earth, dust and ashes, reinforcing the very idea of humanity's humble origins but, on the other hand, these ashes could also be interpreted as alienating humanity from the soil, for they afford only a relatively infertile substance.

Certainly, the ashes of cremated remains afford a powerful medium for expressing a variety of messages, not only those expressing the relationship between the

---

[26] In Mormonism, for example, it is 'spirit' that is believed to animate resurrected bodies and not 'blood'. For, as scripture literally says, 'flesh and blood cannot inherit the kingdom of heaven'. 1 Co 15. 50. So, if not 'blood', then 'spirit' would be properly appropriate.

[27] Gen 2. 9.

dead person and the surviving kin but also the interests and experience of the dead. These come to the fore when relatives decide how to dispose of the ashes of their dead for, while they may bury them in family plots or keep them at home they may also locate them in places expressing the life-interests, work or leisure pursuits of the deceased. These ashes are highly symbolic. While it would be inaccurate to say that they resemble the relics of previous catholic religiosity, the privileged remains of sanctified bodies used for devotional purposes, they may serve as a personalized focus of and for deep memories. But, as with relics and most powerful symbols, these remains both conceal and reveal the dead person. This is an interesting process for ashes achieve it in what is both a similar and dissimilar way from that of the corpse. Many people find the corpse of a relative just such a strange entity because it both 'is' and 'is not' the dead person as once known to the surviving kin. This very ambiguity reinforces some people in their belief in concepts of the soul whose departure from the body accounts for that very sense of strange silence and lifelessness they now encounter. For others, however, the difference simply marks the contrast between life and death.

Rapture

Another paradigmatic scene of some significance within the history of Christianity is that of the Day of Pentecost and the outpouring of the Holy Spirit in what has often been identified theologically as the time of the Christian Church's birth.[28] Though this may seem far removed from any theology of death it has served as one major framework for the self-understanding of millions of Christians, first at the beginning of the twentieth century in the Pentecostal movement and then from the 1960s amongst Charismatic Christians, not least in the USA. Based upon these strong biblical and experiential elements there emerged from the 1960s, and in a more directed and politically directed way from the 1970s, a more dramatic form of religiosity grounded in a further biblical scene, that of Christ's Second Coming and of his being greeted not only by the resurrected dead but also by the living who were to be transformed in the process of rising to meet him in the clouds of heaven.

For many conservative Christians this scene of power holds a strong affinity with ideas of death. It brought to the turn of the twentieth and twenty-first century a renewed vigour in traditional eschatological images of Christ's Second Coming and the 'last things' of Christian eschatology. In what was itself a master stroke of the New Testament responding to questioning amongst early believers over the destiny of the dead there emerged a belief that the resurrected dead and the living faithful would join as a group caught up in the clouds 'to meet the Lord in the air'.[29] Marxen, for example, gave much priority to this outlook within the

---

[28] Acts 2: 1–47.

[29] I Thess 4. 17. Though answering issues of the order of precedence at the end times between those already dead and those still alive when the end came, this text retains a potential conflict between the dead God will 'bring with him' and 'the dead in Christ' who will rise first (vs. 14, 16).

earliest streams of Christian thought and saw it as the focus of hope, more so perhaps than even the doctrine of the resurrection which many Jews already accepted.

> Christians felt sure that Jesus would come again during the lifetime of the first generation . . . as the risen or exalted lord, or as the Son of man. That, however, would mean the end of the world. And where men reckoned with the end of the world in their own lifetime, the question of what would happen to the dead simply did not arise.[30]

Time passed, of course, and that did not transpire but these texts were collected into sacred scripture and, as such, were available for future interpretation and deployment. As with any biblical text it takes certain social conditions and popular attitudes before any one of them is brought into prominence. Two such contexts, of the sixteenth and twenty-first centuries, will illustrate just how differently that may turn out. It was, for example, the reading chosen as the epistle for the Holy Communion service that might take place at the funeral rite in the first English Prayer-Book of 1549. This was not associated with any particular religious movement of a millenarian form. Interestingly, with the removal of Holy Communion from burial in the *Second Prayer-Book of* 1552, this text disappeared or, rather, had its essence represented in the form of this prayer, presented here with the original English spelling retained:

> Almightie God, with whom doe lyue the spirites of them that departe hence in the lord, and in whom the soules of them that be elected, after they be delivered from the burden of the fleshe, be in ioye and felicitie. We geue thee hearty thankes, for that it hath pleased thee to deliuer thys N. our brother out of the myseryes of this sinneful world: beseeching thee, that it maye please thee of thy gracious goodnesse, shortly to accomplish the nombre of thyne electe, and to haste thy kingdom, that we with this our brother, and al other departed in the true faith of thy holy name, maye haue our perfect consummacion and blisse, y eternal and everlasting glory. Amen.[31]

The Protestant theology informing this prayer, and which differed from the more catholic influence of the previous, 1549 Prayer Book, accentuates the idea of the elect and the true faith while retaining a sense of a final consummation of things in the coming kingdom of God evident in the 1 Thessalonians text. These religious sentiments remained general and in accord with the other prayers and religious ideas of the day.

Just over four hundred years later this text was revitalized, not by alignment with any Christian sacrament or rite but amongst millions of evangelical

---

[30] Willi Marxsen ([1968] 1970: 176).

[31] *Second Prayer Book of Edward VI* ([1552] pp. 205–206). Retention of the original spelling may also serve as a reminder of the different age in which people then lived but which contributed so much to the contemporary world of current familiarity.

Christians with a strong literalist approach to the Bible. In this much has been due to the strength of a conservative Christian use of popular literature particularly in America where the *Left Behind* novels of Tim Lahaye depict the miraculous redemptive 'rapture' of the true Christian and the peril of the unsaved who are 'left behind' to experience the 'great tribulation'. Already having sold over fifty million at the start of the twenty-first century their appeal has been seen by some as allied to a 'terror rhetoric' that had its own history within a stream of American Protestantism associated with Jonathan Edwards amongst others.[32] Though possessing a strong evangelistic thrust there are evangelical Christians who have questioned the left behind books and film as unwarranted interpretations of biblical texts.[33] But, still, this motif holds power and stands out over those traditional scenes of Christ's Passion, Last Supper, and resurrection that lie at the heart of the Eucharist and pivot around the liturgical point of Easter. So, too, with his birth, baptism, transfiguration and ascension around other points in the liturgical calendar.

The 'rapture' motif, allied with ideas of 'the tribulation', though of limited presence and import within the New Testament seems to have been a free-floating idea available for use when deemed appropriate. Reinforced by general apocalyptic thought and its notion of interpreting 'the signs of the times' and the tribulation that would befall the faithful[34] this idea became increasingly favoured amongst some American evangelical groups at a time when they were also becoming politically active within the USA. Its impact upon American foreign policy has been much debated[35] with some political and religious commentators linking tribulation and rapture ideas with forms of Christian Zionism and the desire to prompt or enable conflict over the State of Israel in the belief that a final battle between the forces of good and evil 'on the great day of God the Almighty . . . at . . . Armageddon'[36] will usher in the Second Coming of Christ. There is a sense, then, that even in the present day there may be an event of ultimate significance that would not only bring the world order as we know it to an end and usher in a millennial kingdom of divine rule, but would also be an answer to death. In other words, there would be a generation that would not 'see death' but would, by radical contrast, 'be changed'. The Pauline language is crisp: it will be 'in a moment, in the twinkling of an eye', and prompted by the divine trumpet blast.[37] The familiarity of these words, as embedded as they have been in many funeral services, because of the favoured choice of Chapter 15 of Paul's First Letter to the Corinthians, should not detract from their significance in rapture theology and this is where we come to the critical point of the relation of that theology to an American way of life that helped foster its acceptance, viz., what has been called the American Way of Death.

---

[32] Brian Jackson (2007: 52).

[33] Gary DeMar (2001).

[34] E.g. Matt caps 24, 25.

[35] Walter Russell Mead (2006: 39–41).

[36] Rev 16. 16.

[37] 1 Cor 15. 52.

The rapture, as a religious view, needs to be understood not only in relation to contemporary politics and notions of evil persons and locales but also in the light of an American attitude to death that is distinctive in its downplaying of the natural process of decay. With roots in Evelyn Waugh's *The Loved One*,[38] and what Jessica Mitford famously called 'the American Way of Death', we have a backdrop of professionalization of the funeral agency, the fees it charged, and its cosmetic approach to the corpse that was made to appear 'asleep'. The revision of Mitford's 1963 exposé some thirty-five years later only seems to have reinforced that scene.[39] What is more, such a context offers one potentially powerful influence upon rapture theology. My suggestion being that rapture beliefs furnish another version of the American Way of Death, offering the absolute and ultimate form of death avoidance. For in it people do not die at all but are instantaneously transformed. What Marxsen proposed for early Christians has its application for those current believers who see themselves at one with their early confreres: 'the question of the resurrection of the dead was not a question which exercised the minds of the early Palestinian Christians',[40] for Christ would come soon and they would be transformed. This interpretation, whilst inevitably, speculative, offers a real suggestion of the ways in which cultural factors at least conduce to the acceptability of a religious motif and, finally, brings us to the point of 'human remains'. In the context of this chapter there are two elements to consider. The first being simply the Christian dead whose bodily remains are resurrected in the traditional form of resurrection belief but the second adding the new dimension that those living at this special time will simply not die but be transformed into new beings. This is the most economic and direct form of coping with death yet imagined within Christian culture history. Perhaps mention should be made, however, of one potential sense of 'remains', albeit odd in referring to the non-Christian world who are, as this scheme has it, 'left behind'. They are, by definition those pertaining to an immoral domain who will now suffer the ravages of Satan who comes into his own for a period of time.[41]

Time and autonomy

This sense of 'time' is one of many that pervade Christian history and are, in different ways, aligned with the forms of treating the dead discussed in this chapter. More widely, still, the very idea of 'time' is of fundamental importance to the spirituality of life and death. Here I do not refer to the technical philosophies of time[42] that have occupied numerous thinkers, not least in relation to death, but to the more practical dynamics of how people see their social past and

---

[38] Evelyn Waugh (1948).
[39] See Jessica Mitford (1998).
[40] Willi Marxsen ([1968] 1970: 176).
[41] As in Tim Lahaye and Jerry B. Jenkins *Desecration* (2001), the ninth volume of the 'Left-Behind' series in which 'antichrist takes the throne'.
[42] Hans-Georg Gadamer ([1960] 1989: 256–57), and his reflections on Heidegger's *Being and Time*.

future and how they conceive of their own identity in life-style and death-style embedded within those dimensions.

The promise of many descendents lay at the heart of Abraham's sense of God's covenant with a chosen people, the faith that was counted to him for righteousness had no resurrection and no need for resurrection in it. The rise of resurrection beliefs by the time of Jesus that involved a sense of the justification of a righteous individual complemented beliefs in Christ's imminent return but, in its delay or absence, went on to be the foundation belief of the increasingly institutionalized Christian church. Its focus moved from an earth-based Messianic restoration of all things in a renovated earth to a transition state preparatory for a heavenly city. Abraham's time-line from patriarch to descendent was transformed into the hope for a personal future in heaven. Thoughts of one's 'future' inevitably take place within the individual heart and mind so who is to say that the ancient Hebrew gaining a sense of purpose and satisfaction in contemplating his descendents was any less 'personally focused' than a modern Christian pondering his personal life in a heavenly future with God? But, with time, and in societies where kinship decreases in significance whilst self-focused interests grow, it is understandable that individuals become concerned with their own 'time', with the 'time they have', its 'loss' and 'saving' and in their own 'time-rich' or 'time-poor' lives. All of these quality-embedded time-dimensions undergird funerary patterns and a sense of self and of relationship with others and with God. They are also intimately allied with ethics and styles of life.

In terms of contemporary spirituality of life and death it is to be asked how 'time-wealth' or 'time-poverty' relate to 'eternal-wealth' and 'eternal-poverty'. And also to ask how they reflect relationships between people and between people and things. Is it possible for a rushed-life to be eternal? Is 'time-poverty' a sure sign of an eternity-weakness? While a great deal of care is needed here lest we slip into over-easy notions of happiness, it is important to have a person's sense of well-being in mind. For those generations born into a delayed-gratification society this can be difficult, yet if the idea of salvation has any practical realization it must include a sense of well-being understood within the constraints of life. All Christians can agree that love, in the sense of an outgoing concern for others, lies at the heart of the faith. Certain attitudes to time and to the quality of eternity pervade the possibilities of love. Anxiety over time, especially over its scarcity engenders fear and makes love hard. Love, by contrast, fosters a sense of having time and parallels the awareness of timelessness in worship. That is not to say that Christian spirituality breeds sloth, or an other-worldly unconcern: the Protestant Ethic, with all its critical opponents, stands surety for that. Love, in conquering a fear of time also helps banish a fear of death. But this assertion, as true as it may be, carries with it the dramatic consequence of the death of one's loved companion. The profound reality of 'embodiment' means that those who love and prove it through long self-giving to the other and for the other's good must come to see the other die. The death of the visible embodiment of one's love, of the one with whom all of one's time was well-spent, is hard to relate to the conquest of death. But there is no avoidance of such times for human beings: when life-long lovers are parted new pathways appear, some lead to a despair, a waiting for death to end the half-life, others to a kind of wisdom of inevitability, perhaps even with a resurgence of life in due course. Here pastoral formulae are few in the light of personal circumstances and the possibilities of faith and friendship.

Death's blessing

So it is that death may be a blessing when timely and a curse when it is not, and that applies as much to our self as to those we love. As human beings we wake up to find ourselves conscious in a world of great complexity. The search for meaning begins as we make noises in responding to our mother, it expands in many directions. Our two major characteristics are those of language and a moral sense, each an attribute of society and each pressed into action in response to the fact of death. Not that awareness of death is often present, nor would we wish to entertain it when forced upon us by the circumstance of bereavement. Yet timely death is a blessing. As to judging that timeliness, that is not easy. Our society has a deep sense that there is an appropriate age for it. We assume that infant and youthful death, that the death of parents with younger children and the death of people in the prime of life are all bad. On the other hand many would see sudden death when a person is old but not senile or sickness ridden as timely. As the twenty-first century begins western European society is on a cusp of changing thoughts on life and death, on suicide and assisted suicide.[43] The long traditional sense that reckoned God, and later, society, to have a right to give and take life and to know what is right and proper for people is no longer taken for granted.

For 1400 years, from the Council of Braga of 561 until the change in English secular law in 1961, and the Catholic Church formally changing its position in 1983, suicide had been sinful and criminal. Pity for those killing themselves might often have been present, along with the hope of God's mercy, but self-death remained wrong. Still, however, modern society holds a strong sense that life needs preserving, not least for those whose may desire to self-destruct in their youth, and is prepared to remove their actual freedom in an attempt to 'cure' them of that kind of wish and to restore them to a rightful state in which they will agree with the majority that life is worth living.

Yet, death may be blessing when severe and incurable illness strikes. 'It is a blessing' we say to each other when finding something to say about such deaths. Many entertain the fear that sickness in old age will render them a nuisance and burden to others as to themselves and would wish an appropriate form of death, preferably sudden and without prolonged pain. Amongst the fears are those of 'indignity', something people who have enjoyed a sense of control in their life worry might beset them in old age. But what is a 'blessing'? Blessings are a form of gift, a high form of gift, one that cannot be repaid. It is a fine example of the inalienable gift. It is a kind of human grace, an expression of good-will and even of love, from one to another: it causes the recipient to flourish and is the opposite of a curse, that negative expression desiring the withering of another. Much in Christian thought has seen death as a curse. Following St Paul, and echoing the

---

[43] James M. Hoefler with Brian E. Kamoie (1994).

second Genesis myth of human creation, death is promised to Adam if he dis-
obeys the Lord God,[44] and it is visited upon him in due course. Adam and Eve
are put our of Eden, not cursed, but to be pained in the labour of wresting a
living from the earth and producing children. With Paul 'death' becomes the 'last
enemy'.[45] But one of the pastoral needs of today concerns the fear many have of
indignity in old age as a kind of 'last enemy'. Here the resources of faith pass
beyond that of the individual to the church community as a community of life,
one with responsibilities that are now increasing as older populations increase.
Once more, death and life-styles cohere.

Here we face a problem of perspective, of the way we view the world in which
we live. The Pauline scheme draws together a cluster of concepts in which sin and
death frame our life: fulfilment will come only after death. Yet even he could see
death in a positive light when regarded as the gateway to 'be with Christ'.[46] But
this kind of otherworldliness is profoundly problematic for many. Doubtless
there are many in the world, whether the increasingly aged or those under duress
and oppression, and they are in the majority, who bring different issues. For them
the idea of a heavenly paradise may offer an attractive hope. But that is not the
case for those whose interest in this life is great and who see this world as full of
opportunity for self-development and for helping to develop the lot of the far less-
privileged. If we add to this an interpretation of the Kingdom of God as a desired
state of a transformed earth and not of some heavenly city then issues of life and
death are dramatically changed.

In all these issues the gearing of theological, cultural and individual interests is
ever a complex aspect of any society's religious life as this chapter has shown
and as the next chapter takes further still. Yet, as we shall see, some sense of the
conquest of death remains possible as Christians appropriate their vocation to be
amongst those who have passed from death to a life fostered when fear no longer
dismays.

[44] Gen 2. 17.
[45] 1 Cor 15. 26.
[46] Phil 1. 23.

Chapter 8

Cremation, Burial and Change

As Chapter 7 showed, theological concerns are seldom isolated from wider social pressures, whether political, economic or philosophical when it comes to the topic of funeral rites. This chapter takes up the linking of theological and social factors in a focus upon cremation and on aspects of death-related doctrine. In particular, it explores some of the complexity involved in the religious politics on death rites within both Catholic and Orthodox Churches, paying particular attention to theological elements that carry particular repercussions for cremation. This particular form of dealing with the dead certainly merits some popular attention since it has received very little within most Catholic and Protestant debates in recent decades, despite the fact that this practice of modern cremation has involved the greatest practical ritual change experienced by Christianity in the twentieth century.

I say 'ritual' rather than 'liturgical', here, to emphasize the lack of theological analysis given to that shift, a lack that is obvious when compared to the theological energy deployed in Eucharistic, ecumenical, political or gender-focused theologies and practice. This comparison is apt because cremation and Eucharist, for example, have largely partnered each other as levels of practical activity within the actual life of many clergy. The Church of England, with other major churches, became increasingly Eucharist-focused between the end of the Second World War and, say, 1980, a period in which British cremation moved from nearly 7per cent in 1945 to nearly 65 per cent in 1980. It was, to be precise, in 1968 that the pendulum swing from burial to cremation as the dominant mode of British funeral occurred. To give a wider sense of this development, the following table shows how cremation grew in Great Britain over the best part of a century. The cremation rate is shown as a percentage of all funerals except for the very first entry of 1885 when three individuals were cremated. The second column, for 1900, shows a percentage of 0.07 which represented some 444 individuals. From the 1950s the British cremation rate increased very steadily indeed at between 1 per cent – 3 per cent each year until 1990 when it came to a plateau at just about 70 per cent of all funerals before moving to just touch 72 per cent in 2000.[1]

Cremation rates in Great Britain (% of all deaths)

1885	1900	1915	1930	1945	1960	1975	1990	2000
3 people	0.07	0.22	0.87	7.8	34.71	56.07	69.81	71.50

[1] Davies, Douglas J. and Lewis H. Mates (2005: 433–456).

Although nineteenth- century European, American and Australian intellectuals, medical doctors and free thinkers who sponsored the idea of cremation met with some initial opposition from some church bodies, as Peter Jupp's history of cremation[2] has ably demonstrated for Great Britain, it is interesting to see that, by the time the two world wars had deeply affected the face of British values, the main denominations entered the second half of the twentieth century as the main ritual operators of the new institution of the free standing civic or privately owned crematorium. The rapid growth of crematoria virtually encompassed most of urban Britain, providing a ritual space of dramatic novelty that passed largely unstudied for nearly half a century.[3] The unstudied acceptance of crematoria and their business offers a remarkable example of ritual development and social change that can be interpreted in a number of ways including cultural adaptation, the invention of tradition, a form of secularization or paradoxically, the sacralization of secular space by religious organizations. Many other factors were involved in the adoption of cremation by churches and allow distinctive insight into the relationship between attitudes to death, theology and the dynamically aesthetic lives of different societies. In Europe, for example, cremation rates throughout the twentieth century serve as a mark between areas that have been traditionally Catholic, Protestant or Orthodox, while the whole episode of the holocaust threw cremation into problematic areas, not only for Jews but also for Germans.[4]

Catholic forces

The Catholic attitude was deeply influenced by secular forces, largely initiated by Italian Freemasons in the last third of the nineteenth century. Freethinking and anti-clerical, they elected to use cremation as a means of disposing of the dead in specially architected 'cremation temples' in many key cities.[5] Although the Catholic Church had encountered issues of cremation of Catholics in India,[6] of which it did not approve, it was this Italian provocation that elicited its strongly negative response.[7] Though aware that not all interested in cremation were anti-Catholic, the Vatican decreed in 1886 that cremation was improper for Catholics, describing it as a 'detestable impious custom'.[8]

This was reinforced in Canon Law in 1917[9] when a church funeral was denied to any seeking cremation or even to those supporting cremation organizations. Here ecclesiastical politics in relation to unbelievers played a dominant role over

---

[2] Peter C. Jupp (2006).
[3] Hilary Grainger (2005).
[4] Tim Purcell (2005: 168, 286, 323).
[5] Marco Novarino (2005: 207–210).
[6] John Newton (2005: 108).
[7] Marco Novarino (2005: 207–210).
[8] Marco Conti (2005: 109–110).
[9] 'De sepultura ecclesiastica': See Anna Salice (2005: 111).

a ritual practice. It was only in 1963 that attitudes changed allowing cremation for Catholics but with the retention of the 1917 Law against cremation if it was used with anti-Christian design.[10] Peter Jupp has rehearsed the way in which Britain may have had a serious input into further changes when Monsignor John McDonald, Cardinal Heenan's representative on the Council of the British Cremation Society, took a resolution from the Society asking that catholic priests be allowed, contrary to current ruling, to attend at the crematorium service. Heenan 'took it to the Pope' and whether for this or some other reason, 1966 witnessed a change of directive allowing such attendance.[11] Additional developments included, for example, the Canadian Catholic Church seeking permission from the Congregation for the Doctrine of the Faith and The Congregation for Divine Worship to allow cremated remains to be present during celebrations of requiem masses. This was granted in 1985.[12] More than a decade later, in 1997 similar permission was granted to the USA National Conference of Catholic Bishops. In describing these changes John Newton noted that the archdiocese of Chicago explicitly discouraged the use of the American term 'cremains' for human ashes, preferring 'cremated remains' as an expression of the dignity to be accorded to the remains of a human body.[13] In the American Catholic context there is a strong objection to the scattering of remains and a preference for their burial or being entombed. In the Anglican Church in Wales a similarly strong directive exists for the burial and against the scattering or any other form of dispersal or location of remains. Within Catholicism there has also been an awareness of the potential for 'violently destroying the corpse by fire' as Monsignor John McDonald once described it,[14] a theme recurring below for Orthodoxy. But, beyond the sphere of any particular church we find the Cremation Society of America in 1944 referring to people as having 'no right to crush, grind or pulverize human bone fragments'.[15] Certainly, churches have seen the emergence of cremation and cremation-aligned rites as problematic. Sometimes it has been the theological politics of these events that have been used to demarcate ideological boundaries, not least against secular attitudes and States. This has been particularly the case, for example, with the Greek Orthodox Church and its longstanding opposition to cremation. This merits comment for many may be relatively unfamiliar with this context and because it raises important general issues of theology influencing both life-style and death-style.

Orthodox forces

Certainly, Greek Orthodoxy's objections resembled Rome's in having a strong political element, with the Greek Church using cremation both as a boundary

---

[10] 'De cadaverum crematione'.

[11] Peter Jupp (2005: 141).

[12] This took the form of an 'indult' or special permission for local use different from common custom.

[13] John Newton (2005: 112).

[14] John F. McDonald (1966: 2).

[15] Stephen Prothero (2001: 150).

marker of Greek Orthodox identity and as an attempt to make that identity co-terminus with that of the Greek State. In the former USSR something similar occurred when the Russian Orthodox Church had to cope with the Soviet introduction of many kinds of rituals intended to replace traditional church rites associated with most aspects of family and community life, including a major thrust to replace burial with cremation.[16] But other factors also influence local divergences from norms that once made perfect sense in the ongoing life of traditional village or town contexts. So, for example, it is reported that the poor physical condition of some large Russian cemeteries in Moscow and St Petersburg leads some to prefer cremation, with the Church acquiescing. In Japan, where the broad culture is almost entirely cremation based, the Orthodox follow suit as they also do, though for quite different reasons, when elderly Canadian Orthodox individuals die while wintering in places such as Florida. It is quite usual for them to be cremated and have the proper funeral back home in Canada, focused on the cremated remains.[17] In Britain, too, with its standard cultural practice of cremation it is known for the Orthodox to be cremated for a variety of family and economic reasons. One way of coping with the tensions involved in such contexts where, perhaps, the will of the dead or the family runs contrary to the expressed will of the Church, is for a religious funeral service to be held in the church, as for burial, but for the remains then to be 'be handed over to the relatives', for a cremation.[18]

Alongside these social factors lie the theological issues of Orthodoxy which we approach here through the clear focus brought to much relevant material by Bert Groen.[19] These are worth rehearsing and developing not simply because, as a cluster of views, they may be unfamiliar to most non-Orthodox Christians, but also because they embrace such a variety of themes of wider relevance to funerary theology at large. There are four foci to the overlapping issues he identifies in relation to cremation: these may be identified as, Resurrection Flesh, Body and Relics, Body and Temple, and Burial and Tradition.[20]

First we have the formulation of Christian belief that the dead should rest in the graves until Christ's return and its associated day of judgement when 'new, heavenly flesh' will cover the resurrected bones, as happened to Jesus through his resurrection. The very idea of cemeteries (*koimeteria*) is one of a place where the faithful sleep,[21] with death being identified as sleep (*koimesi*) or as repose (*anapausis*), until the appropriate divine time of resurrection and, as such, burial 'proclaims and foretells the resurrection of the dead.' Even so, as Panagiotis Boumis, writes,

---

[16] Christopher Binns (1980–1981. 2005: 369–371).

[17] Bert Groen (2001: 206).

[18] Anastasios Barkas (2005: 226–227).

[19] Bert Groen (2001), wrote from The Institute of Eastern Christian Studies in Nijmegen.

[20] I present these in a slightly different order from Groen who places 'relics' after 'temple'. No change in theological significance is involved.

[21] 1 Thess 4. 13 'those who sleep'. The text of 1 Thess 4. 13–17, is part of the Orthodox funeral liturgy, partnered by John 5. 24–30, a key text on resurrection.

Neither the authentic tradition of the Orthodox Church, nor the inspired Holy Bible, nor the infallible decisions of the ecumenical Councils, doctrinal definitions and sacred canons give us a straight answer on the question of whether cremation is either prohibited or necessary, or even allowed.[22]

Even so, custom has developed an interpretative approach including this complex idea of resting in sleep, accompanied by the decay of the earthly flesh until such time as it is replaced or reclothed by the heavenly flesh.

This theme of heavenly flesh is clearly rooted in Paul's biblical argument concerning the continuity yet transformation associated with God's re-ordering of the world at Christ's second coming with its aligned resurrection of the dead. The comparison of now to then is expressed as a difference in the orders of things on the analogies of differing kinds of light emanating from sun, moon or stars, or of the flesh of humans, birds and fish. As Paul said, 'not all flesh is the same flesh'.[23] The Orthodox emphasis upon this particular element of flesh is more specific than the broader Catholic and Protestant discourse on a generic resurrection body. One practical and related feature of this is tied to the fact that, traditionally, and in many places until very recently, it was customary for the grave to be opened some time after burial, when in local terms it was considered that the corpse would have decayed, for the bones to be exhumed and placed in appropriate ossuaries. The decay of the 'human' and 'this worldly' flesh thus gained a prominence that was not the case in many other contexts, even where graves might be used for subsequent burials and bones removed to crypts. Within such a process and notwithstanding the pressure of tradition, we should not ignore the human distress, referred to by social psychologist Magdalini Dargentas as the 'trauma for the bereaved', involved in exhumation, not least when it might occur after only three years for those with rented grave spaces.[24] Here the extent of decay was the issue.

In the Greek context, popular belief often saw the decay of the flesh as a sign that the soul had truly left and was safely in its appropriate afterlife domain prior to the resurrection. Lack of decay might indicate one of two things, either unforgiven sinfulness or saintliness. These two states can be viewed in terms of what might be called the moral-somatic status of the dead, indicating the relation between the moral status and the physical condition of an individual and reflecting an underlying Christian theological commitment to a set of deeply interlinked ideas of embodiment, sacramentality and incarnation. In short, the human being is a deeply integrated person grounded in and as a body within a material world that is, in turn, perceived as the created medium of divine concern and operation into which Jesus entered and which he validated, as the divine son and saviour. To this must be added the complementary sense of sacraments as the material means through which these doctrines operate and affect Christian individuals, the Church and the world at large.

[22] Panagiotis J. Boumis (2005: 225–226).
[23] 1 Cor 15. 39.
[24] Magdalini Dargentas (2005: 223–225).

As for the Greek dead, it would be the immediate community of the deceased that would have to bear in mind the quality of life lived when arriving at the interpretation of whether the uncorrupted body was a mark of sin or glory. If the former, then a further rite was available in which the priest could pray that sins be forgiven by God so that the body might properly decay and the soul, hitherto of intermediate 'position' might pass on its way to rest. In the case of funerals of those who had been subject to 'a curse or excommunication' there are special Episcopal prayers 'not only to lift the curse or excommunication, but also that the body may dissolve into the elements from which it was made and the soul be with the saints'.[25] If the latter, non-corruption, is the case then a different outcome could be expected and this brings us to the second broad reason for opposing cremation, that concerning holy remains.

Secondly, then, we have the relationship between the body and relics, albeit of a restricted and elite group. Were cremation allowed then there would be no basis of knowing the moral condition outlined above and, certainly, in modern cremation, there would be no proper bone remains of saints or martyrs to preserve and venerate in the ways held dear by Orthodoxy, not that this affects the vast majority of today's dead. The fact of the martyred or saintly dead present among the living faithful fosters an attitude to embodiment, to death and destiny that was once also very strong, and remains to a degree, in some Catholic contexts but which Protestantism firmly rejected at the Reformation. The Protestant preference would, however, bear a degree of affinity with the next reason for Orthodoxy's dislike of cremation.

Thirdly, we have the belief that the human body is not, primarily, the possession of its human holder but is, following New Testament ideas, the temple of the Holy Spirit. Though the texts concerned could be interpreted as referring to the collective 'body' of the Christian community or church they also have an application to individual members of it.[26] As Groen indicated, this kind of interpretation leads to seeing that 'cremation is a destructive act of violence against the body' and is 'lacking in respect'.[27] We have already seen above, that both some Catholic and non-religious sources have wondered about this and it is worth pondering especially since violence is easily set against the profoundly important contemporary notion of dignity.[28] Throughout the twentieth century and in close parallel with the rise of the notion of human rights, the theme of the dignity of individuals has assumed increasing importance. In part this has been due to a general demise in a widespread and shared Christian conviction over what was once expressed as the Fatherhood of God and the Brotherhood of Man. In other words, the essentially ethically-based notion of human dignity is invoked to replace the essential Christian ethic of the value of each person before God. In many contexts it seems as though 'ethics' replaces 'religion' in a general secularizing context. Other echoes of this may, perhaps, be seen in Britain and elsewhere as people

---

[25] Burt Groen (2001: 210).

[26] 1 Cor 3. 17. 2. Cor 6. 16.

[27] Bert Groen (2001: 204).

[28] Douglas J. Davies (2005: 165–167: 'Dignity and Violence', in Davies and Mates 2005).

decry those, especially politicians, who do not 'listen to them'. Dignity involves being heard: indignity involves disregard. For many Christians there is an important dynamic here in relation to prayer, one way of looking at which lies in Christians believing themselves 'heard by God'. Indeed that might almost be a definition of prayer, much more so that the possibly more naïve view of prayer as 'talking to God'. In a secular context where prayer does not serve as such a basis for life the power vacuum of feeling significant leads to people wanting the powerful or socially significant to 'listen to them'. Much of this is enshrined in the word 'respect' that has gained tremendous currency in the self-reference of many advanced societies, or rather in the economically marginal who seek 'respect'.[29] Not to 'get respect' is to feel a lack of dignity and a general sense of worthlessness. Indeed some have even argued this kind of case for some disadvantaged black youths in Britain in relation to violence and a sense of disregard for life, but its import is wider still. And, just as dignity and respect are sought for or abandoned in life so too in death. The corpse becomes the vehicle for these values and at least should give us pause for thought to ask the question of whether we have the right to burn a body. Though simple, this question allows us to see unfamiliar dimensions within apparently familiar scenes. This is one reason why I devote this chapter to cremation, not because cremation became the most popular form of bodily disposal in twentieth century Britain, and in much of north and west Europe, but because it poses questions for a Christian theology of death that often pass unasked. And these very questions may further the depth of our approach to at least some aspects of death. Certainly, within Orthodox theology that body, whether in life or in death, is a valued temple of the Holy Spirit. It would be hard to think of a stronger validation of human beings than to talk of them as hosting the divine presence. And, as in life, so in death, and this makes it easy to see why cremation could be rejected as a process of indignity and violence. Burial, by sharp contrast, resonates with the scriptural account of Christ's death and deposition.

Fourthly that very point of resonance underlies the Orthodox commitment to tradition as such. This Church possesses as its basic mode of discourse, self-understanding, and theological interpretation, the tradition of previous doctrine. What Church Fathers have said and the liturgy they all helped create is the world of current living. To break with tradition is to violate the logic of theological discourse. What is more, that kind of abstract understanding of a way of thought and life has been framed and under-girded by the traditional patterns of life in urban and, not least, in village Greece. Monastic traditions, too, foster and invigorate pragmatic maintenance of custom. The very existence of graves in village cemeteries, along with memorial rites at various periods following burial, ensure a continuity of relation between the living and the dead. But times are changing and already some have argued that the formal content of Orthodox funeral rites 'do not exclude cremation', with even the exhumation of bones being a relatively late cultural development related to over-full cemeteries and not intrinsic to any theological idea or, indeed, to any established liturgical textual tradition, even

---

[29] Richard Sennett (2003) offers an incisive analysis of and an inspiring testimony to *Respect*.

though at places such as Mount Athos exhumation has been practised for centuries. The use of columbaria for the retention of remains or, indeed, their burial could be facilitated by cremation. In arguing this case for change to allow cremation in Greek Orthodoxy Groen pinpointed two significant issues, viz., body-soul relations, and the form of burial rites. These are valuable within the wider discussions of this book.

First, he speaks of a certain 'tension, maybe even a contradiction in Greek Orthodoxy' between the body as quite unimportant, given the emphasis upon the soul – which he thinks might be a remnant of Platonism[30]– and the body as very important in the sense of its future resurrection. Though he does cite authors who stress 'the belonging together of body and soul',[31]much as in the Catholic view of the soul-body unity discussed elsewhere in this book and reflecting the profound influence of Aristotelianism as in the theological-philosophical work of Thomas Aquinas. This problem area recurs through discussions of death not only because the issue of how to conceive of 'soul' in relation to 'body' lies at the heart of so many theological formulations but also because the idiom of 'soul' comes to be a means of pondering the issue of self-consciousness, identity and vitality itself. Even in a solidly materialist view of human life as the life of the body ideas of awareness and consciousness can come to be used in ways that resemble ideas of the 'soul'. In his Orthodoxy argument Groen speaks more in Platonic than Aristotelian ways of the soul as capable of having a life of its own and of cremation as facilitating that life free of its bodily arena.

> At death, body and soul are separated. It is the soul of the deceased that is important, its salvation, not the body, which is consigned to decay and to become nothing.[32]

This resembles the way many lay-people in Britain have responded to ideas of the afterlife, with technical philosophical issues of how identity requires an embodied expression and the like not being particularly germane. Indeed, one of the advantages of cremation for many people without any formal theological interest or a traditional belief they feel they must reflect, is that it simply removes the body and any future thinking about bodily things. If they believe in an afterlife at all it is, more directly, expressed in terms of the 'soul passing on' or some-such motif.

Secondly, and with a different direction of thought, Groen ponders the generic form of Orthodox Burial rites and identifies for main themes that logically follow each other. They begin with (i) a prayer for the repose of the deceased and for forgiveness of sins, followed by (ii) the affirmation of Christ as the Lord over life and death, and (iii) the vanity of earthly life with its mortal body, and (iv) the sorrow of the relatives and the eternal memory of the dead. One of his important

---

[30] Though, realistically, any simple use of Platonic–Aristotelian emphases within Orthodox thought ought to be avoided as simplistic.

[31] Burt Groen (2001: 216). Note 50. Includes references to Anthony Bloom (2000).

[32] Burt Groen (2001: 216).

considerations is the fact that, while the liturgical texts accentuate the human pain and fear surrounding death and grief, the biblical and Byzantine Greek texts of the services are 'unfortunately hardly accessible to most of those present'. They may, therefore, miss the final sense of the texts as they 'accentuate the transformation of the pain of those left behind in the light of the resurrection' as well as the Gospel texts of the comforting of mourners and the fact that 'the deceased will not be forgotten, neither by God nor by those left behind'.[33] The interplay of theological and pragmatic elements in the rite ensure that Christ as Lord of all, who had even descended into hell in his death conquest, is set alongside the body that decays and is even eaten by worms. To reiterate, Groen notes that while there are extensive themes both on the pain of grief and its transformation in a resurrection hope much of this can be lost in the rite because most present have little access to its biblical and Byzantine Greek medium.

Death politics

This Greek Orthodox example shows the complexity of interplay between theological, social and political factors surrounding death rites, and it is not without its parallel in Russian Orthodoxy where cremation served as a medium of ideological warfare between church and state during the Soviet era of the USSR. On a wider, non-Orthodox front, the contemporary Peoples' Republic of China sought to replace traditional forms of burial by cremation and shifted, for example, from a 36 per cent cremation rate in 1991 to that of 51 per cent by 2001. Within that period, the increase from, for example, 27 per cent in 1997 to 40 per cent in 1998 reflects the July 1997 'Administrative Rules of Funerals and Interments' that advocated cremation over burial.[34] Though there has been nothing of that imposition within Europe the following table[35] illustrates the influence of its Catholic–Protestant traditions.

Cremation rates in selected countries

	1950	1960	1970	1980	1990	2000	2004
Ireland					2	5	7
Italy					1	5	8
Spain					3	14	18
France				1	6	17	24
USA		4	5	10	17	25	30
Sweden	15	26	40	51	61	70	73
UK	16	34	56	64	70	72	71

[33] Burt Groen (2001: 216).
[34] Zhu Jinlong and Liu Fengming, Zuo Yongren, Gao Yueling, Zang Honchang, and Li Jian (2005: 122) for reform; Davies and Mates (2005: 455) for statistics.
[35] Davies and Mates (2005: 433–456).

This table only notes figures once they reached a one percent rate in each country. Here I take Sweden's State Lutheran Church[36] and the Church of England to be, essentially, Protestant. Indeed, cremation rates provide one of the easiest short-hand distinctions between that religious divide. It is also interesting to ask to what extent cremation rates might also serve as one potential measure of secularization? Time alone will tell this since as the twenty-first century commences cremation rates are beginning to advance relatively rapidly in previously staunchly Catholic countries. Here, too, I also include the USA, fully recognizing the complex division of Protestant and Catholic America as well as the influence of Orthodoxy and Judaism, both strongly preferring burial. For the USA, too, the issue of secularization remains important despite its apparently strong religious profile as the twenty-first century begins.

These changes taking place in Spain, France and the USA are notable and offer a challenge to theologians and pastors when pondering people's attitudes to death. In Chapter 4 we contrasted two schemes identified as the eschatological and the retrospective forms of fulfilment of identity, indicating that the latter had strong connections with cremated remains and what is done with them. This is important when considering the ritual associated with cremation and with the liturgical forms it may take. The modern theology of cremation in Britain has been outlined by Peter Jupp and shows, for example, how the Church of England's debates, focused in the period 1937–1944, included the decision that the actual practice of cremation held 'no theological significance' as such. Behind the debates lay issues of changing attitudes to the doctrine of the resurrection of the body. Some thought that people at large no longer held that view and that it was the soul that took precedence. Others argued that the creeds spoke of the resurrection of the dead and not of bodies as such, leaving open the mode of the person that would follow the divine act of resurrection. He also describes how opinions varied on prayer and key points of the service focused on the question of what is done at which point? Should the prime focus fall on a service in the crematorium chapel and, if so, what of the resulting cremated remains? The practice of remains being interred or scattered by crematorium officials had become widespread and was devoid of any formal prayer. Jupp posed the issue in the question, 'At what point was the committal prayer most appropriate?'[37] The assumption here seeming to be that in the burial service there was a single 'committal' and, in the sense that there was a focused moment when the coffin was interred and prayers said, that is correct. Michael Perham has also explored this topic of committal for the later twentieth century noting the uncertainty of if and when it might have occurred in the context of some contemporary British cremation rites conducted by the Church of England.[38]

But there is another aspect of this issue meriting detailed theological comment, albeit lying outside Jupp's nineteenth and twentieth century focus and it

---

[36] It became disestablished only in 2000.
[37] Peter Jupp (2006: 139). Jupp's valuable account relates historical aspects of theology and wider social policy over cremation.
[38] Michael Perham (1997: 167).

concerns ideas of the body and the soul at other periods of Christian history. Here, for comparative purposes we draw on some sixteenth and seventeenth century examples of this almost interminable and ongoing theological problem in the philosophy of Christian religion and also restrict it to Anglican deliberations during the English Reformation to show something of the Catholic–Protestant interplay of thought.

Commendation and committal

Here we approach soul and body through the ritual acts of commendation and committal because, as we shall see, the former tended to be applied to the soul and the latter to the body in the three historical Prayer Books of the Church of England of 1549, 1552 and 1662. This focus is valuable as a foundation for analyses of subsequent funeral rites because it identifies the dynamics of theological and liturgical thought at work during a period of rapid religious and social change, and one different from that of Orthodoxy.

In the First Book of 1549, one still reflecting Catholic perspectives, there are three points of interest. The first comes as the priest casts earth 'upon the Corps' and says: 'I commende thy soule to God the father almightie, and thy body to the grounde, earth to earth, asshes to asshes, dust to dust . . . '[39] At this point the single verb of commendation refers to both the soul as it goes to God and the body to the ground until the resurrection when the 'vile body' will be transformed by Christ to be like 'his glorious body'. The second moment comes in a prayer that follows almost immediately and which takes the form: 'We commende into thy handes of mercy (most merciful father)[40] the soule of this our brother departed, N. And his body we commit to the earth . . .' Here we have a commendation of both soul and body followed by a commendation of the soul and a committal of the body. But then, in a prayer of thanksgiving to God for delivering the deceased from, 'the miseries of this wretched world, from the body of death and all temptacion,' we encounter a formulation expressing the trust that God has brought the departed soul, 'into sure consolacion and reste', with the further and crucial description of that soul as already having been committed to God by the dying person himself. God is one who has, 'brought his soule which he committed into thy holye handes'. So the departed person, whilst presumably in the act or process of dying is seen as having played a part in the committal of his own soul to God. This is, indeed, an interesting transitional prayer that places a degree of responsible action upon the ordinary believer, and not leaving all to the priest. There is, here, a richness of theological possibilities that soon becomes truncated in the more Protestant version of 1552 where some considerable change occurs, and not only in its new-found brevity. Now, as earth is 'cast upon the body, by some standing by', and it would seem not by the priest, he says:

---

[39] I retain the spellings of facsimile editions of these rites.
[40] Mercy is a characteristic theological and liturgical feature of early Anglicanism.

Forasmuche as it hathe pleased almighty God of his great mercy to take
unto himself the soule of our dere brother here departed: we therefore
commit his body to the ground . . .

The difference between these two schemes lies in the prime role touching both
the soul and body. Now there is no commendation of the soul, for it is God
who has been pleased to 'take unto himself' that soul; neither is there any 'self-
committal', nor yet any commendation of the body, rather there is a simple
commitment of the body to the ground. The 1662 book largely follows that of
1552 in the key features mentioned here and though 'committal' becomes the
prime mode of ritual action, there remains a powerful prayer of 'hearty thanks' to
'Almighty God' as the one with whom 'live the spirits of them that depart hence',
and 'with whom the souls of the faithful, after they are delivered from the burden
of the flesh, are in joy and felicity'.

The idea of the dead being at rest is present in the First Prayer Book not only
because of its use of a biblical text referring to those who 'die in the Lord' and
who are blessed as they 'rest from their labours',[41] but also in the Collect that
refers to the living who one day will 'sleep in' Jesus Christ as they now believe to
be the state of the deceased. This point is immediately reinforced by the final
reading from the First Epistle to the Thessalonians that concluded the service and
spoke of those believers who have 'fallen asleep'.[42] The essence of this early Christian 'sleep motif' is retained in the 1552 book, with the I Corinthians 15 chapter
describing the risen Christ as 'the first-fruits of them that slept', followed by the
motif of 'rest' and of those who 'sleep in him'. Though these biblical images of
sleep seem natural enough they were, in fact, much debated in the wider world
of the European Reformation. John Calvin's very first theological writing was
devoted to an objection to ideas of soul-sleep and to the death of the soul. His
analysis embraces many issues. He is fully aware of the similarities and differences
between speaking of 'soul' and 'spirit'; he rehearses the thought of early Church
Fathers such as Ambrose and Augustine on the image of God in relation to the
human soul and not to the body as such, and he is fully alert to the spirituality of
faith whose sense of 'the kingdom of God in the soul is itself a proof that the soul
never dies', rather it 'remains fully alive as it is taken up in the Lord' as George
Tavard describes it.[43] Though written against Anabaptists, sectarians of essentially
Protestant persuasion, Calvin's view would also have left no place for Catholic
ideas of purgatory. The Reformation was famously influenced by theological ideas
concerning the afterlife and the dead, not least, through the indulgences sought
by the living from the treasury of merits controlled by the Church. Protestantism
went far in severing the living from their dead and changing the culture or death.
The issue of prayers for the dead and, most certainly, of any formal rites on their
behalf, was to simmer-on within Anglicanism for centuries and, perhaps, did not

[41] Rev 14. 13.
[42] I Thess 4. 14–15.
[43] George H. Tavard (2000: 80 and 1, respectively). This is an excellent account of Calvin's
study *Psychopannychia*, written in 1534 but probably not published until 1542.

make liturgical reform of funerals a sought-after field. And when the catholic afterlife-world was denied as a domain over which the Church could still exert some influence interest turned to the issue of Christ and his dealings with the 'spirits in prison'. Christological debate was, after all, a crucial focus within Reformation debate as it continued and developed ideas of atonement that also occupied medieval theology.

Descension of Christ

In terms of the themes of survival, fear and love that are of interest in this book, attitudes to death and the dead focus quite dramatically in the attitude of hope. Indeed, hope is a major bond linking life-style and death-style and the way societies engender and foster it reveals a hallmark of each society's character. Concepts such as 'the American Dream', 'Human Rights', Democracy, Sharia Law, and the like, offer their own images of hope for people. For Christian theology hope is, essentially, Christ-focused, most especially in relation to death as one major constraint upon hope.[44]

One aspect of hope lies in the afterlife and what can be done to ameliorate the lot of the dead. Though here, as elsewhere in this book, the notion of the 'dead' is problematic in the sense that it includes those who 'live' or somehow exist in afterlife worlds.[45] Indeed, this is a constant problem when dealing with 'the dead' who are often treated as alive in some sense or another. The Medieval period is well-known as one in which the living and the dead had some form of exchange-communication in and through rites performed on their behalf, as in requiem masses. Prayers for the dead said in chantries established for that very purpose offer concrete architectural evidence for this human concern for their dead. During the English Reformation many aspects of this exchange were removed and, in a sense, the living were deprived of their dead. But that did not mean that the dynamics of the after-world were rendered redundant as is shown in the interest of Christ's activity in that domain.

The new Church of England debates over the phrase in the Apostles' Creed, 'He descended into hell', revisited earlier Christian discussions to reveal a spectrum of belief on the afterlife. One issue was whether ancient figures such as Adam, Abraham, Isaac and Jacob were with God in heaven or in some other location. Because, for Protestants, much hung on ideas of faith and the preached word of God as a necessary prelude for gaining heaven some argued that the ancient patriarchs did, in effect, have the benefits of the gospel long before the birth of Christ because of their faith. 'The Gospel was preached to Adam, now dead, but then alive, when Christ Iehoua preached to him the Seede of the woman'.[46] Some pressed the point that the doctrine of Purgatory was but a new

---

[44] Willi Marxsen ([1968] 1970: 175–188) offers highly informative and pastorally valuable insights on hope as part of his textual analysis of resurrection motifs.

[45] When Richard Carlil (1582: 73), for example, says that 'dead' cannot be used of 'souls' that live in an afterlife he highlights the problem of how to classify 'the dead'.

[46] Richard Carlil (1582: 73).

product of the Council of Ferrara of 1439 and spoke freely, for example, of Adam ascending immediately to heaven as does anyone whose faith leads them to crave pardon and seek mercy. Heaven itself is conceived as the church with Christ as its head and, for example, with Abel as its 'first martyr'.[47] There was a variety of opinion over how Jesus may have engaged with that after-world that included descending to hell whilst still alive on the cross, that he descended only in his power, or that he descended in both body and soul and suffered torments there after his crucifixion.[48] Some, with much citing of early Church Fathers and Thomas Aquinas, even wondered why and by whom the 'descended into hell' clause was included in the appropriate creed at all. Whatever the detail, however, the overall message was that the conquest of evil upon the cross resulted in ultimate repercussions in infernal regions. Satan, sin, death and hell were well and truly vanquished. A major feature of these debates was that the nature of the soul as distinct from the body was also well and truly agreed upon by all and that the life after this life mattered a great deal. Here were grounds for hope.

However, from Calvin and Cranmer's days to ours, it cannot be said that any degree of unanimity persisted within Christian traditions over these issues. Though Catholics and Protestants were one in the sixteenth and seventeenth century in their belief in a soul-body theological anthropology, even though they differed radically on how one might or might not be related to those souls after death, that changed. As we saw in Chapter 2, the twentieth century witnessed Protestant theologians abandoning ideas of the soul in preference for a unified sense of a 'person' and of a newly-created resurrection body that would appear by divine goodwill in due course. In popular Christianity, however, ideas of the soul passing on after death continued to hold sway for the majority of those Britons who believed in an afterlife as in the following table.[49]

Afterlife beliefs in English Anglicans and Roman Catholics (%)

Group	Soul passes	Resurrection	Returning	End of life	Trust in God
Anglican	33	4	14	32	17
Roman Catholic	48	18	11	14	32

[47] Richard Carlil (1582: 12).

[48] Richard Parkes (1604: 24). *A Brief Answer unto Certain Objections and Reasons Against the Descension of Christ into Hell.* Oxford: Joseph Barnes. Key texts were, Acts 2: 27. Psalm 16: 10. 1. Pet 3. 19. Eph 4. 19.

[49] Adapted from Douglas J. Davies and Alastair Shaw (1995: 93). For 1603 people interviewed in their own homes. Some held to several categories as in the Catholic case. Often 'Trust in God' partnered other categories. The percentage scores in each column thus stand independent of each other.

Practically a third of those identifying with the Church of England in this random sample of the general public saw death as, essentially, the end of our existence, compared with some 14 per cent of Roman Catholics. Those accepting an afterlife often held some kind of soul belief, both in an explicit sense of 'the soul passing on' and also in what is here labelled 'Returning', and which referred to 'coming back as something or someone else', a phrase used in preference to 're-incarnation'. Similarly, many opted for 'trust in God' alongside these beliefs. What is obvious is that any direct acceptance of formal resurrection belief was relatively low for both churches whose theologies are strongly resurrection focused. The higher Catholic profile on the single 'soul' motif easily reflects the strength of liturgical concerns with the soul in that church's theology. What is also apparent is that those identifying with the Church of England had a very low interest in resurrection motifs. At the time of that survey, in the mid 1990s, it was these people who had a moderately extensive familiarity with cremation when compared with Catholics whose adoption of cremation after their Church's acceptance of it in the mid 1960s was relatively slow.

For those with such a soul-belief cremation could resonate with the ending of the body and its significance far more than the actual ritual language used at cremation with its references to resurrection. The dissonance between ecclesial language and popular belief in resurrection may well have been one reason why the practice of taking ashes from crematoria developed from the later 1970s and then increased rapidly. In terms of our notion of life-style coherence, while people might have to accept church-based rites at the crematorium they could, privately, do what they liked. Though accepted in Britain as relatively customary, indicating how quickly custom can change in relation to newly invented traditions, many other countries, as Sweden, do not so easily permit the removal of remains.[50]

Theology of Cremation

Such potential confusion in communication between clergy and people included a potential for confusion over the topics of commendation of the soul and com-mittal of the body that were implicated in crematorium rites. If there is no 'soul' what is 'commended' and to whom? Presumably it is the person who is to be commended, but how should we think of a 'person' in relation to his or her 'body', especially a dead body? Certainly, there is a definite corpse present but to what or to whom is it to be committed? How might one best speak of fire, or cremation, or the God behind the fire and cremation process? And what of the resulting remains? Do they constitute a substance that could be regarded as a symbol of the deceased in such a way that commendation language remains applicable at any subsequent rite, or are they simply a symbol of the body that was once committed to fire and now is committed to earth?

These are questions that a new rite creates for an old tradition and they prompt the issue of a potential theology of cremation. Here I assume that it is worth

[50] Curt Dahlgren and Jan Hermanson (2005: 60–64).

asking whether there could and should be a 'theology' as opposed to, or perhaps related to, the traditional Christian commitment to theology rooted in burial. This is interesting since it was not the churches that introduced modern cremation. From a church perspective it was the laity or even the broadly secular populace that accepted the practice with most churches following behind, realizing that they needed to be involved. They did so, however, by retaining an essential 'burial theology' with an absolute minimal change in liturgical language. And even when some verbal changes occurred their theological base remained unchanged. Against that background it is worth asking whether a 'cremation theology' might not be valuable. To do so is to assume that theology involves a creative process grounded in the Christian tradition while also being both responsive towards and innovatory in relation to contemporary contexts. Though here it is only possible to offer the briefest reflection on a theology of cremation it is worth doing so as a further prompt for liturgists whose work has, already, issued some results.

At the outset any theology will dwell upon appropriate symbols since theologies are, essentially, exercises in the deployment and interplay of symbols. Baptism has its water, the Eucharist its bread and wine and, in burial, the earth from which we came is thrown upon our coffin. But what of cremation? The obvious answer is fire: yet in modern cremation fire is a hidden symbol and hidden symbols are problematic. In eastern Europe, for example, this is less problematic due to the use of fire in flame-holders associated with funerals. If not fire, however, what of the crematorium itself as a prime symbol, especially perhaps its mode of separating people from the coffin-contained body? Indeed, there is some empirical evidence to mark the crematorium as some kind of a 'sacred building' and I have analysed that elsewhere.[51] But, the more obvious symbol of cremation, and the one I pursue here, lies in the ashes. Unlike burial, in which the corpse as 'input' in the rite predominates, in cremation it is ashes as the outcome of the rite that come to the fore. Despite the fact that ashes play no part in the cremation rite itself cremated remains have come to be important as the focal symbol of cremation, now itself established as culturally normative in Britain. And ashes are accessible and with potential for use in a great variety of popular ways.

Theologically, however, ashes are a problematic symbol especially if we understand a symbol to participate in that which it represents. In Christianity, the corpse is a symbol both of death and of resurrection life because no corpse can be ultimately differentiated from the corpse of Jesus. Yet, unlike, Jesus, the Christian corpse is, in burial, offered to or made subject of the process of decay. Its ultimate destiny, whether or not involving a soul, or prayers on behalf of that soul, belongs to a divine providence. Ashes differ from the corpse in that they do not carry the double message of a death-process and a future resurrection in anything like a similar way. Current liturgical theology would seem to reject the view. It assumes that ashes are 'like' a corpse and ought to be buried in and through a 'burial theology'. Yet it is here that we encounter a dissonance, for symbols work when they make sense to people, and the making of sense involves complex intuitive

---

[51] Douglas J. Davies (1996).

processes that may well not occur in this case. For ashes are already 'processed'. They are more like a final product than the 'intermediate substance' of a corpse. Certainly, when ashes are buried in a grave and treated as a body this symbolic dissonance can be ignored or even partly overcome, but when people actively, and of their own cultural accord, do not bury them in a formal liturgical fashion, but use them in some private rite then it is highly unlikely that resurrection motifs will predominate.

Four potential ecclesiastical responses to this are feasible. One, that ashes be continued to be buried as though they were a corpse under standard burial theological ideas; the second, that special formal rites be generated for their disposal under some theology of cremation; the third, that some guidance be provided for individuals to use in their private actions and, the fourth; that people be allowed to do whatever they want following on after a church-led cremation service. If the second option is deemed worthy then some theology of cremation might emerge to help people think and feel their way through the cremation of their relatives. What features might enter into such a theology? Though only some basic thoughts can be offered in the scope of this book it is worth pondering some constraints and opportunities such a challenge presents.

Fire

At the outset fire is a problem. Since theology needs relating both to ritual actions and to the materials used in them this medium of cremation appears paradoxical. Traditionally, the key rites of Christendom have deployed very specific materials in water for baptism and also in other rites including the sprinkling of coffins, bread and wine for Eucharists and more popularly and not sacramentally defined, earth in burial. Earth, too, has been used, for example, in the funeral rite preparatory to cremation in the Church of Sweden where it is placed on the coffin, an action fully exemplifying the earth-burial motifs of Christianity and, practically, ignoring or even contradicting the fact of the cremation that is to follow.

As for fire and cremation, it is fire that has to be considered as the ritual material at hand and despite its liturgical use in the Paschal Vigil Service where newly kindled fire and the candles lit from it symbolize the resurrection and the light of Christ fire has had many negative connotations in Christian culture history as in the burning of heretics. In one traditional but perhaps overly logical sense this might not be seen as problematic since earth burial also had its punitive element in that it was disobedient Adam who would be returned to the earth from whence he was formed. Fire, too, could be read as similarly punitive but that would be entirely unfeasible in the modern world and would, in any event, be symbolically wrong on the Adam-earth model. For humanity did not come from 'fire' in order to return to 'fire'. There would be no appropriate traditional framing for destructive and punitive fire. But all is not lost given the cleansing and purgative attributes of fire and the way other fire-motifs have been deployed. Words such as those of the Canticle, *The Benedicite,* for example, offer some background possibilities: 'O ye fire and heat, bless ye the Lord, Praise Him and magnify Him for ever.' This notion of fire as a creature of God offers a real potential here and is, for example, evident in the way Teilhard de Chardin mediated on his death:

> Set me ablaze and transmute me into fire that we may be welded together and made one . . . Teach me to make a communion of death itself.[52]

Poetic theological utterance is of the essence of the flow of worship that captures the mood of the heart to inspire faith. That, at least, was what I took as a motivating assumption when composing the following prayer as a suggestion for use in cremation services at the crematorium. It is entitled 'Prayer of Light' because it seeks to contextualize 'fire' as a subset of 'light', and to identitfy 'light' with Christ.

> *Prayer of Light*
> O Lord by whose word the heavens were made,
> Whose love made us from dust,
> Receive the mortal remains of (N) now departed this earthly life.
> Dutifully we give his body for cremation,
> As ashes to ashes, dust to dust,
> In the hope of life eternal, through Christ our Living Lord.
>
> That as the flames of earth consume our mortality
> So in the fullness of time the flame of your love
> May remake us eternally in the glory and stature of Christ
> Who alone is the Light of the World
> The light no darkness can end,
> Who with You and the Holy Spirit
> Is God for ever and ever. Amen.[53]

Certainly there are examples of similar funerary alliances of concepts as in the Syrian Marthoma Church where Christ is identified as the 'Sun of righteousness, in whose light the heavenly beings tremble . . . who visits those in their graves with the rays of his radiance, who is the true light that lightens the darkness with his wondrous splendour'.[54] In these, as in all Christian funerary rites it is easy to take for granted and in the process to ignore the significance of the place of Jesus Christ and, in particular, the very fact of the personalizing of the death in hand through its association with the death and life of Jesus. The power of Christian faith lies, to a great extent, in the links that people can make between themselves and this particular person. Though formal theology grounds itself in discussing the nature of Jesus as the divine Son possessing both human and divine natures and set in relation to a Father and Holy Spirit in the Holy Trinity, it is likely that many believers find their sense of Jesus in their capacity to identify with him

---

[52] Teilhard de Chardin (1974: 95).
[53] Douglas J. Davies (1990: 45).
[54] Paul P. J. Sheppy (2004, Vol. 2., p. 107).

in his human life experiences. This sense of affinity is fundamental in faith. When they stop to reflect on their experiences some Christians doubtless invest their image of Jesus with highly 'divine' and supernatural attributes whilst others venture to stress his humanity, but the affinity is, nevertheless, grounded in their human and personal need. The deep attraction of Christianity lies in this rooting of a life-style and death-style within another 'person'.

Crematorium

It is precisely that personal identification, albeit almost unconscious, that has consequences for cremation as a process of transforming the bodily basis of personal identity and for the crematorium as the place where that occurs. Indeed, it is precisely the theme of impersonality that has often emerged in British discussions of cremation as we saw in Chapter 2. It is an important factor given the very high incidence of cremation in Britain for, in addition to the potential depersonalizing of the dead, there has often existed a popular sense of crematoria as production-line, factory-like, institutions that process the dead. Here the coffin becomes a symbol of that process and, as such, is reduced in personal significance. More particularly, the coffin as a box processed by a conveyor belt gained a certain degree of popular expression once cremation became established in Britain after the 1960s. As I have shown elsewhere the material basis for this idea of conveyor-belt processing was hardly justified by the obvious facts of the case since, as survey evidence showed, only a very small number of crematoria employed such a device.[55] However, it is very likely that the idiom of being processed was much more applicable to the congregation's sense of being 'processed' as they had to enter many crematoria by one door and exit by another. This 'flow through' scheme was deployed to speed-up service times during a period when the numbers being cremated were steadily increasing. Some have sought to offset or counteract this implicit sense by actively promoting ritual action directed to or focused on the coffin. The Catholic tradition possesses the relatively easy means of achieving this with holy water with all its evocation of baptism and Christian identity, others employ a touching of the coffin or standing by it rather than speak liturgical words from a distant lectern. To involve family and friends some invite the placing of a flower on the coffin prior to its committal and removal from the crematorium chapel. It is also not unknown for people to 'address' the person in the coffin as though they were able to hear, an act that prompts its own issues over identity, the dead, and the living.

---

[55] Davies, Douglas J. (1995: 20). In this 1990 survey, of the 225 British crematoria, of which 136 (60 per cent), responded, only 6 per cent had conveyor-belts.

Chapter 9

Life-Death Balance

We speak so easily of life and death as a natural pair, but are they always naturally suited? Life and old age or working life and retirement, for example, furnish alternative pairs as might the period of hectic domestic family-life compared with later years when young adult children all leave home. The changing dynamics of our life-cycle reflected in these pairings provide the underlying drive of this chapter as we ponder how the life-styles they express relate to potential death-styles.

One of the most frequent and recent uses of a similar pairing of concepts is that of 'work-life' balance, a phrase much used by those responsible for the 'human resources' – the employees – of many of today's companies and businesses. It reflects the priority of work in the life of many British contemporaries and, albeit indirectly, it invokes death through the implicit idea of stress resulting from a 'work-life' imbalance. In exploring these themes we first adopt a direct appraisal of life as a process demanding death before pursuing a more abstract approach to philosophical and theological perspectives on death in complex western societies.

Ecology of death

Death and life are absolutely one in the basic fact that we need food. Even when the human staple diet is that of corn, wheat, rice or potato, it requires the death of the source plant. Though seldom viewed as 'killing', a term generally reserved for animal life, the processing of food normally involves its death, whether in harvesting or cooking. When we do eat 'living' plants, as in a lettuce just cut from the garden we speak of their 'freshness' rather than of their 'life'. To speak the obvious, here, is to highlight the most basic fact that human life demands death in the spiralling circles of food chains of existence. Many anthropological studies show how a society often views itself as distinct from the world around them in and through the process of food preparation. This divide is often formally categorized in terms such as 'culture' and 'nature' with prepared food becoming the medium for expressing human self-definition. In different cultures some rearrangement of symbolism becomes inevitable if, for example, blood is drawn from living cattle for the herdsmen's daily sustenance. Indeed, such a reminder is valuable in helping us relate the biological necessity of food for existence with the moral values invested in it. Though such cultural schemes have long expressed a clear recognition that human survival requires the death of plants and animals the changes effected by modern industrialized and commercialized food production for urbanized populations has changed such understanding in a radical way. In this change the eater has been alienated from the eaten. Such basic facts of cultural change have deep significance for theological views of the world including the recognition of processes of death that underlie our source of biological life. Nowhere is death-style and life-style more intimately bound than in this.

To talk about lettuce or fresh blood consumption when approaching the theology of death is, then, important because ideas of life and death pervade whole fields of human existence. Here, too, life-style and death-style cohere as the nature of vegetarianism demonstrates. Though seldom given explicit attention, menus and cookery books regularly reflect ideas of the meaning of life itself as espoused within a particular society and, certainly, often reflect the social structure of societies. The best known of these, perhaps, is the Indian food and drink system that deeply embeds the caste system and clearly marks the ritual purity associated with the hierarchical division of society. The case of traditional Judaism is also well-known as a scheme that helped maintain boundaries between God's chosen people and others and also, as some interpret it, helped symbolize the very unity of God, one perfect in every way and devoid of contradictory attributes. So, too, with the purity conceptions inhering in Islamic notions of *halal* foods. In both Jewish and Islamic cultures the animals eaten and the mode of their slaughter relate to the idea of the divine source of life. In the traditional Hebraic conception of 'the life being in the blood' we see, quite clearly, a theological frame placed around the killing of animals for food. The faithful do not 'eat life', for the life is in the blood and must be shed in ceremonial slaughter that reflects a kind of offering to God. The people eat what is now devoid of its own life as a substance that will sustain the independent life of the eater. Here individuals and their society follow divine commandment believing that all life comes from God. But, as in many aspects of life, one idea and practice evokes others so that 'life', in the Jewish case, becomes inextricably rooted in God. God gives it and takes it, God's people must honour and respect it, they must not murder those of their divinely chosen community. It is no accident that the Genesis myths not only link the giving of life to Adam and Eve with the provision of plants for food but also with the 'fruit of a tree' as a source of human death. The killing of Abel the herdsman by his pastoralist brother Cain also finds a place in the network of ideas tying sources of food to divine acceptability. Later prophetic treatment will speak of the lion eating grass like an ox[1] when it comes to pondering the perfect day of the Lord just as priestly writings develop rules for food use as part of a growing ritual domain associated with the temple and the organization of social life.

In quite a different way numerous forms of Eastern traditional thought have, apart from ideas of social status, associated different kinds of food and fasting with bodily, mental and spiritual conditions. In a symbolic sense something similar emerged in later twentieth- century western thought as attitudes to food developed with a growing interest in health and well-being. The intellectual force

---

[1] Isa 11. 7.

of the science of food often came to reinforce this general cultural interest with health and helped raise issues of social class differences in respect of eating habits, incidence of food-related illness and ultimately mortality rates.

All this is relevant here because, although slogans may tend to favour 'food and health' regimes over references to 'food and death', that link is not far removed. Indeed, the issue of obesity has come to assume political as well as medical significance in, for example, the developed societies of Britain and America. Obesity has become a potential symbol of death, with many authorities warning that young and fat generations may well begin dying before their parental generation raised in more austere days. In the opening decade of the twenty-first century fat occupies headline space more often than famine. Paralleling this are the many forms in which food is now also made to carry symbolic messages of health and well-being that, ultimately, relate to avoiding death for as long as possible. Wider aspects of food and death emerge over concerns with issues of food production, population growth and changing ecological conditions. Water, too, is rapidly assuming a place of some significance as an ultimate life resource.

Theology, food and death

As distant as these topics may, at first, appear no theology of death should ignore the social significance of food as a symbolic medium of vitality and mortality as also of death. Certainly, many political and economic aspects of food, life and death reflect biblical motifs of providing food for the starving and a reminder to the rich that a substantial food supply symbolized by feasts or good harvests stored in large barns do not furnish an adequate basis for life.[2] Here it is enough to note that food and death, or rather death's transcendence, are the two foci of the temptations of Jesus in the wilderness at the outset of his public ministry when the devil tempts the hungry man to turn stones into bread and to launch himself from a temple pinnacle to be saved by angels.[3] The subsequent saying of Jesus echoes traditional Jewish passages of divine deliverance in wilderness conditions, that 'Man does not live by bread alone, but . . . by everything that proceeds out of the mouth of the Lord.'[4] The development of both Jewish and Christian ritual, especially in The Passover and Last Supper, bonded the use of food substances with theological beliefs directly related to death and deliverance. And to that we return later in this chapter after, first, looking more carefully at symbolic aspects of life and death and the partnering of terms with which we began this chapter.

'Death' partnered

In his philosophical work on the nature of death in society Jean Baudrillard argues forcefully that 'the *institution* of death, like that of the afterlife and immortality,

---

[2] Lk 12. 17–31. 17. 19–31.
[3] Lk 4. 1–11.
[4] Deut 8. 3.

is a recent victory for the *political* rationalism of castes, priests and the church whose 'power is based on the management of the imaginary sphere of death'. As an argument on secularization he submits that the 'disappearance of the religious afterlife' in more recent times is the result of the State's increased power and control of life, indeed, the afterlife 'passes over into life itself.'[5] For him, of course, 'the Church' means the Roman Catholic Church and that largely in a French context, still, his broad picture holds for countries possessing dominant church organizations in recent times. His philosophical analysis is important for any theological engagement with the meaning of life and death in modern society because his is, perhaps, the best example of one who roots life and death issues in the material organization of economic wealth and political power. If nothing else Baudrillard is important as a restraint on turning death issues into strictly theological debates on resurrection, soul, immortality and eternity or into psychological analyses of grief in bereavement. Were his work theological it could be described as prophetic or as a crisis theology in the sense of serving a judgement on his day and age.

Underlying his approach is a deep commitment to that concept of reciprocity or gift-theory to which we have already referred earlier in his book and which sees human life as a process of give and take in the working out of various kinds of relationships. This he develops in an existential direction with a theory that life must pay its dues to death. Here we overlook the potential criticism that his use of gift-exchange theory is too forced in order to accept his emphasis on the theme of time, and the desire to accumulate 'time'. He argues that 'our whole culture is just one huge effort to dissociate life and death' as evident in religion's deferral of death into the afterlife, in science's preoccupation with 'truth' and in economics with its devotion to 'productivity and accumulation'.[6] It is here that time enters the discussion as a measure of the value of life, not least with strong economic overtones. In the British context, the drive to dissociate life from death emphasizes the hope for a long life whose economic ventures yields an equally enduring and wealthy retirement. The valuing of time begins in the work-place as notions such as 'quality time' cluster around other descriptions such as 'money-rich but time-poor' and are distanced from death because it challenges both time and riches. The distance between the first and twenty-first centuries become negligible as we hear echoes of that fear in the biblical parable of the rich farmer whose death came just when he had built bigger barns to house his wealth as a resource for future years.[7]

Baudrillard's point is that such accumulation is fruitless because it cannot engage in any form of exchange with death. To long to save money, as also to hope to 'save' time, is ultimately fruitless because both time and money are but expressions of a person's real place in society in which fulfilment comes only from actual exchanges with that society. Using this language of 'exchange' is useful as

---

[5] Jean Baudrillard ([1976] 1993: 144).
[6] Jean Baudrillard ([1976] 1993: 147).
[7] Lk 12. 13–21.

long as we appreciate that 'exchange' takes many forms with the greatest benefits accruing from the 'exchange' presented in forms of relationship.

Church and death

However, our concern here is with the engagement of the church with death and with the widening role of other institutions in respect of death. Take Baudrillard's assessment cited above that the power of churches is rooted in their 'management of the imaginary sphere of death'. Though most Christians would probably not appreciate his use of the term 'imaginary' in this context it is, in fact, a very valuable notion because it carries a strong technical meaning in the way he uses it. For him, something is an 'imaginary' – and it is used here as a noun with the indefinite article – when it stands in relation to something else and helps confer a meaning on that partner entity. So, for example, we often speak of 'man and woman' as two paired entities with each significant only because of the other. 'Man' on its own would have no real significance: so, too, with 'woman'. In Baudrillard's technical argument 'man' would be the 'imaginary' of 'woman' and 'woman' the 'imaginary' of 'man': the particular context determining the direction of the emphasis. So, too, with using the term 'imaginary' in relation to life and death. 'Death' on its own has no real significance, neither has 'life', each gains its particular sense and nuanced meaning from the other in a fashion that is especially important for the theology of death. Indeed, for this book, this imaginary pairing highlights the fact that 'death' depends on what we *mean* by 'life' just as we could argue that 'life' depends on what we mean by 'death'. It is this that underlies the constant motif of the paired life-style and death-style idioms in this book. We will explore this pairing here, asking how individuals or groups prefer to run the formula recognising that Baudrillard, himself, stops before posing this question. His concern is only to establish the importance of the relation[8] between the two, viewed more or less as equals but I want to be more nuanced by asking how a particular sense of one of them will influence the other in their paired relationship. Here, again, life-style and death-style cohere. To ask this question and to emphasize this kind of argument is not an exercise of playing with words or simply devising new modes of discourse for the philosophical fun of it: it is to grasp the seriousness of words in religion and their place in the life of faith. Here, then, we explore several imaginary[9] options and their driving assumptions to gain some sense of a spectrum of death views.

---

[8] For him it is precisely the 'structural relation' that is important ([1976] 1993: 133). This reflects the way in which formal Structuralism (as in the anthropology of Claude Lévi-Strauss) posed its analysis and saw the meaning of something as lying in 'the relation between' opposed pairs of other things.

[9] While dropping 'imaginary' for imaginary now that the meaning of the term is established, I still retain '-' around 'life' and 'death', where appropriate in this chapter, to indicate their imaginary status.

Death drives life

First: 'life' depends on what we mean by 'death'. 'Death' is the driving concept so that whatever significance is given to 'death' will influence what we then mean by 'life'. If 'death' means an empty nothingness, a pointless vacuum, perhaps viewed in a strongly philosophical way then its imaginary partner, 'life', should also bear some of those attributes. In ordinary terms someone might then say 'life is meaningless' precisely because they have a deep sense that 'death' is meaningless too. There is much in classical existentialism that would bear that out. But what of that type of Christian case in which people see 'death' as the entry into a heavenly afterlife of bliss with rewards for earthly action? There 'life' assumes a different meaning, often as the context for strong ethical endeavour and a rigid striving to obey divine commandments. Equally, as in the past, it could be a context of fear driven by a sense of 'death' as an afterlife of hell and its punishments. Different again would be an emphasis on 'death' as a present, day by day, 'dying with Christ' and entering into the love of God, with a corresponding sense of 'life' as a daily 'rising with Christ' in a realm of love for others, self and God.

These have all been or are viable theological options, but what of the case that many might identify as secular, of the ecologist who sees 'death' as the proper return of matter into the humus-rich, soil-skin, of the earth. This person, too, is likely to view 'life' in an 'imaginary' way but one not attracting an essentially negative partner. It would be possible to think of numerous other cases too in which the 'death' element drives the 'life' partner and all would reinforce the point that death is not a neutral word and shows the usefulness of 'death' as an imaginary partner concept of 'life' in the structured relationship through which we frame our existence.

Life drives death

Now we reverse the scheme to say that 'death' depends on what is meant by 'life'. In many respects we could simply reverse the points just made and, for example, say that ecologists view 'life' as a complex interplay of processes that reproduce biological systems and in which the cessation and decay of these systems plays a crucial role. The very nature of 'life' requires 'death', at least of complex biological structures, perhaps noting that single-celled entities seem to split into two new entities and causing the single 'parent' to cease to exist as such. In religious terms we might note that long tradition of earlier Jewish history in which 'life' was a covenant with God in which a promised land and a multitude of offspring was the goal and which made 'death' a blessing of old age in which one passed into a shady domain or even ceased to be, except as an ancestor held in respect by one's descendents. Several other theological versions of 'life' are possible and many will be able to develop their own accounts of them and go on to see how each would affect its imaginary partner of 'death'.

This form of argument allows us to see clearly not only that imaginary partner-terms influence each other but also that it is wise to clarify just what such partner-terms mean in discussions of mortality and eternity. This is especially important for the theology of death since we are now in a position to appreciate that there are many theologies of death because 'death' carries many meanings.

But this way of understanding partner-terms raises the question of just which terms better partner each other. We become so familiar with the common expression 'life and death' that they seem to bear an inevitable bond. But what if other partner-terms displace 'death', so that 'life' is not an imaginary partner of 'death' but that, for some people, and perhaps this is the case in some forms of spirituality 'life' is understood in relation to another prime concept. An example might be that of ancient Israel, as mentioned above, 'life' could be seen as an imaginary partner of 'covenant' or of divine blessing and increase.

Death and ?

So what of contemporary British Christianity? While, quite obviously, there is no single answer there are certain clear directions of thought. Charismatic Christians, for example, might well align 'life' with the 'Holy Spirit' as imaginary partners constituting this dynamic form of spirituality. The Holy Spirit as the Lord and giver of life, as the Nicene Creed expresses it, plays a vital part in the religious experience, in worship and in the theological framing of life-activities for Charismatic Christians and doubtless, for others too. In this context where 'life' and 'Holy Spirit' are the imaginary partner-terms of existence 'death' is likely to be understood as 'spiritual death', to be without the Holy Spirit, or ever in a worst case scenario to be influenced by an evil spirit. Here 'death' is unlikely to feature in hymns and charismatic songs as an afterlife motif unless it is an extension of enjoying the presence of divine power.

Then there are Christians for whom faith stresses social and economic justice as in many mainstream American Christian denominations where civil rights holds a high profile and serves as the model for other topics such as the rights of sexual minorities. For such 'life' means freedom to develop as a person within society and church community and without the pressures of oppression and prejudice. The imaginary partner of 'life' may not be 'death' as a biological cessation but 'oppression'. In other words, the apparently ordinary partnership expressed in the phrase 'life and death' is not as self-evident as may at first appear. The fact that Christian tradition has invested 'life and death' with a distinctive meaning and force itself demands specific exploration in particular contexts to allow the complexity of theological ideas to emerge.

Jesus and death motifs

Furthermore, the place of Jesus in such analyses is of fundamental importance for 'Jesus', too, plays an imaginary role as a partner-term in theological and faith-based utterances. The very meaning of his name is determined by its partner-term as in Jesus Christ. Another fine example lies in Teilhard de Chardin's[10] strange, poetic, yet science-inspired view of cosmic evolution focused on Christ enshrined in this prayer-like statement that challenges us to identify imaginary partners for

---

[10] Teilhard de Chardin (1881–1955). French Jesuit, much engaged in geology and palaeontology, especially in China. His rather unorthodox theological writings were only published after his death.

'death', or to consider whether 'death' lies merely in the background while some other concept emerges to partner 'Christ'. In his prayerful reflection Teilhard speaks both to himself and to the divine.

> Accept death in whatever guise it may come to me in Christ-Omega[11], that is, within the process of the development of life . . . Jesus-Omega, grant me to serve you, to proclaim you, to glorify you, to make manifest, to the very end, through all the time that remains to me of life, and above all through my death.[12]

Here we are in no afterlife of purgatorial cleansing, of a Paradise or of a City of God, location gives way to the process that is evolution understood both biologically and spiritually as a development of a universe driven by and towards love. This is a mode of discourse that changes the key and alters both the mood and the images of much traditional alliances of Jesus and the afterlife.

Pastoral challenge

While few may share Teilhard's view of life and Christ, there remain many forms and shades of belief amongst those served by clergy and others in the ongoing pastoral work of churches, making that task a challenging one. It is not surprising that increasing numbers of families wish to make some personal contribution to funeral ceremonies, with music, readings or words about the dead for in these we can appreciate the imaginary partner-concepts at work beneath their approach and choices. Often, it is the meaning of 'life' in imaginary partnership with 'family' that drives their desire to make an event of the funeral, rather than any partnership of 'life' and 'death'.

The task of many a pastor lies in negotiating such perspectives with the traditional language of their church that possesses a deep embeddedness of 'life' and 'death' motifs informed by narratives from Adam to Christ as second Adam, from baptismal rites of 'death' as imaginary partner to 'rebirth' and of marriage rites including the 'death-parting' motif of the vows. To all this may be added, for more regular churchgoers, the Eucharistic language of 'death', resurrection and of the sacramental food that may 'keep you in eternal life'. Against all this lie popular ideas of moral behaviour and the judgement of actions in relation to heavenly rewards, as well as the theological imperative of grace and divine love that often contradicts human expectations of reciprocity.

So, there is an importance in identifying 'life' and 'death' as imaginary paired concepts within an understanding of existence and of knowing how an emphasis upon one of these will influence how the other is perceived. Given that 'life' has

---

[11] 'Omega' fills a technical role in Teilhard's thought. It is the end point of all things, a summary of evolutionary processes and also of the evolution of love, it is God, 'the Centre of centres . . . The *totus Christus*' (See editor's note. Teilhard de Chardin ([1961] 1965: 90)).
[12] Teilhard de Chardin ([1961] 1965: 91).

a greater presence for the vast majority of contemporary people in advanced societies than does 'death' we can see how 'death' becomes the dependent variable whose meaning is influenced by the meaning of 'life'. This has many consequences, not least in terms of how the traditional theological weight given to death in established liturgical forms may differ significantly from current values and perspectives. Informally, this has been acknowledged in the way that ideas of hell and of heaven and, indeed, of much afterlife discourse, have either vanished or been retired to inevitable liturgical corners of church life. 'Life' has new imaginary partners, and these are felt as much by the clergy as by regular and occasional congregational members. The degree to which coherence obtains between them will be the degree to which the services of the church will or will not be sought.

Pragmatic management

Already there is some evidence that such coherence is absent for, as the twenty-first century begins, we find in England that while the mainstream churches still conduct the majority of funerals there is a growing minority that seek their own management of family death, including a more hands-on approach to the body and a decreased dependence on funeral directors. Similarly, an increasingly lay minority now take part in funeral services, giving readings, eulogies, or in providing music favoured by the deceased. The currently small yet increasing role of independent funeral officiants and of the British Humanist Association, for example, reflects a practical secularization both in the sense of a decrease of official church activity and also in the belief driving alternative forms of funerary event. Times are changing fast and with differing consequences. For clergy of established churches with enduring local pastoral commitments decreased contact with people through funerals may well be viewed as a loss, while for those with a more focused concern for a gathered congregation the shift could mean a saving of time for what they may regarded as their real work. In this field of pastoral service, however, 'gain' and 'loss' carry the double meaning of opportunity for pastoral support and of evangelism on the one hand and of economic income through funeral fees on the other and the latter may not be inconsiderable for churches whose financial base is weak.

What is obvious is that pastoral care is linked with both time and money. Part-time, paid, celebrants can devote themselves to a family over the period of initial bereavement and sometimes even afterwards in a way that clergy with large-scale responsibilities cannot. Such celebrants are also able to reflect the values of those they serve more easily than clergy who can be viewed as imposing a scheme or assuming that traditional religious schemes will apply. Contemporary funeral celebrants are more likely to talk to family members about themselves and the dead to arrive at a picture in which 'life' motifs will be linked to appropriate imaginary concepts rather than immediately to 'death'. This explains why the phrase 'celebration of life' has come to be increasingly important in death-related contexts. Even the notion of 'memorial' services has become less frequent. To replace memorial by celebration is to engage in a basic shift of value. It is worth noting that while, in the mid 1970s, Baudrillard cited Marcuse to the effect that 'theology and philosophy today compete with each other in celebrating death as an existential category',[13] we might now want to replacing 'celebrating death' with 'celebrating life': and that is a major shift.

Celebrating life

In the light of life-celebration we now take up the topics of old age and retirement on the one hand and the Eucharist on the other. Though, at first sight these may seem quite unconnected they are joined here under the heading of 'celebrating life' as a means of exploring further the issue of imaginary partner-concepts, in this case involving the interplay between ideas of celebration and thanksgiving. This provides opportunity for further reflection upon life and death and prepares for a further line of thought on 'sacrifice' in the final chapter.

Old age

For aging we return to Teilhard de Chardin and his poetically spiritual appropriation of older age as he pondered how to 'assimilate, utilize the *shadows* of later life'. 'Shadows' he defines as "enfeeblement, loneliness", and 'the sense that no further horizons lie ahead'. One is to 'discover in Christ-Omega how to remain *young*: gay, enthusiastic, full of enterprise', and not to think that 'every form of melancholy, indifference, disenchantment is to be identified with wisdom'. He defines what it means to be 'young' as being 'hopeful, energetic, smiling and clear-sighted', with 'smiling' as an expression of 'facing with sweetness and gentleness whatever befalls one'.[14] In this meditation upon his older age he expresses a piety worked out in relation to an idea of Jesus and a sense of the divine in him that takes the form of a deeply felt personal awareness.

> Desperately, Lord Jesus, I commit to your care my last active years, and my death; do not let them impair or spoil the work I have so dreamed of achieving for you . . . The grace to end well, in the way that will best advance the glory of Christ-Omega: this is the grace of graces. Live under the impassioned desire to help forward the synthesis of Christ and the universe. This implies love of both, and more especially love of the supreme axis, Christ and the Church. Communion in and through death: to die a communion-death . . . What comes to one at the very end: the adorable. I go forward to meet him who comes.[15]

Certainly, Teilhard retains some traditional language but it, too, is transformed: 'deeply and incurably my ills become engrained in my flesh, the more it may be

[13] Jean Baudrillard ([1976] 1993: 150).
[14] Teilhard de Chardin ([1961] 1965: 90).
[15] Teilhard de Chardin ([1961] 1965: 91).

you yourself that I am harbouring as a loving active principle of purification and of liberation from possessiveness'. He speaks of the 'dark tunnel' or 'dizzy abyss' as the future that lies before his aging life yet moves forward in the hope of being 'lost, of being engulfed' in the Lord, of being 'absorbed into your body'. His desire is not to 'receive communion as I die', but to be taught 'to make a communion of death itself'.[16]

In all of this 'life' is not partnered by imaginary 'death', it is partnered by 'Christ', and a 'Christ' whose significance is much less that of traditional creedal formulations of divine and human 'natures' in one 'person', all terms of profound and complex ancestry,[17] than of an evolution-inspired sense of moral meaningfulness in the cosmos as it forms and allows life and intelligent, self-conscious life, to emerge within it. But it also possesses a containment of negative powers: 'Grant that when my hour has come I may recognize you under the appearance of every alien or hostile power that seems bent on destroying or dispossessing me.' He refers to 'the erosions of age' that may 'begin to leave their mark on my body, and still more on my mind', and to the time when he may begin to lose hold of himself and, 'become passive in the hands of those great unknown forces which first formed me.' Then he prays for an understanding that it is the Lord who is 'painfully separating the fibres of my being so as to penetrate to the very marrow of my substance and draw me into yourself'.[18]

In Teilhard we see something that most will not see in their own lives, viz., an acceptance of the fact of pain and decay as a natural part of the ongoing and developing nature of the world itself. Throughout the twentieth century, advanced societies increasingly coped with pain through scientific medicine and came almost to assume that a painless death, probably sedated and unconscious, is a human right. The rise of the hospice movement and of developing palliative care has made some inroads into that territory to seek a sense of 'dignity' around death. That, itself, makes sense when it parallels a life that has been invested with respect. Indeed, as we have already seen, the closing decades of the twentieth century witnessed the emergence of the notion of 'respect' as a distinctive aspect of life sought by many, most especially by the economically or socially disadvantaged. The media tell of street gangs as groups within which youngsters seek 'respect', or of violence done to those not showing 'respect': it is far from a neutral word. Indeed, 'respect' may well be its own imaginary partner of 'dignity' as a person moves from life to death. These are terms that, fundamentally, speak meaning into what is otherwise meaningless, value into what is otherwise cheap or worthless. And this is where the search and need for social significance by the young and socially marginal for whom death may not seem a problem may mirror a similar need among the old.

[16] Teilhard de Chardin ([1961] 1965: 95).
[17] See John Hick (1976: 460–462) for the briefest appropriate note on 'persons' in the Trinity.
[18] Teilhard de Chardin ([1961] 1965: 94–95).

Arc of life

Contemporary social life exists as an arc, from conception and sought-for pregnancy, through birth and childhood, the middle-class person is trained for a good career or job. The curve of significance rises further in marriage and parenthood and in an accumulation of wealth that allows them to engage in socially admired and preferred leisure and domestic activities. Then, unlike many – but not all – traditional societies, where the curve of life rises into respected old age and a meaningful life ended in death, the life-arc curves down into retirement, where respect remains as long as economic wealth and social usefulness remains before passing into a marginalization of the very old. Their death is then as relatively insignificant as were the last years of life. Baudrillard's analysis of old age and retirement follows a similar argument, though much more nuanced by his driving model of reciprocity. He speaks of traditional societies in which, 'Years constitute real wealth which is exchanged for authority or power', compared with modern societies where accumulated years 'have no capacity to be exchanged'.[19] He speaks in an insightful but stark way of old age as a form of territory: 'recently colonized, old age in modern times burdens society with the same weight as colonized populations used to. Retirement or the 'Third Age', says precisely what it means: it is a sort of 'Third World'. Old age becomes a 'ghetto, a reprieve and the slide into death'. Here the challenge for Christian theology and church practice is enormous and, in many respects, not only raises the stake on how 'life' is valued in relation to death but also on the place of death within the life-reflection of older old people.

From another sociological direction Clive Seale's important work offers a driving hypothesis that 'social and cultural life involves turning away from the inevitability of death, which is contained in the fact of our embodiment, and towards life'. He describes the many ways in which language is utilized to achieve this end, especially in how it helps frame an idea of our self-identity that involves a 'hiding away' of death. He develops the notion of what he calls 'resurrective' practices, nothing to do with theology of resurrection, but as behaviour 'that restores a sense of basic security fractured by death' and which 'is also a routine feature of daily life'. This ultimately leads him to interpret the 'resurrection of the dead, usually experienced as a theme of organized religion' in terms of 'a resurrection of hope in survivors about continuing in life'.[20] This is one of the sharpest available expressions of a sociological analysis of the human drive for survival, one worked out in the form of a daily process of meaning-making in the face of the fear of senseless existence. Here there is strong support for my own former argument on the 'words against death' that underpin many aspects of culture and its means of establishing a sense of meaningfulness against the fact of death.[21]

This is, perhaps, precisely where contemporary Christian theology has an opportunity for pastoral support, given its traditional resources and organizational

---

[19] Jean Baudrillard ([1976] 1993: 163).
[20] Clive Seale (1998: 1, 4, 194).
[21] Douglas Davies (1997: 1).

presence in society. What, then, are its resources? First, it has the potential for talking about 'life' and 'death' as imaginary concepts that bring with them a weight of many meanings on life and the worth of persons covered in previous chapters while, secondly, it has ritual events through which to express those meanings and, thirdly, it has all these things embedded within a community. Having already explored baptism and marriage in a previous chapter we now consider the Eucharist as a further complex resource for the Christian life-style and death-style relation.

Eucharist

The Eucharist develops the baptismal theme of Christian identity as a conquest of death rooted in Christ's passion and resurrection. This is particularly obvious in its sense of being a 'thanksgiving' for that conquest of evil and the inauguration of a new life and of a community context for that life. As baptism marks the life of the body washed from sin and rising to life from death as Jesus was raised from death to life so the Eucharist speaks of feeding the new body of the believer by the sacrificed body of Christ which, at the same time, is acknowledged to be a resurrected and transformed body. The rite's many symbolic aspects develop these themes to include Christ's death as both a self and covenant sacrifice, his betrayal by disciples and even an abandonment by God. But, in this rite too, the Holy Spirit plays a key role in blessing and transforming the Eucharistic elements of bread and wine into the life-giving substance for the faithful. It is that Eucharistic blessing that turns bread into something more – just as we thought of cooking as turning 'natural things' into 'cultural' food suitable to eat. At the Last Supper – itself the model for the Eucharist – at least as portrayed in John's Gospel, the divine Father could hardly be more evident as the one from whom and to whom Jesus made his way, while the Spirit of Truth is promised. That Spirit is then given by Christ himself in one of his resurrection appearances.[22] Death lies at the heart of the Eucharist's proclamation of life making it perfectly fitted as the dominant rite integrating Christian life-style and death-style. In all Christian traditions the rite that is variously called the Eucharist, Mass, Holy Communion or Lord's Supper relates to that Last Supper which, in the New Testament, is related in a variety of ways to the Jewish Feast of Passover marking God's deliverance of the Jews from Egyptian captivity following the divine slaughter of the Gentile first-born. Jewish homes were saved from deathly visitation because of doors marked with the blood of sacrificed lambs. Death is the final plague brought to the Egyptians by the Lord such that, 'there was not a house where one was not dead.'[23] This prompts the Pharaoh to give the Jews their freedom and comes to be the mythical charter for interpreting the keeping of Passover until today. Here death and life are inextricably bound and confer mutual meaning upon each other with the symbolic power generated by these

[22] Jn 13. 3, 14. 15, 20. 22.
[23] Exod 12. 30.

associations providing a ready dynamism for the Passover meal in which Jesus uses words that identify him as the sacrificial lamb and the events that were to befall his disciples as a deliverance.[24] This involved his personal agony of self-commitment to the divine purpose, his betrayal, trial, crucifixion and death. His words at that Supper linking the Passover bread and wine with his own body and blood are evident in the earliest of records, as in Paul's outline of the night of betrayal,[25] and became pivotal in the development of subsequent Christian ritual with its growing emphasis upon deliverance from sin.

Whichever Christian tradition one chooses, the death of Jesus is pondered both as a sacrifice for sin and as a means of deliverance into, or participation within, a new and higher form of living. Traditional Catholic doctrines of the Mass may speak more of the priest and a re-offering of Christ's sacrificial death while sharp Protestant memorialist theologies may eschew such notions in order to engage in an act of faith that recalls Christ's act of salvation. The former furnish a ritual context of altar and priest, of crucifix, of distinctive forms of bread and wine and active remembrance. The latter seek to turn attention inwards to the heart of faith framed by a deep solemnity of affect. But life and death and life transformed remain central. Here we have a higher-order life that, symbolically, can be described through the blessing of food already cooked. This food, symbolic of life partnered by a quality of eternal existence rather than by death, is also a food not eaten alone and is not separate from the divine Master providing it.

Communion of Saints

Here food, fellowship and life are embraced by the Eucharist and as we approach this complex network we are alert to the intricacies of personal experiences framing it. These embrace former baptismal, marriage and funeral rites that a person is likely to have experienced in church as well as the experiences of daily life and family association. The liturgical language that variously speaks of this corporate sense includes reference to the Christian family, the body of Christ and, by wider extension, to the entire Communion of Saints. In some traditions this is subdivided into the church militant on earth, the church expectant composed of the dead who are resting or in a state of purgatorial preparation in anticipation of becoming the church triumphant in the full divine presence. And it is to one aspect of this corporate body in relation to death that I now want to re-draw attention by means of some empirical material derived from The Rural Church Project's research in five English dioceses.[26] The issue in question concerns the relationship between the living and the dead, one that has exercised much theological debate for centuries, especially between Catholic and Protestant forms of the faith. Shifting from doctrinal debate to empirical practical theology one study of active communicant members of the Church of England asked if they gained

---

[24] Mk 14. 22–24.
[25] I Cor 11. 23–32.
[26] Data gathered in 1989 (Davies, Watkins and Winter 1991) but on the issue raised here no subsequent research has been done. Previously introduced in Chapter Four.

some sense of the presence of their dead loved ones when at the Eucharist. The following table reveals the results arranged by percentage within age groups.

Experiencing the dead at the Eucharist

Age	18–34	35–44	45–54	55–64	65+
%	50	39	31	27	47

Source: Table from Douglas Davies (1990: 28).

The extent to which people felt able to respond to this theme is noteworthy, as are the dual peaks of early and later adulthood, the former marking the death of the grandparental generation while the latter that of partners and peers. It is, perhaps, not surprising that a liturgy in which life and death are closely combined, that formally prays for the departed, and links the living and the dead in the wider unity of Christians, should evoke such experiences. In a much larger random sample of the general British population approximately a third reported sensing the presence of the dead, most often of parents and grandparents, at some time or other, though this was not related to specific church ritual, and was more likely to be in the domestic context of the home.[27]

These empirical results raise interesting theological questions over the role of liturgical prayer in relation to personal experience and could, for example, be explored much further for those churches in which prayers for the dead are largely forbidden for doctrinal reasons. The dynamics of life are such that the memory of others often helps constitute part of individual identity. Indeed imagination and memory are hardly discrete components of thought and their mutual activation in liturgical contexts informs Christian spirituality to a marked degree.

Food, faith and life

The Eucharist is thus a complex phenomenon, not simply in terms of its theological and liturgical history but also in terms of personal and group psychology. In it we encounter not what might be called 'survival' but 'symbolic' food that carries extensive loads of significance often aligned with ideas of divine sustenance, provision or salvation. This distinction offers one way of exploring the distinction between different levels or qualities of life in relation to ideas of death.

Theologically speaking we can bring this to sharp focus in Eucharistic logic through the biblical language of St John's Gospel where humanity lives, not by the survival food of bread alone but, by the symbolic bread of life who, as Jesus the Christ, is that divine word that was 'in the beginning with God' and which subsequently proceeds from the mouth of God in and through his incarnation.

---

[27] Davies and Shaw (1995: 96–97).

The Prologue to John's Gospel, familiar to so many as the liturgical Gospel for Christmas Day, presents these ideas in an intensity of symbolic association that comes to fullest expression in the notion of 'life'. John makes it absolutely clear that 'in him was life', a life that was also 'the light of men.' It shines in the darkness but the darkness is not able to seize it and put it down.[28] At the very outset this Gospel establishes the issue of life as a concept of considerable force: not simply as a concept of survival but of transcendence or, as we might express it, of super-survival or salvation. We have already seen how John's first chapter compares the water of John the Baptist's immersion rite with the Holy Spirit baptism that Jesus is to accomplish.[29] This comparison of two levels of significance is dramatically reinforced in John's second chapter with its 'sign' of water transformed into wine at the marriage in Cana of Galilee: not only does the water become wine but good wine. For John's Gospel this sign of Christ's 'glory' is an occasion for the disciples to believe.[30] The dichotomy of ordinary water and supernatural wine, of life in the flesh and in the spirit, as well as divisions between earthly and heavenly, the below and the above, run throughout the gospel.

There are two reasons for referring to John's Gospel here. First, because it has often been extensively used as a resource for interpreting later developments of Eucharistic and baptismal theology, stressing the symbolic nature of Christ's body and blood in relation to the ritual use of bread and wine, as well as the power of the Holy Spirit in human renewal and rebirth. Notably, John has the dead Jesus speared so that 'blood and water' flow from his side.[31] The second, and perhaps less obvious value in John lies in the contrast made between levels, degrees, or forms of 'life'. Here, again, the 'below' contrasts with the 'above', the material with the spiritual. John begins his third chapter with the account of ordinary birth and the water that pertains to material life contrasted with the Spirit so that one must be 'born of water and the Spirit'[32] if one is to have the power to enter God's kingdom. To reinforce the point still further his fourth chapter, whilst opening with a note on baptism rapidly moves to a consideration of qualities of 'drinking water' and wells. In his conversation with the Samaritan women at the well at Sychar she speaks of quenching thirst and he of 'living water', of an interior spring supplying an eternal yet personal well.[33] The early preoccupation of this Gospel with water as a medium that speaks of ordinary levels of life and of the higher life in the Spirit continues into Chapter 5 where even miraculous waters at a Jerusalem healing site are transcended by Jesus' own power when he tells an invalid there to 'pick up his bed and walk'. This leads into a theological discourse that comes to focus in the words that the day is coming when the dead will hear Jesus' words 'and will live', because Jesus, as the divine Son, has been granted 'life in himself'. The Gospel moves rapidly from issues of water to those

---

[28] Jn 1. 4.
[29] Jn 1. 24–33.
[30] Jn 2. 11.
[31] Jn 18. 34.
[32] Jn 3. 5.
[33] Jn 4. 7–15.

of food: five thousand are miraculously fed while the disciples are warned about the difference even between food miraculously produced and the real 'food which endures to eternal life'. This, again, leads into the affirmation that Jesus is 'the bread of life' and that the faithful who 'eat the flesh of the Son of man and drink his blood' will be raised up from death in a resurrection at the last day.[34] By the close of his sixth chapter, which includes the note that some found all these ideas too 'hard' and withdrew, and that betrayal would follow one day, this Gospel has presented its prime ideas of a life of the flesh and another of the spirit, the first grounded in death and the second in a higher quality of life symbolized by participation or 'abiding' in the identity of the Son of man and in the promised resurrection. This is one of the clearest grammars of discourse of life, death and higher-order life in the New Testament and furnishes one profound resource for those seeking to engender a Christian life-style and death-style within their meditative life and practical ethical existence. Other formulations are, of course, perfectly possible and might include, for example, Charismatic or Liberation styles of spirituality, each with their valuation of life and death, and with an accompanying ethical vision of living.

Betrayal as death

Any such theological ethics will, inevitably, have to engage not only with the enhancement of life but also with the opposed forces of depletion, one of which needs some comment here, that of betrayal. Betrayal is a phenomenon which is its own form of 'death', in the sense of its onslaught on life and on the flourishing of individuals. This needs attention as part of the intimate alignment of life-style and death-style of Christians not only because betrayal stands at the heart of John's portrayal of the climax of Jesus' ministry amongst his disciples but because of its occurrence in everyday life. Its positioning in the Gospel reinforces its paradoxical presence in association with the Last Supper. This theme is also evident in the Synoptic Gospels[35] and it is no accident that Paul also makes strong reference to Christ's taking bread and wine and defining them as expressing the new covenant in his body and blood when chiding Christians at Corinth for their improper behaviour and, in that sense, for a kind of betrayal of the message they had received from him. Indeed, he frames the Christian ritual meal with the statement that it was, 'in the night in which he was betrayed' that Christ took bread and wine. Paul invests this fellowship meal with some importance as his words indicate: 'For I received from the Lord that which I gave to you.'[36] Here was something central to the tradition and, indeed, to his identity as an apostle. Betrayal, at least betrayal of a kind, was there as an established early theme in Pauline spirituality if we may identify it in his self-description as one in which he had 'persecuted the church of God'.[37]

---

[34] Jn 6. 27, 52–54.
[35] Douglas J. Davies (2000).
[36] I Cor 11. 23.
[37] I Cor 15. 9.

Eucharistic gift

Paul is not alone, for all of the gospels highlight the issue of betrayal.[38] The power of this motif should not be overlooked given the context not simply of a shared meal, but of the Passover meal. Not only did mutual eating in that cultural context mark family unity and a high order of obligation but also the additional dimension of deeply shared identity against an oppressor or even an enemy. With the Last Supper context the ensuing betrayal reveals an enemy within and not without the sacrifice-marked doors. John makes this poignantly emphatic in a text in which Jesus actually gives a specific morsel to Judas, at which point Satan enters him and he goes out into the night.[39] Food becomes the symbol, one might even say the negative sacrament, of betrayal. But, whilst it is focused on Judas, betrayal in some sense comes to extend to the disciples at large in the Synoptic tradition as they flee when Jesus is arrested or, in the case of Peter, verbally deny knowing Jesus at all.[40] The Johannine tradition engages with betrayal in a more complex way, noting both Peter's stark denial and that the disciples will be 'scattered every man to his own home' leaving Jesus 'alone'.[41]

All these ideas, including friendship and betrayal, are part of the theological resources of Christianity available for development across wide areas of the life of faith, not least in terms of old age and death, resources whose interpretation can benefit from the theoretical insights of that gift-theory that we have already partially used and now develop further.

It has become entirely natural to speak of 'gifts' in relation to the flow of Eucharistic action. The elements of bread and wine are seen as gifts coming from God through natural processes of plant growth, then taken and offered as 'gifts' to God before being received back as consecrated gifts to succour life 'in the Spirit'. Underlying the species of bread and wine is the ultimate 'gift' of Jesus as God's Son, given as a sacrifice for the life of the world. We ourselves, then become gifts offered both to God as an act of mundane worship and to the world at large through lives of service.

But such 'gift-language', often recurrent in previous chapters, can often be loose and lose much of its potential significance. To overcome this some degree of technical analysis is valuable, once more, to distinguish between alienable and inalienable gifts. This distinction is of real significance for theology and for understanding life and death for there is a powerful qualitative difference between alienable and inalienable gifts: the former belong, as it were, to the market place, they can be bought and sold and their value is readily easily assessed. We use many such gifts as part of ongoing social life, they constitute presents and mark relationships and different kinds of situation and there is always a degree of appropriateness to the market value of the gift and the relationship marked. Balances come to occur in what Mauss saw as the threefold process of giving, receiving and in a future responsive return gift. One of the beneficial aspects of

---

[38] Matt 26. 21. Mk 14. 18. Lk 22. 21. Jn 13. 21.
[39] Jn 13. 26, 30.
[40] Mk 14. 71.
[41] Jn 13. 38. 16. 32.

these gifts is that they reflect personal relationships of some kind while also being based in a monetary value. They reflect the 'thought' behind the cost of a gift, and that 'thought' is a symbolic expression of a relationship.

But what of inalienable gifts? These Mauss saw as including gifts that humans give to the gods. Other anthropologists[42] have developed these ideas and allow us to see how such 'gifts' are not rooted in market economies but have to do with the deepest values of a society. To give and receive them is to be engaged in profound aspects of being human and being related to others, not least to the past and to the beliefs and values that underpin our very way of life. In popular terms, for example, we often speak of something as having 'sentimental value': that would be an inalienable gift. Within families such objects that we may inherit or are passed on to us speak of family ties, of love and memory and of certain commitments to the future.

For Christian theology it is obvious that the Eucharistic elements or 'gifts' of bread and wine do carry a market cost and have to be purchased for use but that their 'gift' nature lies elsewhere and cannot be 'purchased' when 'received'. The reason for that is obvious, for in the processes of thanksgiving and consecration their status or identity changes because they become intimately aligned with another gift, one that is totally inalienable, the gift of Jesus as the Son of God. This kind of anthropological analysis is very theologically useful because, for example, it completely avoids the traditional and much disputed theologies of how bread and wine relate to Jesus' body and blood. Instead of arguments over transubstantiation, consubstantiation or memorialist thoughts of Jesus and his presence the grammar of discourse, the very way of talking about the significance of these things changes.

The alienable become inalienable through worship. The underlying and dominant power of Jesus as the divine gift transforms other sorts of gift. An increase or metamorphosis in value occurs and this bears directly on any understanding of 'life' and 'death'. For it is the body of Christ, itself a symbol of his death, that becomes the food of and for spiritual life, a theme that countless Christian authors have explored for millennia. This body is inalienable: it cannot be bought and it cannot be sold. It links us to the source of Christian value in Jesus and in his relation with the earliest disciples. This bread and wine then poses the question of what is valuable in and about life? The theological answer running and developing through Eucharistic theology, and we can see this as intimately allied with baptismal theology, is that the alienable gifts of creation, divine as they are, are yet transformed under the influence of the inalienable gift of salvation. The consequence of this for the worth of human life is that the apparently alienable life of creatures becomes the inalienable life of the redeemed. Again, in theological terms, it is the Holy Spirit that makes it so by bringing to us this vision of how things are.

As though to reinforce this vision in the most powerful of all ways the phrasing of some Eucharistic prayers and readings includes the scripture that it was 'in

---

[42] See Jacques Godbout with Alain Cailllé ([1992] 1998), and Maurice Godelier ([1996] 1999).

the same night that he was betrayed' that Jesus took the bread and the wine of the Passover meal and laid a foundation for the rites that would evolve as the Eucharist, Mass or Lord's Supper, according to different traditions. The significance of this is more dramatic when viewed through gift-theory than through the memorialist-transubstantiation debate which itself leaves the depths of the 'betrayal' motif largely untouched. And it is that motif that highlights the question of how the utterly inalienable can be sold for a market price? The infamous thirty pieces of silver become the symbol of all betrayal[43] and mark the paradox of love and love betrayed whose emotions reach into the depths of human hope and despair and touch the roots of death in life.

And this is of direct bearing upon old age and death for it speaks of the 'value of life' and brings that whole domain of worth to the forefront of our concern. The 'work-life' balance mentioned earlier was once socially structured though weekends, holidays and retirement. The rise of healthy older and old age and the prospect of very long retirement before, perhaps, the confinement of care, is rapidly changing that scheme. This means that the social value placed upon people in the different phases of life is also changing. We have seen Baudrillard's social analysis of the 1970s with its extremely negative appraisal of old age as a sort of 'Third World', but already much is changing still further. More people will work into what was once retirement time, but really old age is likely to increase and to pose questions on the arc of life with its favoured endeavours.

The challenge for Christian theologies lies in how to view imaginary 'life'. To see what proper partner-concepts bear an affinity with it. It may be that ecological ideas are already shifting an alienable-gift sense of the material products of the world into something inalienable. The world itself as a gift beyond price and 'life' within it as such too. Just how that 'life' is then related to 'death' in imaginary ways remains to be seen. What this and previous chapters have shown is that Christian theology has many resources within its pool of potential orientations to existence to challenge and sustain thinking and living amidst these issues, and the final chapter extends that resource still further.

---

[43] Matt 26. 15.

Chapter 10

To Live and Live Again

Christian churches own the problematic but inevitable 'double imperative' of maintaining the millennia-long traditions of the Jewish-Christian past whilst fostering the faithful in today's quite different world.[1] Theology is part of the conversational debate sustaining that imperative while a theology of death explores it in a most particular way whether in fundamentalist beliefs of a literal heaven or in an entirely socio-psychological liberalism. Much hangs in the balance and ethos of this spectrum of belief. The nature of human life is such that some believers immerse themselves in the formal tradition with contemporary ideas hardly impinging upon the core of their being while others live the reverse mode. The latter cannot quite understand why the deep traditionalist either ignores or strongly opposes new ideas. To the traditionalist the faith falls if the afterlife is disbelieved. Others either ignore that issue while giving themselves to different themes of Christian living or else give up on 'belief' regarding 'eternal life' in any formal sense.

In so offering tradition as a deep human resource for contemporary living, most especially in relation to death, Christianity offers a blessing and a curse. The blessing lies in the many ways hope – as the ground rock of human survival, and love – the basis for human flourishing, have been combined by past believers and made available for our own contemporary pondering. The curse lies in the sense of dismay when tradition is experienced as an antiquated straightjacket seemingly denying life as many know it today. That pull of the past and of the present creates the 'double imperative' between tradition and modernity.[2] Just which ideas control our approach to this tension varies with, perhaps, two holding dominant place, one embedded in science and the other in social science.

Science, social science, life and death

One basic view of life is that humanity has arisen as part of an evolving world devoid of any ultimate significance. The human mind, prone to making meaning as part of its drive to survive in hazardous environments, over-extends itself when asking about the ultimate meaning of everything. Religion is seen as part of this meaning-making tendency and its over-drive, with its teachings on an afterlife bringing an apparently final meaningfulness to things that, essentially, have

[1] *Mystery of Salvation* (1995: 204).
[2] I use 'modernity' loosely: some might prefer post-modernity.

more limited ends. That outlook can be held as easily by natural science as social science.

Another view is convinced that there is a God ultimately responsible for the cosmos and thus also for humanity. Two paths pass from that standpoint. One assumes that revelations from that divine source must needs control belief today, it gives priority to the Bible and will muster any available means to maintain its apparent meaning, this can include the deployment of scientific ideas as in the FINLON notion discussed below. The other assumes that such scriptures are deeply, culturally influenced by their own day of origin and express the belief of people of that time as they sought to understand and engage with the divine. But this approach also takes responsibility for continuing with that engagement. Various experiences of public worship and private meditation and complex private intuitions, as well as diverse forms of peer pressure, direct the thought of all such individuals while fear, potential meaninglessness, love and a fullness of being pervade all of this thought.

For some, death is obviously the end of life, for others it is the gateway to further existence. The implicit assumption of this book is that Christians ought to recognize that diversity more clearly and mutually accept it. Such an outlook would increase the subtlety of biblical interpretation and acknowledge the diversity it contains while refocusing spirituality and ethics upon life lived today. Emerging from the previous chapters is the sense that life is an inalienable gift to be accepted daily by grace: each day being a day of death – of dying 'in Christ', and of resurrection – of rising with Christ. As such each day is baptismal and Eucharistic, lived within the domain of the Spirit as the Lord, the giver of life. The community base of the church frames this life and so engages with tradition and scripture that the life of Christ is manifest.

Physics and myths

In acknowledging this diversity it is worth pondering the strategies that faith engenders whether we accept them or not. Take, for example, the work of some scientists as they acknowledge the final death of the cosmos – the 'mortality' of the cosmos[3] – as we know it and relate that to their biblical convictions of God's ultimate promise of eternal life. Perhaps the best case is Robert John Russell's Center for Theology and the Natural Sciences at the Graduate Theological Union at Berkeley, and its notion of FINLON: FINLON is the anagram for 'the first instantiation of a new law of nature'.[4] The essence of one of Russell's arguments[5] is that, as modern physics argues, one day the universe will die and, if that is the end of everything, then in true Pauline terms our faith will have been in vain. But, biblical material speaks of eschatology, of final things that will involve an eternal destiny for believers. Since physics speaks of some distant future and

[3] Cf. *The Mystery of Salvation*, (1995: 202).
[4] See Ted Peters (2006: 166) for a brief account of this.
[5] Robert John Russell (2002: 3–30).

theology also speaks of some 'future' it is deemed advantageous for them to be more in dialogue with each other.

Russell sees Christians as holding either a subjective or objective view of Jesus' resurrection: the former amounts to the disciples being influenced by Jesus and constructing a doctrine of his resurrection, the latter accepts that something actually happened to Jesus and that changes the way we need to understand the world of science. He adopts the 'objective' view for the case of his argument. Accordingly, our ordinary understanding that there are laws that govern the past, present and future is faulty, because in Jesus something happened that shows that people do not always die, as common sense views of the past and present and anticipations of the future indicate. FINLON thus applies to Jesus as the first instance of a new order of things. This line of thinking assumes that Christ's real resurrection will one day be reflected in an entire new order based on new laws of 'nature'. The divine fiat will achieve this and, meanwhile theories from physics may be pondered as potential indications.

From a sociological perspective we could argue that this is an interesting example of how beliefs emerge and religious groups form and flourish. While the intellectual capital of science is here brought to bear upon religion we might argue that while physics is good for cosmology, eschatology is much better served by the history of religion and the comparative study of religion. Conservative biblical scholars have, however, often avoided that route of comparison and of widespread human religiosity in order to protect a particular Christian exclusivity, a point made strongly a generation ago by New Testament scholar Willi Marxsen: 'many Christians are afraid of research into comparative religion and therefore, urged on by this fear, simply close their mind to it.'[6] I raise this example to highlight the power of intuitive faith to drive belief into domains where, as I see it, its language fits but poorly.

In my opinion the greatest formal problems over religious knowing, including life and death, come not primarily from science but from the human and social sciences even though the science and religion debate is often given media priority with high profile and distinguished participants. I fully accept that, for example, scientific questions over the origin and potential destiny of the cosmos, alongside our deepening knowledge of our genetic constitution, are basic domains yet to disclose many things. The science and religion debate, however, seems to take for granted the status and value of the submitted religious data, yet it is precisely the nature of that material, about which the human and social science of religion, as well as critical theology, has so much to say, especially in terms of how scriptures may and ought to be interpreted. We can argue, for example, that one prime issue in the creationist – evolutionist debate begins precisely in the nature and interpretation of scripture and in the nature of authority structures of churches and religious groups.

As far as death is concerned it may be that there is some point in discussing the physics of different dimensions of existence and of the possibility of life as 'soul' moving from one to another. Possible, too, of thinking of the divine mind as a

---

[6] Willi Marxsen ([1968] 1970: 181).

computer holding all the information on a person and thus being able to maintain them in some sort of being even after they are physically dead. But, there is much more basic work to do and advantage gained in pondering the nature of human desires to transcend life expressed in the myths, doctrines and rites of many religions. Not a venture for faint hearts, it soon reveals the value of the kind of consideration of Tillich's advocacy of the 'courage to be' in Chapter 6.

There we encountered a kind of argument that might lead some to ask whether Tillich was not engaged in some philosophical or theological trickery by using radical doubt as a form of energy source for absolute faith. From a distant reading this might well be the case but for those whose own life-experience brings them into stark encounter with Tillich it may come as a persuasive relief. Indeed, the mode of rejection or acceptance may well be less a matter of opinion than of life's context and experience. It certainly provides an option for those who have lost any sense of the pragmatic truthfulness of literal biblical narratives and authoritative doctrine but who, nostalgia apart, feel a profound draw upon their life and inspiration for their participation within their religious tradition. Indeed, it may even open up a new sense of what God is in relation to people. This is a positive credo of high practical outcome as someone feels empowered to say 'yes' to the world, even in the face of death.

We live in days in which knowledge of the world and of ourselves is growing as never before, days in which doctrinal-myths[7] need questioning just as the sense of our ignorance needs acknowledging. From a human and social scientific standpoint of what is known about how human communities construct ideas it seems obvious that afterlife beliefs need analysis as the imaginative engagement of self-conscious beings fearing annihilation in death. Into that mythical land can be brought the most sophisticated of scientific-Christian theories of the cosmos, of divine energy, and of the intentions of love but the mythical-theological base should not be ignored in that process. Physics does not turn Genesis myth into anything other than myth. Myth-making is no less myth-making whoever devises the narrative, nor is it any the less important. This must simply be asserted. But, and there is a 'but', as long as there is a sense of God and a commitment to live in that sense and amongst the community of people spirited by it there may be open options for the future that we cannot imagine. Each generation is driven by the knowledge of its day to try and conceive the future. God may give us a life we cannot imagine, one unrelated to any mythical paradise, transformed world or heavenly city. To say that that is impossible is to speak foolishly. To accept that one's life may be lived in orientation to that possibility in and through Jewish creation myths, Messianic ideals and the interpretative concepts of Church Fathers and current church leaders grounded in their diverse cultural roots is simply to accept the facts of life. To affirm that one can live in critical debate with that past is also to affirm the resource that theology provides. All such gospel-roots may be no more than the booster rockets for an ongoing

---

[7] Doctrines often serve as myths, it is often the status of church institutions that prevents its recognition.

entry into other worlds: but even such technical analogies betray our culturally relative lives.

Life without end

We live at the beginning of an age of scientific development whose knowledge of genetics, for example, is likely to change key paradigms of health expectations. Not only will distressing diseases become curable but even now some geneticists are talking with a degree of realistic anticipation of the possibility of human life being extended by considerable periods of time. It is also not inconceivable to think of the human constitution as capable of avoiding death, just as with some other forms of biological life since, 'at the organism level, there are no physiological or thermodynamic reasons why death must occur'.[8] A generation ago this very idea of living forever would certainly have belonged to science fiction. But, what if my ailments, diseases and physical problems can be removed and repaired so that I can live for ever? Ignoring the ethical, economic, demographic and ecological aspects of this scenario what of its theological import? What would happen, for example, to a conservative theology of Genesis and the Fall if there was no death? What would we make of Christ's death and what would become of funerals – on the assumption that someone, sometime, might die of accident? What, too, of baptism and Eucharist? All of these theological topics are pervaded by the language of death and its conquest. One response might be that death, howsoever delayed or occasional, would become increasingly terrifying though, by sharp contrast, some might even argue that the Kingdom of God had arrived. Just as death's removal from its historically central spot in the safe-societies of the later twentieth century made it marginal – much discussed in a secondary fashion but avoided in any primary way – so its future status would be enormously more marginal. Another response might, conceivably, be one of anticipated acceptance or even pleasure as a final destination at the end of a very long journey. We do not know, for example, just what mental capacity the human being possesses for an enormously long life. There might even be a moment when, beyond the capacity of genetics, the mind decides it has no further wish or motivating will to live. Existential weariness might just be a property of human extreme longevity.

Assuming that possibility of a genetically engineered eternal earthly life, would it be worth living? Further, would it be worth being an eternally living Christian? This question really belongs to the first pages of another book not to the last of this, but it underlies the whole tenor of the present volume's emphasis upon the life-affirmation of Christian living. Someone once said that there are people who long for eternal life who do not know what to do on a wet Thursday afternoon.[9] Doubtless it might be argued that the glory of the beatific vision of God and the eternal worship of deity would afford a focus of faith and a centre of gravity of

---

[8] Jeffrey P. Schloss (2002: 83).
[9] From a student essay but with a forgotten source!

being that renders all earthly comparisons stupid, and that may be so. But, for some Christians, even that hope reflects more of human desire for pleasure and humanity's capacity to conceive of wonders ahead than serve as a firm foundation of contemporary life and faith. Certainly, it will be generations before genetic engineering might effect any 'eternal' earthly living, and that probably for social elites. Long before that each of us will be dead. Meanwhile, Christianity surrounds us as we live and as Christian ethics continues to venture for the poor and many other groups for whom death is, itself, all too immediate. For these, as for us all, the call to live in and through the Lord and Giver of Life is a challenging call. It is a reminder of how, when concluding his debate with Tom Wright on the nature of the resurrection, Crossan not only says that whether it should be taken as literal or metaphorical in mode had been 'argued to impasse', but also stressed that its meaning demanded that Christians should 'take back the world from the thugs'. He speaks in terms of a contemporary 'eschatological life of justice-as-the-body-of-love-as-the-soul-of justice'.[10] So to compound a Christian intensification of life is at least practically wise and returns us to a more human-science perspective upon how life-style and death-style are related through complex intuition that combines insight and understanding.

Moving to life

Bereavement can generate situations in which distinctive intuitions may occur. Here, for example, a faithful and regular Christian worshipper disperses the cremated remains of a parent on a lake and, in that process, simply 'sees' and accepts the view that there is no life after death. Doubtless, this is a moment of complex intuition, many inner ponderings will have led up to it and, despite a lifetime of religious teaching and liturgy grounded in 'eternal life', the inner sense of a 'truth' appears and she moves into the future with an altered attitude to life and death. Here is another person, fairly recently bereaved after a long period of illness of the deceased partner, a time of exhaustion and endeavour. One morning she wakes, draws open the bedroom window curtains and, in looking out, suddenly feels that life is possible again, things will work out. Here, again, another person grieves the recent and relatively sudden death of a friend, sad in not having seen that person shortly before his death. In that moment it is as though that friend has come to pay a parting visit: the anxiety and partial guilt is gone. Finally, we have a strongly rationalist and mature male shaving in the morning when, over his shoulder, he 'sees' his recently dead grandparent looking at him. Earlier we described Schweitzer's momentary insight into 'reverence for life', itself more life than death focused. Whatever the psychological, social or theological factors involved in these cases they prove important for the individuals concerned: they are moments of complex intuition that affect that person's life and become highly germane for the way they go on to negotiate with themselves the meaning and significance of life and death. Their experience may mean nothing to others

[10] John Dominic Crossan (2006: 185–86).

and may cut little ice with some church leaders whose doctrinal views either contradict or have no place in them for such experiences. Yet these are the stuff that visions and revelations are made on and that drive individual lives, they conduce to a sense of salvation.

Salvation is, itself, neither an easy term to define nor a single experience to describe. However, having drawn so much from Schweitzer in previous chapters we do so again with his perspective on salvation as nothing less than 'being set free from the world and from ourselves through a fellowship of the will with Jesus, and being filled with power and peace and courage for life'.[11] Survival is abandoned as, with reverence for life, we embrace it daily as a gift. Learning from the Philippians[12] account of Christ, any grasping afterlife can safely be abandoned with no fear of its loss but only a love of life and of those given to us in and through our living. Such a life has, in turn, the opportunity for intensive living. Just if and how this may emerge in an individual none can predict. For some there will be a triggering crisis, perhaps through bereavement or the appreciation of life's brevity, for others the 'crisis' lies in the revelation of the mystery of life. To some this perspective may appear strange, perhaps irrational or overly emotional yet, with Schweitzer,[13] it must be said that there is an insight of discovery that brings to us an understanding of life that cannot be taught. His view was that, 'in the final analysis, our relationship to Jesus is of a mystical sort,' in and through which our will experiences a 'clarification, enrichment and quickening': this he is happy to call a 'Jesus mysticism'.[14] Here there is a mutual unanimity of will and fellowship of those so committed across the generations. Had he been Catholic I suspect he would have developed this in terms of fellowship within the church. For all this, as confessional theology, is impossible without the church's tradition of the life of Jesus, worship and the call to faith and to renewed life 'in Christ'. The faith is a resource for faith even when the form of faith may appear unconventional. Additionally, we can hardly ignore mentioning Schweitzer's commitment to Bach and his music with all its intrinsic evocation of faith,[15] indeed that may even be one way of beginning to appreciate his closing words in the *Quest for the Historical Jesus* – amongst the best known of all theological reflections of being 'in Christ'. Their attractive familiarity itself being dependent upon their affinity with the experience of many that,

> 'He comes to us as One unknown, without a name, as of old, by the lakeside He came to those men who knew Him not . . . He commands. And to those who obey Him, whether they be wise or simple, He will reveal Himself in the toils, the conflicts, the sufferings which they will pass

---

[11] Henry Clark (1962: 203): Original translation from Schweitzer's *Die Geschichte der Leben-Jesu-Forschung*.

[12] Phil 2. 6.

[13] Though much could be added from the psychology of problem solving and discovery.

[14] Henry Clark (1962: 203–04).

[15] E.g. his recordings of *Christ lag in Todesbanden* and *Leibster Jesu, wir sind hier*, of 1936. *EMI Records: HLM 7003*.

through in His fellowship, and, as an ineffable mystery, they shall learn in their own experience Who He is'.[16]

Doctrines and theological critiques do not exhaust our reflections on such things for living is, itself, the domain of discovery with worship and ethical action fostering and revivifying life.

God's today

In terms of certain and empirical knowledge we do not know what happens at death or beyond death. There may be nothing or there may be realities that traditional beliefs could not even begin to think of modelling.[17] In either case a proper lack of high-mindedness is sensible. Nevertheless, the theme of this book has been to make today the day of salvation. To adopt this position is, also, to have to accept the deep ills of the many for whom that is impossible: here, the much discussed 'problem of evil' in Christian theology remains a 'problem', one not passed or passible to another world for resolution. Yet it is precisely amidst this difficulty that believers have so often been captured by a faith in God's today and called to live beyond themselves. That there is a paradox in this way of speaking is not problematic. There is, perhaps, no greater biblical expression of this than in Paul's account in Romans of the uncondemned life in the Spirit that Christ makes possible. To live as dead bodies is the paradox of the Spirit that he advocates.[18] Certainly it embraces contradictions but that, too, has its own paradigmatic scene of disciples doubting whilst meeting the risen Christ.

This form of living the risen life is a life lived in the face of death, anticipating death as a blessing.[19] Though the liturgical motif that often occurs towards the close of funeral rites rhetorically calls us to awake from sleep to live as we ought there is no formula directing how we may live as those who die. While we might want to say that it depends upon the view that people must arrive at for themselves that is an over-easy response. And this is the case, even within a highly individualistic society, because our private experience is much influenced and pervaded by the lives of others and by their experience of and approach to death. More than that, the world in which we live provides us with a variety of options of and for action within which to make our choices and pursue our course. So, for example, while contemporary British society provides many options for people to exercise their bodies, get them suntanned, have dental, medical and many sorts of body-treatment, including shop-front funeral directors ready to provide their own options of dealing with dead bodies, there are no 'shopping' facilities in which we can simply purchase our own immediate death. The whole

---

[16] Henry Clark (1962: 205).

[17] In saying this I do not mean to echo 1. Cor 2. 9.

[18] Rom 8. 10. That Chapter 8 of Romans stands as a strange complement to its twin-themed Chapter 15 in the First Letter to the Corinthians.

[19] C. E. Winquist (1995: 82). Pondering Tillich and Schleiermacher on life's 'end'.

issue of assisted suicide and advance directives over how we wish to be treated, if and when we appear incompetent to comment, is fraught with moral questions that vary in intensity from outrage to an intense desire for its realization.[20] So, too, with life. The ecological crisis now befalling humanity is likely to put pay to any rampant post-modern individualism as a new meta-narrative of survival dispels charming individualism.

Death's rarity

This, itself may be a difficult truth to learn at this stage of social evolution because death is a rare commodity in advanced society despite its wide distribution, though not by choice, in many developing and under-developed societies. Indeed, those very concepts of 'developed' and 'under-developed' might even be a measure of the 'scarcity' of death. Issues of risk, and the fear of harm lie at the heart of a 'health and safety' culture in which the 'duty of care' aligned with social responsibility have come to be key moral factors in the new-morality of institutional organization. Indeed, I use the phrase 'new-morality' here specifically to refer to the way in which work-based contexts rather than traditional religion increasingly serve as the source for ethical codes. Death as an unusual event comes to the fore as that which must be avoided at all costs, including the legal costs that may be incurred by error on the part of management.

But here we encounter a radical paradox. For against that ecological background there exists an increasing emphasis upon individual autonomy and freedom of choice within a consumerist market economy of available goods and services. With the rise of life-autonomy and a shifting ethics we face the issue of a choice to die set over and against social rules preventing easy take-up of any such option. Society continues to see itself as wiser than the individual when it comes to life and death decisions. Death emerges as the absolute point of logical contradiction between the freedom of the individual in a freedom-focused consumerist society and the welfare state with its social decisions over the conditions determining wellbeing. But there is also another dimension, that is provided by practical Christian piety. Marxsen put this as well as anyone: 'We want to be masters of our lives – and are always and everywhere forced to discover that we are not . . . we want to save our lives and can only do so to a very limited extent and for a very limited time.'[21] Faith addresses this desire quite clearly and answers only by a call for self-sacrifice after the example and in participation with the sacrifice of Christ.

Life intensity

Such sacrifice yields the energy of life and the possibility of 'intensive living'. In this book that life-choice has been hinted at through but a few thinkers and we are now in a position to bring some of their ideas together. Schweitzer, Tillich and

---

[20] James M. Hoefler with Brian E. Kamie (1994).
[21] Willi Marxsen ([1968] 1970: 182).

Hutch are particularly valuable at this point because they allow us to develop the idea of intensive living in a faith context. In Schweitzer we saw the power inhering in an ethic of reverence for life that was the outcome of or perhaps it would be better to say the intuitional discovery of theological and philosophical analyses of Christian culture. Alongside that reverence was a realism in how we relate to each other as those who will die and whose membership in the Christian community brings an eternal presence to the present. From Tillich, too, came the sense of a 'courage to be', prompting us to see that it is, 'a great thing to have a future in which to actualize one's possibilities, in which one can experience the abundance of life, in which one can create something new.' In his sermon on 'The Eternal Now', he addressed both the potential deception and the hope involved in facing both the fact of death and also of old age. He speaks of the way we often focus on the near future and put aside that longer future which holds our death, he thinks that while, perhaps, we could not live without doing so for most of the time we will, 'perhaps, . . . not be able to die if we *always* do so'. His rhetorical question remains powerful: 'And if one is not able to die, is he really able to live?'[22] Here Tillich and Schweitzer are unanimous, recalling how false Schweitzer felt it to be when even Christian people avoided the fact of death that faces us all. A generation later, but inspired by and interpreting and developing the thought of William James – Schweitzer and Tillich's famous contemporary – Hutch brought his own guidance on practical saintliness. In Chapter 3 we explored his two laws of the mortal body focused on 'the turnover of generations' and 'gender complementarity'.[23] Saintliness becomes a self-sacrificial process grounded in a realization of death, of natality engaged with mortality. At the heart of Hutch's analysis of William James is the idea of embodiment,[24] a concept that would gain prominence in numerous disciplines towards the close of the twentieth century.[25] Indeed, much of this book has been rooted in the sense of embodiment as the awareness of life lived as and with bodies that enflesh the very values of our society. Theologically speaking, the doctrine of the incarnation, of Jesus as a particular embodiment of the divine values, evokes within us a sense of our own place in the world. It is because we know ourselves as bodies that we find such a strong affinity with Jesus as a body and then a divine embodiment. Indeed, it has often been that vision of Jesus as the divine embodiment that has attracted believers and allowed them to speak of God in this world.[26] Hutch, for his part and from a broader view of embodiment, moves to an understanding of 'life-giving death', to an outlook grounded in the insight that 'our knowledge may compel us to present our bodies as living sacrifices to life'.[27] We noted in Chapter 3 how odd it is to find Hutch speaking of 'laws', but here it makes sense in the context of his 'living sacrifices' motif which is, quite

---

[22] Paul Tillich (1963: 105).

[23] Richard A. Hutch (1997: 88).

[24] Richard A. Hutch (1997: 120).

[25] e.g. Malcolm MacLachlan (2004).

[26] Douglas J. Davies (2002: 19–52): on 'Embodiment and Incarnation'.

[27] Richard A. Hutch (1997: 120).

obviously, an intentional parallel to Paul's famous biblical appeal to believers 'to present your bodies as a living sacrifice, holy and acceptable to God'.[28] For Paul this was the right and proper 'spiritual worship' for Christians even in their current paradoxical state of undergoing suffering in the very body that is also the dwelling place of the Holy Spirit.[29] This Pauline perspective itself comes close to a formal affirmation, perhaps not quite a 'law', but yet a principle of the life of faith.

Many will find it hard to evaluate both Schweitzer and Tillich in terms of their formal Christian orthodoxy as far as the plain meaning of words and creeds are concerned. Some will see them tending to an existentialism that is beyond the Christian boundary, interpreting their piety grounded in 'the Christ' as suspiciously abstract, as the very phrase 'the Christ' might itself be taken to indicate. Others will see their intuitive apprehension as a clear piety focused on Jesus as the 'one who comes to us' or as the 'New Man'. For those who might find these individuals problematic or at least ambiguous greater clarity lies in the difference between Hutch and St Paul, and yet this very divergence highlights the importance of 'self-sacrifice' as a medium for understanding and living in the light of death.

Death denied, ignored, transformed

Hutch's play on Paul's ideas raises the important fact that whether people are Christian or not or, indeed, whether they are Christians with different approaches to afterlife beliefs, there is a practical need for an outlook on death. Here, perhaps, we find a crucial ethical issue, viz., not between afterlife believers and non-believers, but between those prepared to build 'death' into their life-style and those who are not. And it is this issue that brings us back to the key concepts of this book, viz., of intensive living on a Christian base. To do so is also to acknowledge the two options capable of summary as the denial of death and the ignoring of death: each capable of either a religious or a secular version. Though it is possible to deny death in either a religious or a secular fashion, it is also possible to ignore it religiously or secularly. I take the ignoring element first, for it is probably the most common in contemporary developed societies.

Death is ignorable because it is relatively rare, just as toothache was once common and intrusive in daily life but is now relatively rare. Once death's presence occupied a high and frequent profile, with most families experiencing loss of members across a wide age range and living in communities with ongoing losses in other families. To speak of *memento mori* , of formal reminders of death in previous ages and other cultures is simply to reflect such a social life. Christianity, initially, enhanced that awareness through its early focus on resurrection and eternal life as also on martyrdom. With time, its developed systems of sin and punishment with all the images and practices of penitence, purgatory and hell, fostered later in medieval religion, added further dynamics as fear engaged with hope.

[28] Rom 12. 1.
[29] Rom 12. 1. 8. 8, 18–24, respectively.

Death's profile has now, however, withdrawn into the margins of active social life. It occupies the distant scene of older old age, yet images of old people's homes can be seen as attracting elements of the purgatorial to them: few would see them as desired havens of well-deserved rest. Death occasionally intrudes from society's margins through accident or terminal illness for those 'untimely' struck down in their prime or, even worse, as infants or children. Still, for the most part, death can be marginalized because it is already professionalized for the great majority by hospital and funeral director. Since a funeral can be arranged largely within a week it is practically easy to get it 'over and done with'. Cremated remains can be lodged somewhere suitable and life can return to 'normal'. The memories of the dead are quite another thing, but they, too, can be built into one's life story as one recalls relatives 'as they were'. Even when those memories play a large part in an individual's life, as well they may, perhaps especially with aging and a growing memory-likeness between the living and the dead, they are not public memories. Rather after the fashion of secularization theory that locates religious values in the private rather than the public domain, so with memories of the dead. It would be seen as 'morbid' for someone to ply a trade of memories, or rehearse their grave-visits and talking to the dead, in a public context. So, both for real reasons of forgetting about death or keeping silent about private thoughts, death becomes socially ignored.

As for secular denial of death, this emerges from a more reasoned position that we are animals in a world operating through processes of life and death so that it would be wrong to attach any special significance to human death over and beyond that of any animal. In this sense, what is denied is the investing of death with any ultimate significance. Philosophically, it embraces the well-known argument that since death is the end of us we will not be aware of it in its very occurrence and, therefore, it is of no significance to us in the here and now.

But what of a religious 'denial of death'? In many respects this is an interesting and intriguing case. By a religious denial of death I refer to believers who see death as a simple transition from the reality of this world to a reality of an afterlife with God. In some ways we might describe this as an 'easy death' just as it was once fashionable to speak of 'easy grace'. In the words of one popular poem used at many contemporary funerals 'death is nothing at all'. To pass from this world to the next is an expectation that flows from religious experience of God in this life. Some religious groups engage in this transition process so as to redefine death as just such an ease of transition as, in their quite different ways, do both Spiritualism and Mormonism.[30] The latter group spends a great deal of energy in this life engaged in matters of the world-beyond through temple-based rituals of baptism, and numerous other rites, vicariously performed for the dead. The significance of such work is to reduce or transform the sense of death as tragedy into death as part of the overall plan of happiness or plan of salvation overseen by God. Spiritualism, in its own way, has been dangerous territory for major Christian denominations, an attitude that has become customary. But why

---

[30] Douglas J. Davies (2000: 225–233).

should that be? In many respects Spiritualism, along with Near Death Experiences might appear as a powerful ally in reinforcing belief in survival after death. But, on the contrary, they are regularly deemed as problem areas because they offer their own forms of certainty over and against the attitude of 'faith'. A certainty that relates poorly to the core traditional theology of Jesus and his resurrection, for the key rite of emergent Christianity was a memorial meal and not a séance.

Bibliography

Atran, Scott (2002), *In Gods We Trust*, Oxford: Oxford University Press.

Barkas, Anastasias (2005), 'Greek Orthodoxy in Great Britain', *The Encyclopedia of Cremation*, (eds) Douglas J. Davies and Lewis H. Mates, Aldershot: Ashgate, pp. 226–27.

Barrett, C. K. (1955), *The Gospel According to St John*, London: SPCK.

Baudrillard, Jean ([1976] 1993), *Symbolic Exchange and Death*, London: Sage.

Berger, Peter L. (1997), *Redeeming Laughter, The Comic Dimension of Human Experience*, Berlin: Walter de Gruyter.

Berger, Peter L. (1969), *Sacred Canopy*, London: Faber.

Betjeman, John (2003), *Collected Poems*, London: John Murray.

Binns, Christopher (2005), 'Russian and Soviet Transitions', *The Encyclopedia of Cremation*, (eds) Douglas J. Davies with Lewis H. Mates, Aldershot: Ashgate, pp. 370–71.

Binns, Christopher (1980–1981), 'The Changing Face of Power: Revolution and Accommodation in the Soviet Ceremonial System', Part 1, *Man* (NS) 14 (1980: 585–606), Part 11, *Man* (NS), 15 (1981: 170–87).

Blair, Robert (1813), *The Grave, A Poem*, London: Ackermann.

Blenkinsopp, Joseph (2004), *Treasures Old and New: Essays in the Theology of the Pentateuch*, Grand Rapids, Mich.: Eerdmans.

Bloom, Anthony (2000), 'Death and Bereavement', *Living Orthodoxy in the Modern World: Orthodoxy, Christianity and Society*, (eds) A. Walker and C. Carras, New York: Crestwood.

Boros, Ladislaus ([1973] 1976), *Prayer*, London: Search Press.

Boumis, Panagiotis J. (2005), 'Greek Orthodoxy', *The Encyclopedia of Cremation*, (eds) Douglas J. Davies and Lewis H. Mates, Aldershot: Ashgate, pp. 225–26.

Bourke, Joanna (2005), *Fear, A Cultural History*, London: Virago.

Bowker, John (1973), *The Sense of God*, Oxford: Clarendon Press.

Bowker (1978), *The Religious Imagination and the Sense of God*, Oxford: Clarendon Press.

Brodsky, Joseph ([1995] 1997), *On Grief and Reason, Essays*, London: Penguin.

Brown, David (1999), *Tradition and Imagination: Revelation and Change*, Oxford: Clarendon Press.

Brown, David (1995), 'The Christian Heaven', in Dan Cohn-Sherbok and Christopher Lewis (eds) *Beyond Death: Theological and Philosophical Reflections on Life after Death*, London: Macmillan, pp. 42–53.

Brown, Ron M. (2001), *The Art of Suicide*, London: Reaktion Books.

Bultmann, Rudolph ([1964] 1971), *The Gospel of John*, Translated by G. R. Beasley-Murray, Oxford: Blackwell.

Bynum, Caroline Walker (1995), *The Resurrection of the Body in Western Christianity 200–1336*, New York: Columbia University Press.

Calvin, John (1838), *Institutes of the Christian Religion*, London, Cheapside: Tegg & Son.

Carlil, Richard (1582), *A Discourse Concerning Two Divine Positions, That the Souls of the Faithful Fathers Deceased Before Christ Went Immediately to Heaven, the Second . . . Touching the Decension of our Saviour Christ into Hell.* Publicly Disputed at a Commencement in Cambridge 1552. London: Roger Ward by Holborne Conduit, at the Sign of the Talbot, 1582.

Catchpole, David (2002), *Resurrection People, Studies in the Resurrection Narratives of the Gospels*, Macon, Georgia: Smyth & Helwys Publishing.

Chalmers, Thomas (1826), *On Cruelty to Animals*, Glasgow: Chalmers and Collins.

Chardin, Teilhard de (1974), *Hymn of the Universe*, London: Fontana.

Churches' Group on Funeral Services at Cemeteries and Crematoria, (1997), *Guidelines for Best Practice of Clergy at Funerals*, London: The Churches Group on Funerals.

Cicero (1972), *The Nature of the Gods*, Translated by Horace C. P. McGregor, with an Introduction by J. M. Ross, London: Penguin.

Clark, Henry (1962), *The Ethical Mysticism of Albert Schweitzer*, Boston: Beacon Press.

Clark-Soles, Jaime (2006), *Death and the Afterlife in the New Testament*, London: New York.

Cleiren, Marc (1991), *Adaptation after Bereavement*, Leiden: Leiden University Press.

Common Worship: Services and Prayers for the Church of England (2000), London: Church House.

Congar, Yves (1961), *The Wide World My Parish, Salvation and its Problems*, London: Darton, Longman & Todd.

Conti, Marco, *The Declaration of 1886*, in Davies, D. J. and Lewis H. Mates (2005).

Crossan, John Dominic (2005), See Robert B. Stewart (2005).

Csikszentmihalyi, M. ([1974] 1991), *Flow: The Psychology of Optimal Experience*, NY: HarperPerennial.

Cullmann, Oscar (([1946] 1961), *Christ and Time*, London: SCM Press.

Dahlgren, Curt and Jan Hermanson (2005), 'Sweden, Changing Customs in the late 1990s', *The Encyclopedia of Cremation*, (eds) Douglas J. Davies and Lewis H. Mates, Aldershot: Ashgate, pp. 60–64.

Danforth, L. M. (1982), *Death Rituals of Rural Greece*, Princeton University Press.

Dargentas, Magdalini, (2005), 'Cremation in Modern Greece', *The Encyclopedia of Cremation*, (eds) Douglas J. Davies and Lewis H. Mates, Aldershot: Ashgate, pp. 223–25.

Davies, Douglas J. (2002), *Death, Ritual and Belief* (2nd. rev. ed) London: Continuum.

Davies, Douglas J. and Lewis H. Mates (2005), *The Encyclopedia of Cremation*, Aldershot: Ashgate.

Davies, Douglas J. and Alastair Shaw (1995), *Reusing Old Graves: A Report on Popular British Attitudes*, Crayford, Kent: Shaw & Sons.

Davies, Douglas J. (2000), *Private Passions, Betraying Discipleship on the Journey to Jerusalem*, Norwich: Canterbury Press.

Davies, Douglas J. (1996), 'The Sacred Crematorium', *Mortality,* Vol. 1. No. 1. pp. 83–94.

Davies, Douglas J. (1995), *British Crematoria in Public Profile*, Maidstone: Cremation Society of Great Britain.

Davies, Douglas J. (1993), 'The Dead at the Eucharist', *Modern Churchman.* Vol. xxxiv. No. 3. pp. 26–32.

Davies, Douglas J. (1990), *Cremation Today and Tomorrow*, Nottingham: Grove-Alcuin Books.

Davies, Douglas J. (1988), 'The Evocative Symbolism of Trees', *The Iconography of Landscape*, (eds) Denis Cosgrove and Stephen Daniels, Cambridge: Cambridge University Press.

Davies, Douglas, Watkins, Charles and Michael Winter (1991), *Church and Religion in Rural England*, T&T Clark: Edinburgh.

DeMar, Gary (2001), *End Times Fiction: A Biblical Consideration of the Left Behind Theology*, Nashville: Thomas Nelson Publishers.

Doctrine Commission of the Church of England (1996), *The Mystery of Salvation*, London: Church House Publishing.

Douglas, Mary ([1999] 2000), *Leviticus as Literature*, Oxford: Oxford University Press.

Droge, Arthur J. (1997), 'The Crown of Immortality', *Death, Ecstasy and Other Worldly Journeys,* (eds) John J. Collins and Michael Fishbane, New York: State University of New York Press, pp. 154–69.

Duffy, Eamon (1992), *The Stripping of the Altas*, New Haven, CT: Yale University Press.

Edwards, David L. (1999), *After Death. Past Beliefs and Real Possibilities*, London & New York: Continuum.

Erickson, Victoria Lee (2001), 'Georg Simmel: American Sociology Chooses the Stone the Builders Refused', *The Blackwell Companion to the Sociology of Religion*, (ed.) Richard K. Fenn, Oxford: Balckwell.

Feuerbach, Ludwig ([1841] 1957), *The Essence of Christianity*, London: Harper and Row.

First Prayer-Book of King Edward VI (1549), The Ancient and Modern Library of Theological Literature, (no date). Reprinted from a copy in the British Museum, London: Griffith, Farran, Okeden & Welsh.

Gadamer, Hans-George ([1960] 1989), *Truth and Method*, London: Sheed & Ward.

Gilhus, Ingvild Saelid (1997), *Laughing Gods, Weeping Virgins, Laughter in the History of Religions*, London: Routledge.

Girgard, Rene, (1977), *Violence and the Sacred*, Baltimore: Johns Hopkins University Press.

Glaser, B. G. and A. L. Strauss (1965), Awareness of Dying, Chicago: Aldine Publishers Co. Ltd.

Godbout, Jacques with Alain Cailllé ([1992] 1998), *The World of the Gift*, Translated by Donald Winkler, Montreal and London: McGill-Queen's University Press.

Godelier, Maurice ([1996] 1999), *The Enigma of the Gift*, Cambridge: Polity Press.

Grainger, Hilary J. (2005), *Death Redesigned: British Crematoria: History, Architecture and Landscape,* Reading: Spire Books Ltd.

Grigg, Richard (1985), *Symbol and Empowerment: Paul Tillich's Post-Theistic System*, Macon GA: Mercer University Press.

Groen, Burt (2001), 'The Christian East', *Periodical of the Institute of Eastern Christian Studies at Nijmegen,* Jaargang 53, 2001, 3–4, pp. 202–18.

Gunther, Thomas (2002), 'Resurrection to New Life: Pneumatological Implications of the Eschatological Transition', *Resurrection,* (eds) Ted Peters, Robert John Russell and Michael Welker, Grand Rapids, Mich.: William B. Eerdmans Publishing Company, pp. 255–69.

Henderson, Archibald (1911), *Mark Twain*, London: Duckworth.

Herz, Robert ([1905–06] 1960), 'A contribution to the collective representation of death', *Death and the Right Hand*, (eds) Rodney and Claudia Needham. New York: Free Press.

Herzfeld, Noreen (2002), 'Cybernetic Immortality versus Christian Resurrection,' *Resurrection,* (eds) Ted Peters, Robert John Russell and Michael Welker, Grand Rapids, Mich.: William B. Eerdmans Publishing Company, pp. 192–201.

Heywood Thomas, John (1961), 'The Theology of Paul Tillich', *Breakthrough*, 1961, pp. 14–15.

Heywood Thomas, John (1965), *Paul Tillich*, London: Lutterworth.

Hick, John (1976), *Death and Eternal Life*, London: Collins.

Hoefler, James M. and Brian E. Kamoie (1994), *Deathright, Culture, Medicine, Politics, and the Right to Die*, Oxford: Westview Press.

Hutch, Richard A. (1997), *The Meaning of Lives: Biography, Autobiography and the Spiritual Quest*, London: Cassell.

Jackson, Brian (2007), 'Jonathan Edwards Goes to Hell (House): Fear Appeals in American Evangelism', *Rhetoric Review,* Vol. 26, No. 1, 42–59.

Jupp, Peter C. (2006), *From Dust to Ashes, Cremation and the British Way of Death*, Basingstoke: Palgrave Macmillan.

Jupp, Peter C. (2005), 'Cremation Society of Great Britain', *The Encyclopedia of Cremation*, (eds) Douglas J. Davies and Lewis H. Mates, Aldershot: Ashgate, pp. 135–43.

Kingsley, Charles (1886), *The Works of Charles Kingsley, Volume XXI, Village Sermons and Town and Country Sermons*, London: Macmillan and Co.

Kraemer, David (2000), *The Meanings of Death in Rabbinic Judaism*, London: Routledge.

LaHaye, Tim and Jerry B. Jenkins (2001), *Desecration, Antichrist Takes the Throne*, Wheaton, Ill: Tyndale House Publishers.

Lambourne, Alfred (1917), *The Cross, Holly and Easter Lilies*, (No publisher. Memorial edition of one hundred art copies).

Leeuw, Gerardus van der ([1933] 1967), *Religion in Essence and Manifestation*, Gloucester, Mass: Peter Smith.

Lüdemann, Gerd (1994), *The Resurrection of Jesus*, London: SCM Press.

Mable, Norman (1945), *Popular Hymns and Their Writers*, London: Independent Press.

MacLachlan, Malcolm (2004), *Embodiment, Clinical, Critical and Cultural Perspectives on Health and Illness*, Bristol: McGraw Hill Education-Open University.

Marxsen, Willi, ([1968] 1970), *The Resurrection of Jesus of Nazareth*, London: SCM Press.

Mauss, Marcel ([1925] 1954), *The Gift, Forms and Functions of Exchange in Archaic Societies*, Translated by I Cunnison, London: Cohen and West.

McCane, Byron R. (2003), *Roll Back the Stone, Death and Burial in the World of Jesus*, London: Continuum.

McDannell, Colleen and Bernhard Lang ([1988] 2001), *Heaven, A History*, New Haven: Yale University Press.

McDonald, John F. (1966), *Cremation*, London: Catholic Truth Society.

Mead, Walter Russell (2006), 'Religion and U.S. Foreign Policy', *Foreign Affairs*, Vol. 85, No. 5, pp. 24–43.

Mehl, Roger (1970), *The Sociology of Protestantism*, London: SCM.

Mitford, Jessica (1998), *The American Way of Death*, London: Virago.

Mystery of Salvation (1996), The Doctrine Commission of the Church of England London: Church House Publishing.

Needham, Rodney (1981), *Circumstantial Deliveries*, Berkeley, University of California Press.

Newton, John (2005), 'Cremation, Death and Roman Catholicism', *The Encyclopedia of Cremation*, (eds) Douglas J. Davies and Lewis H. Mates, Aldershot: Ashgate, pp. 107–109.

Nickelsburg, G. W. E. (1972), *Resurrection, Immortality, and Eternal life in Intertestamental Judaism*, Cambridge, Mass: Harvard University Press.

Novorino, Marco (2005), 'Freemasonry in Italy', *The Encyclopedia of Cremation*, (eds) Douglas J. Davies and Lewis H. Mates, Aldershot: Ashgate. pp. 207–10.

Olyan, Samuel M. (2004), *Biblical Mourning*, Oxford: Oxford University Press, p. 131.

Parker, T. H. L. (1969), 'Predestination' *Dictionary of Christian Theology*, (ed.) Alan Richardson, pp. 264–72.

Parkes, Richard ([1604] 1607), *A Brief Answer unto Certain Objections and Reasons Against the Descension of Christ into Hell*, Oxford: Joseph Barnes, and London: George Eld.

Parsons, Brian (2005), *Committed to the Cleansing Flame: The Development of Cremation in Nineteenth Century England*, Reading: Spire Books Ltd.

Perham, Michael (1997), *Anglican Funeralites Today and Tomorrow*, in Peter C. Jupp and Tony Rogers, Interpreting Death, London: Cassell, pp. 157–170.

Peters, Ted. (2002), 'Resurrection: the Conceptual Challenge', *Resurrection*, (eds) Ted Peters, Robert John Russell and Michael Welker, Grand Rapids, Mich.: William B. Eerdmans Publishing Company, pp. 297–321.

Peters, Ted. (2002), 'Introduction: What Is to Come', *Resurrection*, (eds) Ted Peters, Robert John Russell and Michael Welker, Grand Rapids, Mich.: William B. Eerdmans Publishing Company, pp. viii–xvii.

Peters, Ted. (2006), 'The Future of the Resurrection', *The Resurrection of Jesus*, (ed.) Robert B. Stewart, London: SPCK.

Pittinger, Norman (1967), *After Death, Life in God*, London: SCM.

Polkinghorne, John (1994), *Science and Christian Belief*, London: SPCK, p. 163.

Prothero, Stephen (2001), *Purified by Fire: A History of Cremation in America*, Berkeley: University of California Press.

Purcell, Boyd C. (1998), 'Spiritual Terrorism', *American Journal of Hospice and Palliative Medicine,* 1998, No. 16, pp. 167–73.

Purcell, Tim (2005), 'Dresden', 'Judaism', 'Nazi Cremation', *The Encyclopedia of Cremation*, (eds) Douglas J. Davies and Lewis H. Mates, Aldershot: Ashgate, pp. 168–69, 284–86, 323–34, respectively.

Radford Ruether, Rosemary (1993), *Gaia and God*, London: SCM.

Rahner, Karl (1972), *On the Theology of Death*, London: SCM.

Rappaport, Roy (1999), *Ritual and Religion in the Making of Humanity*, Cambridge: Cambridge University Press.

Rowell, Geoffrey (1977), *The Liturgy of Christian Burial*, London: SCM and Alcuin Club.

Rowell, Geoffrey (1974), *Hell and the Victorians*, Oxford: Clarendon Press.

Russell, Robert John (2002) 'Bodily Resurrection, Eschatology, and Scientific Cosmology', *Resurrection, Theological and Scientific Assessments,* (eds) Ted Peters, Robert John Russell, and Michael Welker, Grand Rapids, Mich.: William B. Eerdmans Publishing Company, pp. 3–30.

Salice, Anna (2005) 'Italy', *The Encyclopedia of Cremation*, (eds) Douglas J. Davies and Lewis H. Mates, Aldershot: Ashgate, p. 111.

Scarre, Geoffrey (2007), *Death*, Stocksfield: Acumen.

Schleiermacher, Friedrick ([1864] 1975), *The Life of Jesus*, (ed.) J. C. Verheyden, Philadelphia: Fortress Press.

Schloss Jeffrey P (2002), 'From Evolution to Eschatology', *Resurrection,* (eds) Ted Peters, Robert John Russell and Michael Welker, Grand Rapids, Mich.: William B. Eerdmans Publishing Company, pp. 56–85.

Schweitzer, Albert ([1931] 1933), *Albert Schweitzer My Life and Thought*, Translated by C. T. Campion, London: Allen and Unwin.

Schweitzer, Albert (1936), 'The Ethics of Reverence for Life', Christendom, I (Winter 1936), No. 2, pp. 225–39, in Henry Clark (1962), *The Ethical Mysticism of Albert Schweitzer*, Boston: Beacon Press, pp. 180–94.

Schweitzer, Albert (1919), 'Reverence for Life', *Reverence for Life*, Translated by Reginald H. Fuller ([1966] 1974), London: SPCK, pp. 108–17.

Schweitzer, Albert (1907), 'Overcoming Death', 'Reverence For Life', Translated by Reginald H. Fuller ([1966] 1974), London: SPCK, pp. 67–81.

Schweitzer, Edward (1970), *The Good News According to Mark,* London: SPCK.

Seale, Clive (1998), *Constructing Death, The Sociology of Dying and Bereavement*, Cambridge: Cambridge University Press.

Second Prayer-Book of Edward VI (1552), The Ancient and Modern Library of Theological Literature, (no date). Reprinted from a copy in the British Museum, London: Griffith, Farran, Okeden & Welsh.

Sennett, Richard (2003), *Respect, The Formation of Character in a World of Inequality*, London: Penguin.

Sheppy, Paul P. J. (2003–2004), *Death, Liturgy and Ritual*, Aldershot: Ashgate.

Social Trends, (2003), No. 33. (eds) Carol Summerfield and Penny Babb. London: TSO.

Stanner, W. E. H. (1959–60), 'On Aboriginal Religion', *OCEANIA*, Vol. 30, 108–127, 245–278.

Stewart, Robert B. (2005) (ed.) *The Resurrection of Jesus, The Crossan-Wright Dialogue*, London: SPCK.

Stroumsa, Guy G. (1997), 'Mystical Descents', *Death, Ecstasy and Other Worldly Journeys,* (eds) John J. Collins and Michael Fishbane, New York: State University of New York Press, pp. 139–54.

Tavard, George H. (2000), *The Starting Point of Calvin's Theology*, Grand Rapids, Mich.: William B. Eerdmans Publishing Company.

Temple, William (1935), *Nature, Man and God*, London: Macmillan.

Terkel, Studs (1975), *Working*, Harmondsworth: Penguin Books.

The Political History of the Devil (1739: fourth edn.), Anon. London: Cornhill: Joseph Fisher.

Thornton, L. S. (1956), *Christ and the Church*, [Part Three of the Form of the Servant] Westminster: Dacre Press.

Thornton, L. S. (1950), *Revelation and the Modern World*, [Part One of The Form of the Servant], Westminster: Dacre Press.

Thornton, L. S. (1928), *The Incarnate Lord*, London: Longmans, Green & Co. Ltd.

Tillich, Paul (1963), *The Eternal Now*, London: SCM.

Tillich, Paul (1959), *Theology of Culture*, New York: Oxford University Press.

Tillich, Paul ([1951] 1953), *Systematic Theology*, London: Nesbitt.

Tillich, Paul ([1952] 1962), *The Courage to Be*, London: Collins, Fontana Library.

Tylor, E. B. ([1871] 1958), *Primitive Culture*, New York: Harper.

Walls, Jerry L. (2002), *Heaven, The Logic of Eternal Joy*, Oxford: Oxford University Press.

Waugh, Evelyn (1948), *The Loved One*, London: Chapman and Hall.

White, Vernon (2006), *Life Beyond Death, Threads of Hope in Faith, Life and Theology*, London: Darton, Longman and Todd.

Williams, Rowan ([1982] 2002), *Resurrection, Interpreting the Easter Gospel*, London: Darton Longman and Todd.

Winquist, Charles E. (1995), *Desiring Theology*, Chicago: University of Chicago Press.

Wright, Tom (2003), *The Resurrection of the Son of God*, London: SPCK.

Wright, Tom (2003b), *For All the Saints, Remembering the Christian Departed*, London: SPCK.

Zhu, Jinlong and Liu Fengming, Zuo Yongren, Gao Yueling, Zang Honchang, and Li Jian (2005), 'China, Developments in the Twentieth Century', *The Encyclopedia of Cremation*, (eds) Douglas J. Davies and Lewis H. Mates, Aldershot: Ashgate, pp. 121–22.

Index

Biblical References

Genesis

1.1–2.3	5
1.28	116
2.4ff.	5
2.5–7	119
2.7	112
2.9	120
2.17	127
2.23	45
3.14–23	41
3.17–19	119
3.19	112
4.10	41
6.11–14	41
8.8–12	40
9.3	116
38.8	45

Exodus

12.30	159

Deuteronomy

8.3	149
25.5	45

Psalms

16.10	141
42	95

Isaiah

11.7	148

Ezekiel

18	27
37.7–14	119
47.12	26

Matthew

3.16	40
10.38–39	53
24 & 25	123
26.15	166
26.21	164

Mark

1.10	40
8.31–37	53
10.8	45
12.25	45, 46
14.18	164
14.22–24	160
14.71	164
15.30–32	23

Luke

3.21	40
4.1–11	149
9.23–25	53
12.13–21	150
12.17–31	149
16.19–31	84
17.19–31	149
22.21	164

John

1.4	162
1.5	108
1.24–33	162
1.32	40
2.1–11	46
2.11	162
3.5	162
4.7–15	162
5.24–30	131
6.27, 52–54	163
11.6	28
13.3	159
13.21	164
13.38	164
14.15	159
16.32	164
18.34	162
20.17	21
20.22	159

Acts

2.1–47	41, 121
2.27	141